How To Write For Children & Young Adults

A Handbook
REVISED EDITION

Jane Fitz-Randolph

REVISED BY THE AUTHOR AND BARBARA STEINER

Johnson Books: Boulder

An earlier edition of this book was published in 1969 by Funk & Wagnalls under the title *Writing for the Juvenile and Teenage Market*.

Printed in the United States of America by
Johnson Publishing Company
1880 South 57th Court
Boulder, Colorado 80302

Library of Congress Cataloging in Publication Data

Fitz-Randolph, Jane.
  Writing for children and young adults.
  1969 ed. published under title: Writing for the juvenile and teenage market.
  Includes index
  1. Children's literature—Authorship. I. Title.
PN147.5F5   1980   808'.068   79-2747
ISBN 1-55566-021-5

---

1 2 3 4 5 6 7 8 9

Contents

Preface

Nearly forty years ago an astute teacher, Odessa Davenport, identified the patterns of children's stories and described them so that others could use them. Her painstaking analysis of hundreds of published stories revealed the skeleton structures so basic and natural that writers and editors who had never been aware that any "patterns" existed had instinctively selected and used them again and again. Like the skeletal structure of an animal species, these structures are timeless and universal. Although each piece of fiction employs different details to tell a new and individual story, nobody is going to come up with a new plot pattern five, ten, or fifty years from now—any more than someone can come up with a "new" dog skeleton.

Yet the patterns are by no means formulas, which would stifle creativity. Rather, they are guides to help the writer shape his or her own original ideas into successful stories and books—to avoid producing a monstrosity with two heads or three legs.

After proving Mrs. Davenport's patterns and other fundamentals that she taught in my own writing, I used them in my teaching. Students who mastered them enjoyed consistent success, and editors, too, recognized their validity.

Two case histories will illustrate: A student with a physical handicap could spend only two to three hours a day out of bed. Over the years she had sold her stories, but her output was small and she was selling only about a third of what she wrote. I introduced her to the plot patterns, the "story-in-one-sentence" discipline, and the "basic essentials" technique—all explained in this book—and suggested that she *plan* her stories while flat on her back, so that she could make every moment at the typewriter count.

Within a year she had tripled her output and had sold every story she had written by this method. Reprints of some stories had brought added income, and she had advanced to better-paying markets than she had been able to sell to before.

The second experience was with the editor of a leading children's magazine, who was attending a conference where I had introduced the plot patterns. Like others present, she had never heard of plot patterns and asked for more details. I told her I thought it was probably better for editors to look at stories from a *reader's* viewpoint, and not be too concerned with the skeleton underneath. "But," I said, "you're an able editor, and my guess is that you rarely buy a story that does not fit one of the patterns perfectly."

She had with her a year's issues of the magazine, a monthly with four to six stories per issue. That evening we read all the stories in the twelve magazines; all but two could be readily classified in one or another of the basic patterns. Those two, the editor said, she had been reluctant to buy but had accepted to fill out needed seasonal material.

The plot patterns and other principles explained in this book are not "rules" thought up by writing teachers or editors, but should be seen as "natural laws" of communication. The student who masters them will find them extending rather than restricting his self-expression. One should remember that anyone may break any rule, provided he does it *effectively*. But of course he must know and understand a rule to know whether he is breaking it effectively or simply blundering.

Many of the examples referred to throughout the book, and all but one of the sample stories in Appendix A, are from my own work or that of my students. There are two reasons for this: I know the background of these works, and so can comment on them more intelligently than I could on some with which I am less familiar. And in the case of the sample stories, the authors graciously donated permission for their use. Every effort has been made to provide a wide variety of representative examples.

—Jane Fitz-Randolph

Preface to the 1987 Edition

One day in 1967 a student in one of my writing classes at the University of Colorado requested a conference. She had, she said, reached a crossroad. A highly successful elementary school teacher for six years, she felt she must now choose to go on to further graduate study to qualify herself as an administrator or leave teaching and become a writer. What did I think were her prospects as a writer?

I'm sure I did my best to discourage her. She would, I pointed out, have none of the perquisites enjoyed by teachers—secure job and salary, paid vacation, insurance and pension plans, and so on. A writer's income is never predictable, and it would be *years* before she could earn anything like what she was earning as a teacher.

Barbara Steiner chose the more demanding path. She's the kind of person who works harder than most people think possible at whatever she does anyway, so it might as well be what she really wanted to do. Beginning with magazine stories, articles, and poems, she quickly moved on to writing books. She now has more than 30 books for young people to her credit—fiction and nonfiction, picture books, novels for middle-grade readers, and teenage romances. Two of her books have been Junior Literary Guild selections, and with Kathleen Phillips she is co-author of a book for teachers to use in teaching grade school children how to write. She did not give up teaching, except briefly and is a popular star at writing workshops in the schools and at writers conferences. She teaches writing courses in the University of Colorado Continuing Education Program.

It's a joy to have Barbara Steiner's help and additions in revising this book. Because the principles and methods it presents are timeless, we have made very few changes, except for some updating. A chapter on writing poetry for children, written by Barbara Steiner, has been added; and the lists of helpful resources "For Further Reading" have been completely updated and revised. We both wish our readers every success.

—Jane Fitz-Randolph

I
Young People and You

1

What Can You Expect?

Why write for children? Everyone who does it is asked the question, as if it were in some way a lesser ambition than to write for adults. "But you write so *well,*" someone says—even a fellow writer. "Why do you write for children?" One author, several of whose books have won outstanding recognition, replies bluntly, "Who, more than children, *deserves* good writing—the very best we can give them?"

Richard Adams, British author of *Watership Down* and other delightful fantasies, objects to the classification "children's books." There are simply *books,* he insists—some of which appeal to children of various ages more strongly than others. His plea is for writers to respect their audience, whether children or adults, and not to offer immature readers something that a well-read adult would find without substance and poorly written.

Other writers well known for their adult works agree. Men and women like Isaac Bashevis Singer, May Sarton, E. B. White, C. S. Lewis, Isaac Asimov, Elizabeth Yates, Elizabeth Coatsworth, Rumer Godden, and Ray Bradbury, to name only a few, have made a place in their busy lives to write beautiful and memorable things for children to read. A child's mind—and "child" refers to openness, wonder, and joy, the *spirit* of childhood, rather than to age—is flexible, curious, interested, searching, eager, responsive. Writing for such minds is the most important writing anyone can do.

It's also the most fun. Looking at life from the fresh

viewpoint of a child keeps you young, makes your life interesting and challenging. Writing for children is a happy profession, for childhood is traditionally a happy time—a time of hope and growth, a time of wonder, filled with exploration, adventure, new experiences, love, warmth, security.

It's true that people of all ages are more aware of the dark side of life now than they were a generation ago, and editors welcome stories and nonfiction that deal realistically with problems familiar to today's young readers. Many magazines for teenagers and even some younger readers use stories and articles about broken homes, ethnic problems, drug and alcohol abuse, and so on. Books for readers 11 or 12 and over explore such once taboo subjects as mental retardation, the battered child, extreme poverty, premarital sex and pregnancy, homosexuality, severe illness and death. Nothing is off limits if it is handled skillfully and honestly. Television, movies, and easy access to all kinds of print media have ended whatever age of innocence our children may have enjoyed in the past. Yet despite—perhaps because of—this very situation, children's literature continues to be based on the enduring verities and still seeks to promote timeless values: love, loyalty, justice, honesty, integrity, truth, courage, industry, cheerfulness, unselfishness, good sportsmanship, self-reliance, self-respect, responsibility.

There are other reasons why writing for children is fun. Granted that writing is a lonely profession that requires one to spend a great deal of time in solitary confinement. But the contacts one does make—with other writers, librarians, editors, and young readers—are a constant surprise and joy.

Children's editors are generally wonderful people to work with—helpful, friendly, understanding, and dedicated to bringing children good, well-written reading material that will challenge, inform, enlighten, amuse, and inspire. A great many editors of children's magazines, and many book editors too, will go to almost any length to encourage and help the writer who they think truly has something worth working on and the ability and perseverance to see the project through.

Then there's the fan mail, which is priceless. "I liked your book about our country's flag," a third-grader writes. "I liked best the flag with the snake on it that said, 'Don't tread on me.' Please write your next book about snakes." Children are wonderfully direct. "Thank you for writing such a good book," a ten-year-old says. "All my life, ever since age six, I have wanted to be a writer. I hope someday I can write a book as good as yours."

Or maybe it's "just a little story" in a children's magazine. And one day you receive a letter that says, "My mother died last summer on my birthday. I am twelve. A friend gave me the magazine with your story in it, and reading about Brenda and how she looked after her little brother and sister helps me not to feel so lonesome and to help Daddy take care of my brother Peter . . ." Then you know why you chose to write for children.

There are several conceptions and misconceptions about writing for young readers that we may as well explore right at the outset. One is that writing for children is easy. It's true that in some ways it's somewhat *simpler* than writing for adults, but it is *not* easier. Plots are simpler, characters are less complex, and the stories are shorter. The apprenticeship is generally not so long. But anything written for publication must have form, and form requires knowledge of technique. To tell a good, well-plotted, suspenseful story about a simple situation in a few words may require more real skill than to write a novel. To say that writing for children is easier than writing for adults is like saying that playing tennis is "easier" than playing golf—or vice versa. Each has its own requirements and skills that one must master to succeed.

Closely related to this first belief is another—that one doesn't have to *learn* to write, especially for children. Or more unfounded still, that writing can't be taught. It is persons holding these beliefs who flood the market with impossibly amateurish manuscripts, cluttering editorial offices with material that wastes editors' precious time and so creates a very real threat to the whole freelance system of marketing.

In a sense, of course, writing cannot be taught; you must take the tools, techniques, and principles and *teach yourself* to use them effectively. But the techniques and principles definitely *can* be presented and demonstrated. It is the purpose of this book to do so, and to help you use them successfully in your own work.

A third widely held belief is that the market for material for young readers is poor. The fact is that about 80 periodicals in the United States and Canada buy fiction and nonfiction for children and teenagers. Children's books are a vital part of the business of many large publishing houses, and some firms publish nothing but children's books. More than 3,000 new titles appear each year. Everybody wants children to read more—teachers, parents, librarians, publishers, law-enforcement personnel, counselors. Truly, the children's writer has everyone on his side!

"But the payment is so low," someone will say. Admittedly, the chances of getting a quarter-million-dollar offer from a major movie producer for the film rights to a children's book are slim, although producers do occasionally make films or TV shows from children's books and pay well for the privilege. Instead of the $1,000 to $2,000 or more that top adult magazines pay for a short story, you may receive only $40 or less for your children's magazine story. But you may receive $200, or even $600 or more from some of the best-paying publications for teenagers.

Once you master the craft, you will probably produce

far more marketable material than do most writers for adults, and you will sell a larger proportion of what you write. You may well write a $100 story in a single afternoon.

The children's magazine market has been enhanced by a practice almost unheard of in the adult field—the multiple submission of manuscripts. Several editors of Sunday school publications of various denominations, realizing that their audiences do not overlap, are willing to buy the same stories purchased by other similar publications. About 15 such publications buy material either sent to them at the same time it's sent to other church publications or submitted later, after the story or article has been printed elsewhere. This procedure will be discussed fully in Chapter 23. A writer should not even consider this kind of multiple marketing, however, until he has thoroughly mastered the craft of writing for children and has demonstrated this mastery by making several sales through conventional marketing.

The belief that payment is poor is equally fallacious with respect to books. Children's books don't become best-sellers, but they do often sell over a long time. Succeeding generations of children read many of the same books, and it's not uncommon for a good children's book to remain in print and keep selling for twenty years or more after its first publication. Youngsters wear books out, and libraries order replacements year after year. Children's book authors receive royalty terms that compare favorably with those for other authors; and with children's book clubs and paperback publication of young people's books holding a steady market, the children's book author can earn as good an income as any other writer.

The belief that Sunday school papers comprise the largest part of the children's magazine market and that one must write "religious" or "goody-goody" stories for them has turned some writers away without even an investigation. A survey of Sunday school publications today will show that the stories and articles in most differ very little from those in secular publications, and that the only taboos of either are simply matters of good taste. Editors of both religious and secular publications look for stories that give children a wholesome and hopeful, but realistic, outlook on life and on problems and situations they may have to meet. Saccharine sweetness is as unacceptable to editors as to writers. Some publications do have their own particular angles and restrictions, which an author who wishes to write for these particular periodicals must respect. But these are not unreasonable, and if an author does not wish to adapt to them, there are plenty of other markets.

Some persons are stopped before they get a good start by the belief that the competition is too great. They may have received a few rejection slips when they hear that a certain editor receives five hundred manuscripts a week and immediately decide that their chances would be better in the sweepstakes. The fact is that *at least* 95 percent of those manuscripts—and this is a conservative estimate—are not competing even remotely with the work of the even fairly talented writer who *knows the techniques of writing and studies the markets*. At least 95 percent of the manuscripts an editor receives are completely unacceptable, so poor that he could not use them even if nothing else came in! This fact should alert you to the need to *learn how* to write for children, and to *master* the skills of the profession.

People who make up and tell stories to children—their own, their neighbors', or school or playground groups— often believe that this experience fits them to write stories for publication. "I told this story to my niece and nephew," a student says confidently, "and they just loved it." The fact is that this is no basis at all for judgment. Almost any disjointed, rambling story that has action and progressive movement will hold audience interest if it's told with enthusiasm. Group psychology helps—the fact that the audience is doing and experiencing something together. So does the fact that there's a real live grown-up, often a well-loved grown-up, giving his or her whole attention to entertaining children. To add interest there is the visual aid: the storyteller's changing expression and gestures, personality, the sound of the voice with its modulations, emphasis, and variety.

None of these aids is present in the printed story. Nor does the writer have a captive audience. If the reader's interest flags, he can put the story aside. Or if the beginning fails to interest him immediately, he may never even get into the story. Furthermore, unlike the writer, the storyteller is under no compulsion to please parents, psychologists, librarians, teachers, and editors before his story can ever reach the child. Regardless of his success in his own field, the storyteller will best start from scratch to learn to be a story *writer*.

Many beginning writers believe that a true experience is certain to result in a believable and interesting story. In all probability, it is neither. The true story is interesting to the person to whom it happened or who witnessed it, not because of its intrinsic interest but because of his personal connection with it. And because it actually happened, it has no literary form and so is inartistic. The central event may be a priceless germ idea for a story, but only an experienced writer can shape and use it effectively. For reasons we shall discuss later, the true story almost always sounds less believable when written as fiction than does the wholly "made-up" story. So best save your true story until after you've sold at least a few stories built from more reliable bases.

Another erroneous belief that some beginning writers entertain is that someone may steal their priceless and novel ideas or a story. There are three good reasons why no one is likely to steal your literary property: The professional writer already has more ideas than he can possibly develop in a lifetime; as you yourself gain experience, you will discover that ideas beget more ideas, and you too will have more than you can use. And a reputable editor would no more think of stealing your idea than he would of stealing your wallet. Editors are eager to find new *writers*—much more than to find a new *story*—and stealing from a writer would be a poor way to cultivate that writer! The third reason—hard as it is to face—is that at this stage of your development as a writer, your ideas are probably not worth stealing. Added to all this is the fact that the Copyright Act that became effective in 1978 protects an author's work from the moment of its "creation." So theft of a story or an idea is truly the least of a writer's worries.

Finally, there is a popular belief among new writers that if only they had a good agent, they could sell. The fact is that until a writer has made some significant sales, an agent is only another hurdle between writer and editor—one more person who must approve the story before it can succeed. A reputable agent—and surely no writer wants any other kind—is the first to admit that he or she cannot sell a story that the writer himself cannot sell. Reputable agents work on a straight commission basis, receiving a fee only when they make a sale; so few of them will spend time and effort reading and marketing the work of a writer who has not yet sold anything at all. Agents simply can't afford to work with children's magazine materials, and more children's books are bought directly from the author than through an agent. When you reach the point where your income from writing is $10,000 a year or more, and you are confronted with book contracts that mention foreign sales, movie and television rights, et cetera—then you may wish to ask for an agent's help. But until then you are better off without one.

"How soon can I expect to sell?" Naturally you want

to know, and no question is more difficult to answer because the answer depends entirely on you. Your aptitude, motivation, willingness and ability to dig in and *work,* your background of education and experience, the time you can give— all these variables and many others make it impossible to say when, or even whether, you will sell.

In adult writing, experienced teachers generally agree that about four years of more or less constant effort constitutes a realistic apprenticeship. With similar background, interest, ability, and dedication, the aspiring writer for young people can expect to cut that time to perhaps one-fourth. Some of my students have sold their first story within the semester that they began their study. And some of those who seemed at the beginning to be the least likely successes were the first to sell.

No one can say when you will sell, but if you write publishable material you will sell a large part of it eventually—if you persevere in submitting it. Long experience and many case studies demonstrate this beyond any shadow of a doubt.

POINTS TO REMEMBER

1. Writing for young readers is a noble profession, worthy of a writer's finest effort.

2. There is a good market for well-prepared stories, articles, and books of professional quality.

3. As with any other profession, one must be prepared to learn the techniques and master the skills before he is ready to offer written material for acceptance and payment.

QUESTIONS AND EXERCISES

1. An important part of your preparation to write for children is reading *current* children's literature and getting acquainted with children's

librarians and anyone else you can find who is knowledgeable about children's literature. Visit your local library and browse through the children's section. Look for familiar names among the authors. Try to get some idea of what kinds of books each writes. Give special attention to the *new* children's books by new authors—those published within the last three years.

2. List the qualities, traits, interests, background, and experiences you have that you think will help you write for children and teenagers. Include present and possible contacts with young people of various ages.

3. Write out a statement of why *you* want to write for young readers. Give it the time and thought it deserves, and be as honest with yourself as you can.

Then save your statement in your notebook, where you can refer to it when you feel uncertain, aimless, or discouraged—or when you've just made a sale and are tempted to feel that you have "arrived."

2

For What Audience
Will You Write?

A Thanksgiving Day cartoon pictured a happy family in an automobile passing over a fine modern bridge in a rural, forested area. Their obvious destination, in the distance, was a complex of high-rise apartment houses. The caption read: "Over the river and through the woods, to Grandmother's house we go."

It is perhaps necessary to explain to the present generation of writers that these were the opening lines of a much-loved children's song in the early twentieth century. The cartoon dramatizes the enormous changes in American living since that time. To the average child reader today, the world that included Grandfather's farm with its horses, calves, and ducks, the swing in the apple orchard, and the attic full of trunks, old pictures, and mysteries is more remote and infinitely less realistic than the world of outer space— or even than the prehistoric world of dinosaurs and giant insects.

Why? Because children are *familiar* with these worlds; television brings them into their living room. In all probability their own grandparents, who live in a condominium, talk more about communications satellites, hydroponic gardening, and the possibilities of life on other planets than they do about the old family home.

"Futurity" is more important, more relevant than "history," some educators are saying; there is little precedent

13

in the past for what our children will face in the future. The six-year-old entering first grade now will be only in his thirties during the first decade of the twenty-first century. Probably we, as writers, cannot even envision the possibilities and probabilities the new century may hold, but we *can* help children to develop a healthy attitude that looks forward rather than back, that looks at the world and withholds judgment until the facts are examined.

Don't let all this scare you. Just be alert to it, and remember that you are writing for children *today,* not for the children you knew when *you* were a child. Much, of course, remains the same—the small child's interest in immediate surroundings, joyous anticipation of special holidays, the longing for a pet, a bicycle, or a best friend; the need to prove oneself, to choose and prepare for a career; the basic problems of growing up that we all encountered in our own experience. But these must be translated into today's vernacular and patterns of living if they are to reach today's young people.

Americans love to organize, to establish standards and put things in pigeonholes, and editors are no exception. Somewhat arbitrarily they have divided young people into three age groups: "children" 3 to 8, "juniors" 8 to 12, and teens or "young adults" in the early and middle teens. You will find much blending and overlapping of these groups, with books listed "for readers 10–14," for example, or "for children 2–4." Some editors use school-grade levels as their standard, and some look for material based on a dual standard, such as books for "reluctant" readers with, say, subject matter to interest seventh to ninth graders, but written at a third- or fourth-grade reading level.

We all know that children grow in their reading skills and preferences the same way they grow in other respects, with sudden leaps to higher levels followed by flat plateaus, sometimes with rapid strides toward maturity, sometimes back-sliding or taking off on some tangent that makes us despair of their ever developing any literary "taste." The twelve-year-old comes home from the library with something he loved as a nine-year-old and wants to read again, an adventure story about a boy his own age, a book from the reading list at school, and perhaps a book about computers that's far beyond his grasp, but he's "interested in computers." He asserts that he's "too old" to go on subscribing to the children's magazine he's loved, but spends half of a sunny afternoon when he should be outside playing or mowing the lawn poring over dog-eared back issues. It's impossible to cut him out neatly with a cookie cutter and lay him on a tray of twelve-year-olds. In general, however, the writer will find the three accepted age groups serve as reliable guidelines, helping him to plan stories, articles, and plays that meet editorial requirements.

Very young children have small vocabularies and short interest spans; stories for this age group must be short—rarely over 1000 words—and must be told in short sentences and simple, familiar words.

Children 8 to 12 have usually become very conscious of themselves as boys or girls. During the past decade some editors have made significant efforts to publish "nonsexist" stories and books that show girls in active and interesting roles that used to be thought of as strictly boy activities. Some show boys enjoying traditional girl activities, such as cooking and other domestic roles.

But even today editors know that although girls in this age group may avidly read "boy stories," most boys reject stories that have a girl as the main character. So most stories and books for this age group continue to be for and about boys—often with a sister who plays a more interesting and important role than she would have a few years ago. And a growing but relatively small percentage of books and stories are specifically for girls.

For the same reasons of self-identification, the main character is likely to be twelve years old. Younger children will read stories about children slightly older than they are, but a twelve-year-old scorns a book about a child of eleven. Subjects range from family living and school situations to adventure in out-of-the-way places, and include stories that show life in foreign cultures and lands, experiences with pets, insights into various occupations and industries—all the many things that alert, searching young minds are interested in.

Magazines for young teenagers tend to divide the sexes even further, with more magazines for girls than boys. A few are planned to appeal to both. Many of the teenage magazines are "commercial"; they not only carry advertising but, like adult popular magazines, depend on it for their existence. This fact influences the "personality" of the magazine as well as the contents. Because of its larger budget, such a magazine often contains beautiful graphic art and photographs, sometimes in color; stories and articles may be coordinated with the advertising, with one issue featuring fashion and makeup, another sports and physical fitness. Most teenage magazines resemble adult publications in format and content more than they do children's magazines.

Story subjects for teenagers are different from those that appeal strongly to children. Teenagers are likely to be more introspective than they were as children; there is a good deal of self-searching, and of searching the innermost thoughts of others to assure themselves that their own thoughts and feelings are "normal." They think about their own uniqueness and identity. A psychologist at a large university says that of the 4,000 freshmen who come to him for counsel each year, three-quarters of them are asking essentially, "Who am I? Where am I going? How do I get there?"

Unquestionably there are thousands more who never consult anybody but who are looking for answers to these same questions, consciously or unconsciously, in everything they see, experience, and read. So we find stories for teenagers often more subjective, more "mental," than stories for younger readers. Teenage readers readily identify with a first-person main character, enjoying the intimacy of knowing this character's most private thoughts. So we find more first-person stories for teenagers than for children, and often some very good "stream of consciousness" that readers this age readily identify with. Many books written for junior high and early high school readers are similar to adult books except that they have teenage characters and deal with teenage situations. Many appeal to both boys and girls; but again, those that attract boy readers almost invariably have a teenage boy as the main and viewpoint character. There are also many books for girls in this age group: mystery and suspense stories, school and social activities, girl sports stories, and light romances. For boys there are outdoor adventure, science fiction, suspense and sports stories—and *no* romance! Career books and stories for girls or boys are popular.

Older teenage readers have graduated to adult books or magazines, frequently in nonfiction as well as fiction, though there are many fine books and magazine articles directed to young adults that even the most critical readers will find rewarding. These include biographies, science books, explorations of occupations and career opportunities, books that help young persons in their search for values, and many others.

Some "culturally deprived" teenage readers can be lured by both fiction and nonfiction written in a style simple enough for them to understand but directed to their interests. This is not said disparagingly. There is a great need for such books, not only for teenagers but for younger children, too. We shall discuss this market more in later chapters.

This has been only the briefest survey of the various age divisions and demands of each; we shall explore them fully as we take up the plotting of various kinds of stories. Writers often feel more at home with one age group than another, but before you settle down to live with just one, you should at least investigate the possibilities of all, just as you should stretch your mental muscles by at least *trying* some fiction and some nonfiction, some short pieces and some serials or book-length scripts, and a play or two before you decide that any one of these is your special dish.

The viewpoint is often expressed that if one could just go ahead and write for children, everything would be fine, but before a writer can ever reach this child audience, he first has to please adult editors, librarians, and teachers. This complaint is only partially justified. It's true that adults are the censors and the first consumers, in that they select the raw material and make the decisions about how the finished product is to be made available to the child. And adults control the purse strings.

But this is just as true of children's toys or clothes. And anyone who has lived with children knows that toys that don't please are not played with and clothes that don't please hang in the closet until they are outgrown. Editors and their staffs exercise absolute power over what they accept and publish. But there is a very wide variety of thought among editors; if one doesn't like a certain manuscript, the next may think it the catch of the decade. And of one thing we may all be certain—*all* editors are eager to find stories and nonfiction that will please their readers, and this goes for teachers and librarians as well; certainly no editor or librarian is looking for stories or books they think their readers *won't* like!

So although you'll want to remember that it's the adults and not the children who buy your product, in general you can feel that these adults are on your side, cheering you on, willing to help, rather than viewing them as hurdles you have to jump to reach your young audience. Concentrate on the ultimate consumers—today's children, living in today's world.

Now, how are you going to find out who publishes what for young people? If you have carried out the suggested Questions and Exercises of Chapter 1, you have already gained some familiarity with children's books; this will grow as you continue your study.

Probably you will find a good selection of children's magazines at your public library, which you may or may not be permitted to check out; some libraries insist that the periodicals be read at the library. Other librarians do not subscribe to children's magazines because they feel that the pages to color, cut out, or work puzzles on are simply a frustration to the child who is told that he must not mark or mar.

Many of the secular magazines are available on the newsstand, though some of the most important, such as *Boys' Life* and *Highlights for Children*, are not. Friends may give or lend you copies of these. And perhaps you can round up some back issues of church school publications through contacts with local churches and Sunday schools. Use your ingenuity to scout the local sources.

At your public library you probably will find at least one book that lists markets for writers. The two best known, most reliable, and most comprehensive, are *Writer's Market,* published annually by *Writer's Digest,* in Cincinnati, Ohio; and *The Writer's Handbook,* also published annually, by *The Writer,* in Boston, Massachusetts. The April issue of *The Writer* each year includes a list of children's and young people's periodicals. *The Dobler World Directory of Youth Periodicals* is published by Citation Press and updated as needed. It contains all foreign children's publications as well as those printed in the United States and Canada. You will not want to invest in all of these immediately, but you should be familiar with them; look them up in your library.

These sources will give you an idea of the editorial needs and requirements of the many children's periodicals. But you should never submit to a periodical that you have not actually held in your hands and studied! Market lists cannot convey the personality of the periodical, the style of writing, the tempo, pacing, and subtle individuality. So use the market list as a guide only, to learn about the existence of publications you may wish to write for and their general needs. Some you will rule out at once, as being too far removed from your own interests or knowledge. Others will fall into a "maybe" category. And you will undoubtedly find several that definitely appeal to you.

Of these, some will be available locally and others will not. For those that are not, write to the editorial address, asking for a back copy or copies and enclosing at least a dollar for postage and handling. If you say you are interested in writing for the publication, it is likely you will also receive a helpful leaflet stating editorial policies and needs and including useful hints and information for writers.

The two large market books mentioned earlier also contain comprehensive lists of book publishers, including, of course, publishers of children's books. And both your public library and local bookstores will be glad to let you look at their publishers' catalogs to see the kinds of books published by the various firms.

The more you can find out about your markets and the children who consume the products of these markets, the better prepared you will be for your study of writing for young readers.

POINTS TO REMEMBER

1. Think and write in terms of the present and future, rather than the past.

2. Young people's literature is divided into three generally recognized age groups: 3–8, 8–12, and teens. These blend and overlap.

3. Don't overlook the possibilities of writing for slow readers or the culturally handicapped.

4. Although your work must be acceptable to adult editors, librarians, and teachers, the ultimate consumers are children; concentrate on them.

5. Become as familiar as possible with the market.

QUESTIONS AND EXERCISES

1. Make a list of ten or more valid problems that young people in various age groups have today. Be as specific as you can.

2. Make a list of at least ten interests that children in various age groups have today. Be as specific as you can.

3. Collect ten to fifteen or more children's and young adults' periodicals, both secular and religious, and for different age groups. The better the selection you collect, the better will be your preparation for the study that follows.

3

Let's Get Started

Writing, like most other skills, requires specific, directed, and dedicated *practice*. It should be a consolation to the beginning writer to know that being away from the typewriter for a few weeks or even a few days leaves even the seasoned writer feeling "rusty." But like most persons starting to learn a new skill, most beginning writers resist the discipline of practice. It would be so much pleasanter just to know everything at once and start right out on a complete story for one of the best-known magazines.

But this isn't the way it's done. High aims are certainly commendable, and every writer should set his sights as high as his aspirations can reach; but still he must be realistic enough to set goals within the realm of possible achievement, and must be prepared to do the necessary practicing and serve the necessary apprenticeship, being content with minor sales from time to time and building up gradually to more significant sales. The person aiming to be a violin virtuoso does not expect after only a few lessons to appear on the concert stage. He knows he will first have to spend many solitary hours practicing sometimes tedious finger exercises before anyone will want to listen to him, let alone pay to hear him play. A writer who sends a story to a magazine, no matter how small and insignificant, in effect is asking to appear on the concert stage, for pay.

So for the time being you are just practicing. This thought will give you a certain amount of freedom—freedom from worry about whether the story should be told this way or that, freedom from concern about whether it is good enough to sell, freedom from worry about failure, and freedom to experiment, to try it this way and that, to try new ways of expressing ideas, new forms, and different styles. How do you know you wouldn't like writing for very young children or for teenagers? How do you know you can't write mystery stories or inspirational articles unless you *try* one?

Here you are, with a nice fresh sheet of paper waiting for your words. You aren't going to run out of words, and all you can spoil is the paper, which is neither expensive nor irreplaceable. Relax and enjoy yourself, like a child slithering his fingers through finger paint, pushing, patting, zigzagging, circling—getting the feel of the medium, learning its characteristics, limitations, and possibilities.

Let's stop here to talk about tools, equipment, and working habits, which are as individual as a thumbprint. You will find a discussion of manuscript preparation in Appendix B. For the present, we are talking just about rough drafts.

Some writers compose at the typewriter; others seem to feel freer writing first in longhand; some even like to tell the story to a tape recorder and type it later from the tape. Since your work must be typed ultimately, and since typing is faster and requires less physical effort than writing longhand, you may well discover that you'll save time and effort by developing the habit of doing your thinking and rough-drafting as well as your final copy on the typewriter. But don't feel you *have* to work this way; many full-time professional writers compose in longhand.

If you type, always double space everything, for this is the way it must appear in final copy, and writing your rough draft the same way gives you a feeling for length and proportion; it also leaves space for corrections and write-ins. Leave inch-and-a-quarter margins at the top and bottom of the page, one-inch margins at the right and left. Use one side of the paper only; you will soon be practicing the "scissoring technique," cutting out lines or paragraphs and rearranging others, and if you have used two sides of the paper, you've set a trap for yourself.

Some writers like plain sheets of inexpensive white or yellow paper for rough drafts; others want lines to write on. Some find they write best very early in the morning, before the family are up and about; others wait until the children are off to school or down for their naps or even tucked in bed at night. Experiment. Try different tools, different equipment, different places in the house to work, different times of day. When you find the combination that's best for you, use it.

Whether you work best in the early morning or late at night, write always at the same time and in the same place. Write something every day, whether you feel like it or not, whether you have a good idea or no idea at all. Writing professionally is not something you pick up now and then when you can find a few spare moments. If you're serious about becoming a writer, you will clear out a place in your life for writing, so that you can work at it consistently and regularly. You will arrange a schedule that you allow nothing of less immediate importance to interrupt. Part-time and occasional writing is like weekend golf or horseback riding—you go around with constantly sore muscles, and you neither achieve proficiency nor gain the pleasure that comes with mastering a skill. But if you establish the habit of regular work, you yourself will soon *see* your progress, and you'll find yourself looking forward eagerly to your work each day.

Now, since the plot or structure is so absolutely basic to a story's success, we shall begin by studying plotting. More stories, novels, and plays—for both adults and children—fail because of weaknesses in plotting than for any other reason. No matter how timely the theme, how novel or suspenseful the situation, how individual the characters, or how charming the writing, unless the *plot* is right, the story is almost inevitably so weakened that it cannot succeed. And conversely, the story that is built on a strong plot can often succeed in spite of weaknesses in other areas.

No sensible person would start to make a dress, build a house, or cook a dinner without a clearly defined plan, made out in advance and usually put down on paper—a paper pattern, a blueprint, or a collection of recipes. Furthermore, a skillful cook who makes something that does not turn out right is able to tell from the taste and appearance exactly what is wrong and knows what changes to make in the recipe or procedure next time for an improved result. But an inexperienced person who makes a cake that fails has little alternative but to throw out the cake and the recipe, and next time try a prepared mix. There is no prepared mix for a story.

In just the same way, some would-be writers go on turning out story after story that will not sell. Occasionally they happen on a happy combination of ingredients that results in a sale; but because they cannot *recognize* the combination, they cannot repeat the success. Or they may learn just one kind of plot, and then they are like the pianist who can play just one laboriously memorized piece.

A writer who learns to plot—and plotting really is not difficult to master—will consistently write stories that sell and will be able to rescue many potentially good stories that have somehow gone astray in their plotting. He will spend far less time in fruitless labor writing stories that could not possibly sell no matter how well they're written.

There are five—and only five—basic plot patterns in stories and books for young readers. All are also used to plot stories for adults. These are not arbitrary plots thought up by editors or writing teachers; the classification results simply from analyses of hundreds of successful stories. Very rarely will you find a published story that does not fit readily into one of these five patterns, and when you do, it is very likely to be weak and lacking in interest and drama.

Let us hasten to point out here that we are not talking about "formulas" for writing stories. Formulas strangle whatever creativity a potential author may have. The plot patterns we shall study are never restrictive, for within any one of them the writer has unlimited freedom, as you will see when you begin to work with them. Plotting and writing a story is much the same as planning and making a dress; the dress must fit the form for which it is planned, but the dressmaker has unlimited choice of material, color, style, design. You will find that these plot patterns are not artificial; they follow the lines of real life, yet help the writer to cast material into literary form. Writing for either children or adults is an art. Life, exactly as it is, is not artistic. Life is the raw material to which in the concentrated time and space covered by a story the writer gives the artistic form, significance, and unity which real life rarely has. So look upon the plot patterns as one of the tools that you are going to learn to use skillfully. The more you use them and the better you learn how to think of your story in terms of its plot, the more clearly you will understand how the patterns help you and free you to do your very best work.

Here, briefly, are the plot patterns we shall work with throughout our study of technique—and then on throughout our writing lives. Do not try to understand them fully from these descriptions for we shall take them up in detail later on.

1. *The Incident Story.* This is the simplest—but not the easiest—of the plot patterns. Almost always it is a brief (less than 1,000 word) story for the very youngest children; occasionally one finds a longer Incident story for older readers. There are two divisions in this kind of story: The *Incident-Excursion,* which takes the main character into fa-

miliar territory and situations; and the *Incident-Adventure,* which takes the main character into unfamiliar territory and situations.

2. *The Story of Purpose Achieved.* In this story, the main character has a well-defined purpose or desire at the very beginning of the story, and he struggles throughout the story to achieve that purpose, sometimes gaining a little, sometimes being thrust back. In the end, he achieves his purpose—or at least brings about the achievement, through his own courage, his own ingenuity, some special ability or capacity, or a combination of these. These three means of achievement make three divisions of this type of story.

3. *The Story of Wish Fulfillment.* In the beginning of this story also, the main character has a strong desire or wish, one that is apparently impossible to fulfill. He *may*—though he seldom does—make one or two efforts to get his wish, but fails and accepts as fact that he cannot have his wish, though he may feel very unhappy about it. Then, as a logical result of what he *is* or because of something he *does,* but not in an effort to get his wish—often some thoughtful or unselfish act—he gets his wish or an equally acceptable or better substitute.

4. *The Story of Misunderstanding, Discovery, and Reversal.* In the beginning of this story, the main character misunderstands something: a motive, a situation, an action, even himself. The misunderstanding continues throughout the beginning and middle of the story, and the main character acts or plans to act on the basis of his misunderstanding. But at the end, the action of the story shows him he is wrong; he discovers his mistake. And as a result he reverses his belief and consequent action.

5. *The Story of Decision.* In this story, the main character—almost always a teenager—is faced at the outset with a moral decision. It looks to him, and the reader, as if making the morally right decision will bring him unpleasant

results, whereas the other choice will bring immediate gain and satisfaction. He is strongly tempted to make this choice, but after battling with himself makes the "right" decision, acts on it, and finds that the moral choice was the better one, and he has grown as a person.

As rapidly as possible, you will want to learn to identify readily the plot patterns of stories you read as well as those you wish to write; this is basic to planning your own stories. And along with this you will want to develop another skill and habit, that of stating the story in one sentence. Before you start to write a story—any story—you should *write down* the whole story in one sentence. Not the story situation, not what the story is about, but the bones, the skeleton, of the whole story. Unless you can do this, either you do not have a story or you have not thought about it and "shaken down" your material sufficiently to know exactly what story you wish to tell. Developing the habit of telling your story in one sentence will help you not to waste valuable time and effort writing a story that cannot sell.

At the beginning of each of the model stories in Appendix A of this book, you will find the story-in-one-sentence. Two principles are involved in doing this correctly: 1) Be sure your sentence is reasonably short, and that it is complex rather than compound; this means it will have only one independent clause, with one or more dependent clauses. One can go on indefinitely stringing together independent clauses, joined with *ands, buts,* and *sos,* and come up with an unwieldy marathon sentence. This only defeats the purpose of the story-in-one-sentence. 2) Try to make the sentence also show the plot pattern. For example, a story of Misunderstanding, Discovery, and Reversal might be stated thus: Misunderstanding Joey's reason for not walking to school with him, Dan plans to let the air out of Joey's bike tires, but discovers Joey had to take his dog to the hospital, so offers to go with Joey after school to get the dog and help him bring the dog and the bicycle home.

At first this practice may seem difficult, but you will soon see how to do it quickly and easily. If you form the habit of stating the story-in-one-sentence this way, for each story you read as well as for those you write, you will find it one of the most helpful exercises in fiction writing that you can possibly do.

One more point before we take up actual practice with plot patterns: By far the greatest demand among both readers and editors is for here-and-now stories—stories about boys and girls living today in typical situations and circumstances, about their interests and common, every-day problems. Later in this book we shall take up other kinds of stories—fantasies, animal stories, legends, historical stories, and so on. But since these are all much more difficult to write *well* than the here-and-now story—in spite of the fact that they often *appear* simple—we shall confine ourselves for the moment to stories of boys and girls in typical present-day American settings, who have interests and problems common to their culture and time. When we have thoroughly studied and practiced the five basic plot patterns by writing at least one here-and-now story of each kind, we shall be ready to think about some of the specialized types. So if you have a story about an Indian boy of long ago, or a witch or a deer or a little cloud, that you are simply bursting to tell, please open the safety valve and deflate a little. Put that story aside for a while, until you have mastered the basic plotting techniques that will prepare you to tell it better.

POINTS TO REMEMBER

1. Accept the discipline of considerable long and lonely practice before you are ready to submit stories for editorial consideration; then

be willing to appear in the lesser markets before you are ready to compete in the top markets.

2. Experiment with tools, equipment, and working habits until you discover the combination that works best for you.

3. The five basic plot patterns are these:
1. Incident
    a. Excursion
    b. Adventure
2. Purpose Achieved
    a. By courage
    b. By ingenuity
    c. By special capacity
3. Wish Fulfillment
4. Misunderstanding, Discovery, and Reversal
5. Decision

Accept them as helps rather than restrictions, and let them lead you to sure successes.

4. Determine right now to establish the habit of writing out a story-in-one-sentence for each story you read or write.

5. Limit your writing to here-and-now stories until you have fully mastered the basic plot patterns.

QUESTIONS AND EXERCISES

1. Read the stories in Appendix A. Note carefully the plot pattern of each, and study each story-in-one-sentence.

2. Read half a dozen or more stories in the children's magazines you have collected. See whether, from the brief descriptions of the plot patterns given in this chapter, you can identify the plot patterns of some of them. Then try to write out a story-in-one-sentence statement for each of these stories.

3. Think about several possible physical setups for writing in your home; then arrange one of these, complete with the tools and equipment you will need, and agree with yourself on what specified times you will spend working there.

II

Plans That Work

4

The Incident Story

Every good piece of writing, whether it's a single paragraph, a story of 500 or 5,000 words, or a whole book, consists of a *beginning*, a *middle*, and an *ending*. This may seem obvious, but the important point is that each of these sections has its own essential functions. In every well-conceived story, regardless of its plot pattern, the *beginning* section includes the time and setting, introduces the principal characters, and sets up the story situation or problem. No new material is introduced after the end of the beginning zone. No important characters are added, no angles of the situation that existed *before* the main action began are introduced.

The *middle* is simply an expansion and development of the material introduced in the beginning. It consists of dramatic action and complication that build toward the *climax*, which marks the end of the middle zone.

The *ending*, which should be as brief as possible, ties up any loose ends and rounds off the story. You might think of planning a story in terms of making a cake: the beginning is assembling and blending the ingredients; the middle is the action of the ingredients on one another as the cake rises and bakes in the oven; the ending is the frosting.

Let's consider a typical Incident story—the simplest of our basic plot patterns. First we'll state our story-in-one-sentence: Tommy and his puppy go with Tommy's father for a sail on the lake, where they have several interesting adventures, and then return home.

Summarized, the story might go something like this: Tommy, Tommy's father, and the puppy are on the porch of the cottage where they are vacationing. Tommy asks his father to take him and his puppy for a sail on the lake. Tommy's father agrees. This is the end of the beginning zone.

The middle zone would tell of their starting off and develop with their experiences, with the most interesting and dramatic one coming last.

The ending would relate their return home. It would be very brief: "Oh, Mommie," said Tommy. "We went all the way to Hunter's Point! I saw a mamma duck with her three babies, and Skip fell in the water. Dad bought me a b-i-g strawberry ice cream cone. Going for a sail is lots of fun." (Of course, if Mommie is going to be used in the ending, she should be introduced in the beginning.)

In the strictest sense, the Incident story is not a plotted story at all, in that no character pits himself against odds to achieve a goal, or even strives to make things happen. Rather, the main character is simply aware of and interested in what happens and responds to the happenings. An Incident story may relate almost any happy experience of childhood. It may tell about a trip to the store, a pleasant time at home, a visit to a fair, zoo, or beach, and so on. The child may go with another child, if that is suitable, or with an adult. It is difficult, but not impossible, to tell an interesting story if he goes alone and does not meet interesting people or animals as he goes. Try to avoid having your main character alone except for brief intervals, for in this situation you will have no opportunity for dialogue, interchange of ideas, variety, or contrast—all valuable aids in creating and holding interest.

Incident stories are generally quite short—less than 1,000

words—and are mostly for children under eight. Occasionally a good Incident story is 1,200 to 1,500 words or even longer, and for older readers; but these are rare. The Incident story likely to bring you the most immediate success will contain from 300 to 700 words. Remember that the interest span of the very young child is short, his world simple, his interests few.

In the first type of Incident story, the Incident-Excursion, the main character—a child, of course—goes into an environment more or less familiar to him and has several interesting experiences, usually of the same general nature. The most interesting and exciting is last. Then the child usually returns to where he started, though not always, and briefly recounts the pleasures of his experiences.

For very small children, a sequence of events of interest to the child, rising to the final and most exciting of all, is enough. The child need do no more than go from his house to the garden, where he may see a caterpillar in action, a butterfly hovering over a flower, a bird building a nest—all exciting experiences to a small child. Or he may go down the village street, buy a box of crayons, deliver a note from his mother to the grocer, help his neighbor carry her groceries to her car, then return home. The writer must remember to make each incident one that the child will find interesting, and that is within his power to undertake and accomplish.

The Incident-Adventure story follows the same line, with this difference: the child goes into an *unfamiliar* environment. Remember that the word "adventure" here means adventure *from the very young child's point of view*. The dictionary defines an adventure as "a daring enterprise; an exciting experience." Think what would be a daring adventure, or an exciting experience to a child of six, and you will have good material for an Incident-Adventure story. This story pattern provides a good opportunity for introductions to "firsts"—first visit to a bank, a humane society, or a dentist; first talk with a policeman or fireman; first ride on a ferris wheel or burro; first walk on the beach, in the snow, at night, and so on.

You must not, of course, take the child into real danger or show him in a truly frightening experience. He may feel some fear, which he almost immediately discovers to be unfounded. For example, on his first visit to a farm (an unfamiliar environment) he may fear that a rooster is going to attack him but finds that the rooster only wants the corn he holds in his hand.

Both types of Incident story *must* have an interesting sequence of events that build to a climax, and both *must* have unity. Getting and holding interest without a main character who has a strong motivation to achieve a certain goal presents some difficulties, but these can be overcome if you remember to:

1. Use a number of short incidents, each interesting in itself, and each closely related to one unifying thread.

2. Keep the action fast, the tempo swift. Velocity of events is most important in holding the child's interest. Keep the story progressing.

3. Choose action and experiences in which the child will have an immediate and intrinsic interest.

4. If your material permits, use animals or toys, always sure to hold a child's interest. Do not confuse your own interest with that of a child!

There are several ways to achieve the all-important unity. One is to have the main character return to the point from which he set out and briefly recount his experiences, as suggested in the story of Tommy and his puppy. Or he may arrive at the destination for which he set out and there recount his experiences. For example, his mother might permit him to go down the street and around the corner to visit his aunt, a trip he has never taken alone. So the going itself is an adventure. On the way he pats a neighbor's cat, circles out of reach of a large dog tied to a tree, and meets the mailman, who lets him carry a magazine addressed to his aunt. When he arrives, he tells her briefly about these happenings.

Supplying one or several ingredients common to each of the experiences in the story also helps the story to cohere into a unified whole. In one ingenious story, for example, a small boy shows members of his family how familiar objects look through his new magnifying glass. The fact that everyone in the story, including the main character, is cross because the weather is hot helps give unity to the story. Each member of the family receives help in his task by looking through the magnifying glass, and stops being cross. The main character has no consistent *purpose* in what he does; the story simply unfolds, incident by incident, to the episode where he helps his mother, which is the climax.

Another important technique that helps to give a story unity and also serves to add interest is the use of sound, repetition, rhythm, and rhyme. In the classic children's story "The Three Little Pigs," for example, we have, in each episode, the Wolf calling out, "Little Pig, Little Pig, let me come in," and the pig in each case replying, "No, No, not by the hair on my chinny chin chin." Then the Wolf says, "Then I'll huff, and I'll puff, and I'll blow your house in." This little dialogue repeated each time the Wolf comes to a pig's house delights the child; and by the time the Wolf has huffed and puffed, blown two houses in, and consumed two pigs, the suspense is *tremendous* when he makes the threat at the door of the third pig! And not just for one reading—the suspense actually grows with repeated readings.

Children from about 4 to 8 love all kinds of sounds. They not only enjoy hearing them, they want to imitate them. Writers should be alert to this love for sound, repetition, rhythm, and rhyme. Editors buy many stories that feature them, and such stories are lots of fun to write.

One brief example will perhaps get you thinking about the possibilities. This story was about a little girl who listened to all the household machines. The refrigerator said, "Shi-r-r, whi-r-r-r"; the electric mixer said, "Zzzzz-zig, Zzzzz-zig"; the vacuum cleaner started with, "Zzz-whir, Zzz-whir," and when it was shut off it said, "Ouwh, oough." Then the refrigerator got sick and said, "Thrump, thrump, thrump." There was a little story running through the account, of course, and some of the sounds were repeated several times. The idea for this story was good because most children have many if not all of these machines in their own homes and so can recognize the sounds by the way they are spelled.

The Incident story is one that enables the writer to make use of material that does not fit any other plot pattern and that can be made interesting in no other way. It is well suited to the presentation of information. Editors are always on the lookout for well-written stories that help the child to become aware of and understand the complex world in which he lives. Even the simplest bit of authentic information can serve as the basis for these stories.

One such story was written around the fact that turtles eat in the water. A small boy visits a friend who has two "coin" turtles in a terrarium. His friend gives him some pellets and asks him to feed the turtles while he himself attends to other chores. The boy holds one of the pellets in front of the turtle, and the turtle goes into its shell. Disappointed, the boy tells his friend that the turtles aren't hungry. The friend tells him he must drop the pellets into the water. When he does this, one of the turtles slips off the rock into the water, and swimming up under one of the pellets, pulls it under the water and eats it. Delighted, the boy returns to his friend and tells him of his success.

As you can see, the Incident story can be given considerably more depth and substance—more in the way of permanent value—if in addition to its entertainment value it supplies some kind of new information or helps the child to arrive at a more mature concept of life, such as a greater respect for his own or other people's possessions, or the realization that a cheerful disposition is more acceptable than a cry-baby disposition. This added depth increases salability.

The Incident story pattern often lends itself well to writing an adventure story, in that an adventure is usually not "planned" but simply develops as the main character follows its thread wherever it may lead. A memorable Incident-Adventure story for older readers related a teenage girl's brief visit with a gentle young man from outer space, on the Stanford University campus. But the writer should remember that the other plot patterns are all intrinsically stronger than the Incident pattern, and should cast a story in one of the other patterns if at all possible. If he decides that the Incident pattern is best, he can overcome its inherent weakness to a degree by doing all he can to keep the tempo fast and the action exciting; the older the child for whom the story is written, the faster and more exciting the action must be.

The main character in an Incident story is almost always a child under 8 years old. Occasionally you will find *two* main characters instead of one in this or other types of stories; in these instances the two characters are always of equal importance, with identical wishes, purposes, or problems, so that in effect they are really just one character. It is much easier to establish reader identity when you have just one main character, and unless there is some truly vital reason for having two, you will have a much stronger story with just one.

You will also find Incident stories, of course, in which the main character is an animal, a "make-believe" character, or an inanimate object. But since we are limiting ourselves for the present to here-and-now stories about children, we shall withhold discussion of these characters until later.

The qualities editors want in stories for young children are pretty much the same for all magazines and book publishers. You are on the safe side if you use no slang at all for this age group, though a few editors will allow an occasional "gee whiz" or other mild expletive. Words must be simple, sentences short. No baby talk by either adults or children. Don't let your characters speak incorrect English, and don't use incorrect English in the narrative portions of your story in an effort to create atmosphere. Some writers think they cannot write "naturally" unless they use the incorrect English sometimes typical of the speech of young children, but this is a mistaken idea, as a little research of published stories for this age group will show.

Keep your story events chronological and any time lapses between events as short as possible. For very small children, the story should take place within an hour or two, less if possible. There are exceptions, but make this a general rule. As children grow older, their interest span lengthens. But always check to make sure that the time span of your story, regardless of the age for which you are writing, is as short as your story material will permit. This practice will help to give your story unity and coherence, to speed its tempo, and therefore to increase its interest.

Two devices that are always important in writing for young children, no matter which plot pattern you are using, are appropriate to mention here because they greatly enhance the Incident story. First is the use of as much specific, concrete detail and as much sensory appeal as possible. Instead of "some cookies," say "three round sugar cookies on a blue plate." Paint word pictures that help the child to visualize. And then don't stop with telling how things look; help the child to hear sounds, smell odors, feel texture, temperature, wetness or dryness; help him taste the fresh-ness, sweetness, or "differentness" of the foods the child character in the story eats. Even a baby, when he first en-counters something new, wants to experience it in every possible way; he not only looks at it, but shakes it to hear it rattle, feels it, puts it to his face to smell and taste it. As writers, we want to keep this awareness and searching alive.

And second, while you're developing your own conscious-ness of sensory details, become conscious also of the many "magic words" that waken an immediate response in child readers—words such as party, surprise, mystery, prize, pres-ent, circus, journey, Christmas, birthday, and other good-time holidays, ice cream, cookies, peanuts, and other good things to eat. . . . With these for starters, you can keep building your own list. Refer to it occasionally, and see whether you are always making the best use of words.

Starting off right gives you a big advantage. We have covered many ideas in this chapter, and of course you can't possibly keep them all in mind while you are writing your first Incident story. Don't try to. Just go ahead and write, while the creative impulse is strong, without giving thought to technique as such. Then when you've finished the first draft of your story, go back over this chapter and see how well you've done and what you can do to improve your first draft.

POINTS TO REMEMBER

1. Every good piece of writing consists of a beginning, a middle, and an ending. Learn the functions of each part and plan your own writing accordingly.

2. The most marketable Incident story is 300 to 700 words long, written for children under 8 with a child under 8 as the main character.

3. Whether the story is Incident-Excursion or Incident-Adventure, it must have unity and strong, rising interest that builds to a climax.

4. Interest depends on building a number of short, interesting incidents around one unifying thread, keeping action fast as it builds to the most interesting incident of all, and using animals and toys wherever possible to add to the interest.

5. Unity is achieved by supplying one or more ingredients common to all incidents, and by having the main character either return to the place from which he set out or arrive at the destination for which he set out, and there briefly relate his experiences.

6. Sound, repetition, rhythm, and rhyme can add greatly to the interest, unity, and effectiveness of the story.

7. The Incident story pattern provides a good vehicle for supplying information or character-maturing ideas; including such information or ideas adds significance and substance to any Incident story and makes it more salable.

8. The Incident story pattern can be used for some adventure stories for older readers, though any of the other plot patterns is generally preferable.

9. Use simple words, short sentences, and correct English. Keep the time span covered by the story as short as possible, preferably under two hours.

10. Increase the charm and salability of your story by using specific, concrete details, appeal to all five senses, and "magic words."

QUESTIONS AND EXERCISES

1. In the children's publications you have collected, try to find three or more Incident stories. Identify them as Incident-Excursion or Incident-Adventure. State each as a story-in-one-sentence, and identify the beginning, middle, and ending of each.

2. How long is each of these stories? Who is the main character? How old is he or she, and if the age is revealed, how is it revealed?

3. What do you think was the special appeal in each of these stories that caused an editor to select it in preference to other stories received at the same time?

4. Does any of these stories make use of sound, repetition, rhythm, or rhyme? If not, keep looking to find one that does. Analyze the effectiveness of these devices.

5. Do some of these stories convey information or show some character growth on the part of the main character? Analyze how this was achieved.

6. Study the words in these stories. Underline with different colored pens or pencils the words that add to sensory appeal, those that help to paint word pictures, and "magic words."

7. Plan an Incident-Excursion story for children under 6 that includes some bit of new information for the main character, and therefore, hopefully, for the child hearing the story read. Write the story-in-one-sentence. Then write the story in 300 to 700 words.

8. Plan an Incident-Adventure story for children 6 to 8, making the action as exciting and suspenseful as you can. State the story-in-one-sentence. Then write the story in not more than 1,000 words.

NOTE: Of course you are eager to try your wings, to send your stories out. But restrain yourself. Remember, so far you are just practicing. So file these stories away for the present, and go on to the next chapter.

5

The Story of Purpose Achieved

By now you have gained some appreciation for the necessity of planning your story before you write. This necessity becomes much more apparent in working with the remaining basic plot patterns. Your story is not going to create a unified and pleasing effect by accident. Never write a story without first thinking through the plan for it, and then, having written it, wonder which plot pattern it follows.

The story of Purpose Achieved is probably more difficult for most writers to write *well* than any other type of story. Yet when it *is* done well, it is in many ways the strongest and most interesting of all, largely because we all enjoy seeing someone we like succeed, in spite of tremendous difficulties, in solving a problem satisfactorily. This story pattern immediately involves the reader's attention and holds his interest with tension, conflict, and suspense.

The short story has been aptly defined as "an account of a character with a problem and what he does about it." Let's modify this to say "A short story is an account of a character with a problem *or purpose* and what he does about it," and we'll have a very adequate description of the story of Purpose Achieved.

The first requirement, by our definition, is for a main character—just *one*—with a clearly defined problem or purpose. (Often, of course, these are in essence the same, for his purpose is to solve his problem.) He will immediately begin to do something toward solving the problem, and throughout the story will struggle against equally well-defined odds to achieve his purpose, sometimes making headway, sometimes being thrust back by the opposition, up to the point of crisis and climax. Then in the end he will achieve his purpose, or at least bring about the achievement *through his own purposive action,* thus fulfilling the second part of our definition.

Let's make up an example. We'll title it "A Game of Wits." First we'll state the story-in-one-sentence: When Fred Abbott returns to the deserted playground to find his jacket and discovers a much bigger boy whom he recognizes as the neighborhood "tough" wearing it, he formulates a plan that will require the boy to take off the jacket, thus making it possible for Fred to reclaim it.

In summarizing this and the remaining types of stories, it's good to form the habit of writing the synopses in terms of *situation, problem,* and *solution. Any* short story, play, or novel can be summarized in 250 words at most, and writing out such a summary will help you to see exactly what story you wish to tell; if you cannot summarize your story in 250 words after you've had a little practice, you have not "shaken down" your story material enough so that you yourself know what you want to do with it. Stop right there, and do some better planning before you go on.

The summary or synopsis of "A Game of Wits" shapes up like this:

Situation: Twelve-year-old Fred likes his new windbreaker. So when he comes home at noon from his tennis lesson without it—the third jacket he's lost this year—and his mother tells him to go back for it and not to come home without it, he hurries back to the now deserted playground. The jacket has his nametape sewed in it. Fred looks, but cannot find it. Then he sees a big boy he recognizes as the neighborhood "tough guy" wearing it.

Problem: How can Fred recover the jacket and regain his mother's confidence?

Solution: Fred talks with the boy, getting his name and address, hoping if he can't get him to return the jacket, his mother might be willing to go to the boy's house. Then he reasons that if he can get the boy to take the jacket off, he'll have a better chance of recovering it. He challenges the boy to play tetherball, knowing he can't play in the tight-fitting jacket. The boy agrees and sheds the jacket, dropping it on the ground. They play. Fred maneuvers the boy around the pole so that he is nearer the jacket than the boy is. He wins the game and quickly stoops and picks up the jacket. He asks, "What did you say your name is?" The boy replies, "Bud Jenkens." Fred says, "Then how come it says '*Fred Abbott*' in this jacket?" The boy is speechless as Fred puts on the jacket, trembling but happy, and rides home, where mother welcomes him with a special lunch.

Note that the *problem* is distilled into just *one sentence, stated as a question.* This is very important, for it crystallizes the main character's purpose exactly; your whole story turns on this axis; once this question is answered, the story is *over* and must end very quickly, taking time only to tuck in any loose ends. The *solution*, then, is the answer to the question stated in the *problem*.

Now, why is it difficult to plan and write such a story well? Because the plot is very demanding. It cannot be contrived, but must evolve naturally and reasonably from the situation and the characters. The action that solves the problem must be dramatic and believable, and it must be within the possible achievement of the main character. It must also be achieved by one of three means, or a combination of these:

1. *Courage.* Everyone likes a character who overcomes his fear and accomplishes his purpose by means of courage. Stories for quite small children rarely use this means, but even a preschool child may be faced with a situation that requires courage to meet successfully. For example, it may

take courage for him to admit that he told an untruth, or to go into a strange place or talk to a strange person.

But many of these stories are stories of derring-do. A boy rescues his puppy from drowning in the stream. A girl saves children stranded in the snow in a school bus from freezing to death by keeping them playing active games and by conquering her own fear. The courage displayed can be, of course, either physical or moral, or both.

2. *Ingenuity.* Equally admirable in a hero or heroine is the ability to think of a clever plan to achieve a purpose, and this is the means most often used in Purpose Achieved stories—though it may also require courage to carry out the plan. Readers take pleasure in "being on the inside" with the main character and following the unfolding of the plan. When using this means, the writer must be sure that the plan never takes the form of trickery or lying; readers do *not* like that. The plan must be really clever and succeed because of what the main character does. Real-life happenings often provide the raw material for fresh and original stories of this kind. "A Game of Wits" came from a real-life happening.

3. *Special Capacity.* Sometimes a story hero or heroine emerges victorious because he or she has some ability or physical characteristic that no one else who is present has. Sometimes this takes the form of something the individual had, up to now, considered a handicap. The child who is always "too little" to participate in most group activities is suddenly exactly the right one to climb through a window and unlock the front door. Or the crippled child saves the day by using her crutch to reach down from a boat and give an exhausted swimmer something to hang onto until help arrives.

A special capacity or ability may be either natural or acquired. Examples of the former are an especially keen sense of hearing, being a member of a particular race, or unusual physical strength. Acquired capacities include ability to speak a foreign language, sail a boat, draw pictures, swim well, knit, perform mathematical calculations, and so on. Or the hero may simply have a bit of information not commonly known.

All three means, of course, may be combined in a single story. The story of Purpose Achieved has other special requirements. The problem must be *valid,* not a "tempest in a teapot" kind of problem that could be solved easily if the characters involved would just sit down and talk it over on page 2. It must be a realistic and integral part of the main character's total experience, a natural and logical outgrowth of his situation and way of life. It must never be contrived.

When the author is sure the problem is valid, he must see that the solution, too, is valid, that it grows from the situation and the character and is never simply imposed on the main character to fulfill the necessities of the plot. The author should never simply pull a second problem out of thin air at the crucial point to provide an opportunity for the main character to prove his worth. Let's suppose, for example, that the main character is an inner city teenager who has recently moved to the suburbs and his purpose is to win the acceptance of his peers. He has been invited to a picnic in the mountains, but everything goes wrong. He's inept at finding suitable firewood for the cooking fire, doesn't know the songs the others sing, and falls into the stream trying to cross on a log that the others negotiate easily. He is miserable. But as they hike down the canyon road, they find a stalled car which turns out to be that of the family of the girl the group's leader is interested in. Our hero, who has worked in a garage in the city, quickly finds the trouble, and he and the group leader repair the damage so the grateful family can proceed. The leader now admires our hero, and so all accept him.

The plot is contrived. In the previous chapter we said that plotting a story is like making a cake: *all* ingredients must be assembled and blended in the *beginning*. You can't put the baking powder into the cake after the cake is in the oven. If the hero is to prove himself through his knowledge of automobile engines, let's have the boys *drive* to the picnic instead of hike. Then let's plant in the beginning of the story that the hero hears a sound in the engine that makes him suspicious that something is wrong. He warns the driver, but the driver and the others laugh, saying everything is all right. After the picnic, when they are ready to go home and a storm is closing in, it's their own car that is stalled—on a lonely side road. *Then* his solving of the problem through his knowledge of automobile engines will be a natural outgrowth of the total situation.

One other caution about plotting this type of story: Be sure it does not just slide into its ending. The main character must keep *struggling* to achieve his purpose, right up to very near the end. If the main character thinks of a clever way to achieve his purpose and then proceeds to carry it out just as planned, the story will lack interest and suspense.

The secret of building suspense is, right from the beginning of the story, to build toward not just one, but two possible endings. Show clearly the desired ending, and also the "alternate ending," or what will happen if the desired ending fails to take place. Then throughout the story, keep the reader hoping strongly that the actual ending, the desired ending, will come about, but fearing equally or more that the alternate ending is surely going to happen, that the main character can't solve the problem or achieve his purpose. The likelihood that the alternate ending will happen should grow stronger as the story reaches its *crisis,* which is where the story stands in the final balance, immediately before the climax. This is often called the Black Moment.

The crisis can always be stated as a double-headed question, naming the two possible endings: Will Fred be able to prove his ownership of the jacket and reclaim it, or will the bigger boy take it away from him?

The *climax,* then, is always the answer to the crisis question: Fred picks up the jacket, challenges the bigger boy with the nametape in the jacket, and makes good his own claim.

It will help you to plot successful Purpose Achieved stories if you ask yourself—and write out answers to—these questions before you start to write the story:

1. What does my main character want?
2. What prevents him from getting it?
3. What does he *immediately* do about this?
4. What happens because of what he does?
5. What Black Moment does all this lead to? (This is the crisis.)
6. What, finally, does he do to achieve his purpose? (This is the climax.)

Let's try one:

What does my main character want? Kelly wants recognition and friendship from her fourth-grade classmates at her new school. A bright, intelligent extrovert, she's used to acceptance and participation.

What prevents her from getting what she wants? Besides being new at school in the middle of the year, she's going through an awkward stage that she knows makes her unattractive. She's tall, skinny, has big teeth, wears glasses. The others tend to snub and ignore her.

What does she immediately do about this? She tries out for a good part in the school pageant, joins a small clique at lunch as if she belongs, and approaches Lynn Davis, who seems to be one of the class leaders and who is wearing a Scout uniform, about joining her Scout troop.

What happens because of what she does? At recess, led by Lynn, Kelly's classmates shout a familiar childhood chant: Kelly bumbelly, te-helligo felly; tee-legged, tie-legged, bow-legged Kelly. Aware of the ugly, taunting tone, their teacher suddenly appears on the scene.

What Black Moment does all this lead to? Kelly knows that if Lynn and the others get in trouble because of her, they'll like her even less.

What does she do, finally, to achieve her purpose? Determined to win acceptance, Kelly laughs at the rhyme and joins the others in shouting it, but happily. She even goes on with a second silly verse that the others have never heard; they become quiet, to listen. The teacher, seeing that he's not needed, walks away. When Kelly finishes, the others laugh and cheer, begging her to teach them the second verse. She does so, this time using Lynn's name. Lynn laughs, and asks Kelly to join her troop.

Always, the main character *must* succeed by his own efforts; otherwise the story is weak. Another character may help, or do something that the main character cannot do; a child might enlist the help of an adult to do or help with something he himself can't do alone, for example. But the suggestion or idea must come from the main character. Never let adults take over the spotlight or center of interest in any story for young people; keep adults in the background as much as possible.

It helps to think of your story as a tennis game, with the main character as one player and the opposition as the other. It's always the main character's serve. In the beginning of the story he initiates the action by doing something toward achieving his purpose, winning the game. This action brings a *reaction,* or return, from the opposition, which in turn demands the main character do something more. *Always* it is the main character who initiates the action, who forces the issue; everything the opposition does is *reaction* to what the main character does. If you remember this, you will not fall into the error of letting someone else in the story—or some "accident," either fortunate or unfortunate—take over the initiative, with the main character then reacting or becoming a mere observer instead of initiating all action.

It takes real ingenuity to meet all the requirements of the Purpose Achieved story realistically and come up with a story that is interesting and convincing and that does not seem contrived. In the planning, you must be alert to see that you don't paint yourself into a corner by getting your main character involved in an intriguing and exciting problem—and then not be able to find any way out for him, any solution to the problem. When this happens, your story will stop right there; or not realizing what the trouble is, you may settle for some poor, weak, contrived ending that invalidates the whole story.

You can avoid this possibility by thinking during the planning stage in terms of a character with a purpose, rather than a character with a problem. If you know his purpose, and know that in the end he is going to achieve his purpose, then you have your ending, and it is not too difficult to think of logical obstacles that keep him from achieving his purpose easily.

At this point you may feel that there are just too many things to keep in mind when planning this type of story. But as you practice, you will become familiar with them all and will learn to manipulate them skillfully. It's much like working a jigsaw puzzle: fitting the pieces together, filling in holes, eliminating everything that doesn't play some vital part in the plot.

You will find the results well worth the effort, for there is no limit to what you can do with this plot pattern. Most *novels* are built on the Purpose Achieved pattern, largely because it is the strongest of all plot patterns, offering the best possibilities for sustained interest and suspense. Readers of all ages like to read about a main character with whom they can identify, who has a valid problem with which they can also identify and who solves that problem through his own efforts and action.

This plot pattern, once you master it, is really no more difficult than any of the others. When you understand what it is you are trying to do and have a firm basis for knowing when you're doing it right and when you're in trouble, then you are in a position to correct errors and weaknesses and mold the story properly. And because many writers do not understand the principles or will not make the effort really to master the requirements of this most versatile of all plot patterns, you will find a ready market for your work if you do it well.

POINTS TO REMEMBER

1. Always plan your story thoroughly before you start to write.

2. Learn to write synopses in terms of situation, problem, and solution, being sure always to state the problem in the form of a single question.

3. The main character must always achieve his purpose by means of courage, ingenuity, special capacity, or a combination of these.

4. The main character's purpose must be valid, and very important to him. If he doesn't care vitally about the outcome, the reader won't care either.

5. The main character's purpose must be set up in the beginning and must look difficult, if not impossible of achievement. Keep the main character struggling throughout the middle, and do not allow him to succeed until very near the ending; for when the purpose is achieved, the reader is no longer interested in what happens.

6. To insure suspense, build toward both the actual ending and the "alternate ending," making the reader hope for the one but fear that the other will surely happen.

7. Build to a Black Moment, where the reader fears that all is lost, that the main character cannot possibly achieve his purpose.

8. Be sure that the main character always initiates the action, and that he succeeds through his own efforts.

QUESTIONS AND EXERCISES

1. In the children's publications you have collected, try to find three or more stories of Purpose Achieved. State each as a story-in-one-sentence, and note the means by which the main character achieves his purpose.

2. Write a synopsis of one of these stories in terms of situation, problem, and solution.

3. Analyze the plotting of each of these stories. Is the problem or purpose clearly established in the beginning? How far into the story must one read to know what the problem is? Are the obstacles to an easy solution clearly established? How far must one read to find these? Is the alternate ending made plain? What is it? Is there a feeling of real danger that the alternate ending may happen? How is this achieved? Is there a definite Black Moment? What is it? Does the main character achieve his purpose through his own action? How?

4. Select one of these published stories, other than the one you synopsized, and write answers to the six questions on page 50.

5. Plan a Purpose Achieved story of your own, for children 8 to 12. State the story-in-one-sentence, and then write a synopsis, in less than 250 words, in terms of situation, problem, and solution.

6. Write this story in not more than 1,200 words.

7. Same as Exercise 5, but plan this story for readers over 12.

8. Write this story in not more than 1,800 words.

NOTE: You are still practicing. So write these stories as well as you can, but file them away for the present and go on to the next chapter.

6

The Wish Fulfillment Story

Wishing is as old as man, so it is not surprising that one of the most popular and enduring story plans for children of all ages—and for adults, too—is the Wish Fulfillment story.

Like the story of Purpose Achieved, this story begins with a main character who has a strong wish that is very important to him but that seems extremely difficult or impossible of fulfillment. For this reason, some students confuse it with the story of Purpose Achieved. But it is easy to see the distinction, for in the Wish Fulfillment story the main character's wish appears so impossible to him that he almost never makes any effort to make it come true. In some stories he may make one or two brief and ineffectual efforts to achieve his purpose, the results of which only make both him and the reader more convinced that the fulfillment of the wish is impossible. If the main character does make such efforts, he makes them in the beginning of the story, and has given up trying before the story is well under way.

Dramatic and interesting action follows this, apparently having no relation to the fulfillment of the wish. This takes up the middle of the story. But in the ending the main character gets his wish—or more often a more acceptable substitute—as a *logical result of what happened.*

There are two types of Wish Fulfillment story, and it is at the end of the beginning that the variation starts.

1. The main character gets his wish because of what he

is. The story of Cinderella is the classic example. Cinderella wished she could go to the ball, but she had no suitable clothes and no way to get there. All the activity involving the godmother, turning mice into horses and lizards into footmen, is, of course, highly interesting to children. And in the end Cinderella gets her wish and wins the prince not because of any effort she makes to go to the ball, but because she is sweet and forgiving, obedient, and has small feet.

2. More popular—probably because it's more realistic— is the story in which the main character gets his wish because of unselfish or "right" action, done *with no thought of getting the wish by this means.*

Let's plan such a story:

First, as always, our *story-in-one-sentence:* When Tracy's mother inadvertently destroys Tracy's hopes of getting a cherished job as photo retoucher by "volunteering" Tracy's services as a decorator at the same hour as the job interview, Tracy creates such a beautiful and unusual centerpiece for Mother's luncheon that it attracts the attention of the owner of a gift shop who offers Tracy a job as window dresser.

Then the synopsis:

Situation: For weeks Tracy has sought a summer job that will enhance her art talent. Almost despairing, she sees an ad for a photo retoucher. Employer will teach. Report Saturday (tomorrow) morning for interview. Confident that she can qualify, Tracy hurries home, only to find that the woman responsible for decorations for Mother's service club luncheon tomorrow is ill, and Mother has said Tracy will do them. Tracy wails, and Mother is sorry. But both know there's no way out.

Problem (or Wish): How can Tracy fulfill her mother's commitment and still get to the job interview?

Solution (or Fulfillment): Tracy collects materials for a spring theme, holding a thin hope that she may finish in time to get back to the interview, across town. But next morning she finds unexpected delays as she directs two club members who come to help. With no hope of making the interview, she becomes engrossed in creating an exquisite head table centerpiece, with tiny figurines in a dainty garden swing suspended by ropes of forsythia blossoms over the anniversary cake. Alone, she finishes just before guests are due.

At home she thinks of the lost opportunity as she cleans up and puts materials away, but feels good about the decorations. Mother returns, reporting that women were ecstatic about beautiful tables. The phone rings, and Mrs. Beresford, who was at the luncheon, praises Tracy's work and offers her a job doing window and counter displays for her fashionable gift shop. Tracy knows she'll like this work better than photo retouching.

In the story, Tracy outdoes herself not because she hopes it may get her a job—that never crosses her mind. She gives her best because she loves to create beautiful things and wants to help her mother and the other club members.

The great danger in planning a Wish Fulfillment story is making the story too "preachy," too obviously moralistic. Except for a very few religious magazines, no young people's publication will accept a story that shows the moral too obviously. A story must never be used as a mere vehicle to teach a lesson. Writers refer to this practice as "peddling fish," or "bearing a torch." Usually there is a moral in the story, but it must be implicit in the action, where the reader sees it for himself. In this or any other type of story, if the writer isn't sure whether he's made the moral too obtrusive, he should ask himself, Would this be a good story—a story interesting enough to hold the reader's attention—*without* the moral? If he cannot honestly say yes, then he's peddling fish. Always, the moral must be woven into the story so naturally and unobtrusively that the reader who wishes to see it will see it, and one who does not wish to see it will still have a good story to read. The way to avoid moralizing is to *show* what happens instead of *talking about* what happens. The author should let the action speak for itself instead of passing judgment on what happens.

The second danger that threatens the Wish Fulfillment story is having the wish come true in the form of a present or an obvious reward, or by the main character's winning a contest or a prize. These ways are too coincidental; the reader will not accept them. The writer must be cleverer, more creative, more subtle than this. The wish of the main character must come true as a *logical,* but unforeseen, result of what he is or of the "right action" he has performed.

It's human nature to be pleased and happy when someone we like is made happy by getting what he wants and has worked hard to get—as in the story of Purpose Achieved. This satisfaction is just as strong when someone we like gets what he wants because of what he *is,* or because he has done a brave or kind or otherwise admirable act without hope of getting anything in so doing. We feel that such a person "deserves a break." Even though we may feel that this seldom happens in real life, we feel it *should* happen, that goodness should be rewarded. The Wish Fulfillment story appeals to a universal sense of justice, a belief that a good person should be happy, that virtue should be and is compensated—that truly we do reap what we sow, "good measure, pressed down and shaken together, and running over."

Therefore this type of story enables the reader to achieve a strong sense of self-identification with the main character in the story. But remember that the reader's emotion cannot rise higher than that of the main character, and it is by and through emotion of one kind or another that you hold the reader's interest. You must do all you can to create and sustain reader sympathy for the main character by making him as likable as possible, and often by putting him at a disadvantage in the situation; it's human nature to be for the underdog. But avoid letting the main character feel sorry for himself more than momentarily, for self-pity is as reprehensible in a fictional character as it is in real life— and cheerfulness in the face of disappointment or injustice is as commendable.

The wish must always be a *strong* one that the main character cares vitally about; unless the main character cares deeply, the reader will hardly care at all. The wish must also be one the young reader will feel is valid—that is, a wish that he himself might have, for something that would mean great happiness to him. This may be an unselfish wish, for the giving of happiness to someone close and dear is a very strong desire in the lives of most children. Many Wish Fulfillment stories are written around the idea of a child's strong desire to give a present to his mother, teacher, or friend.

Inexperienced writers have a tendency to assign a wish to a child that is really an *adult* wish *for* the child, but which no normal child would ever think of. Editors frequently get stories in which the main character wishes to save money for music lessons or even so that, many years later, he may go to college, and other similar wishes that are highly unlikely to motivate any young child. Think of what the *child* wants, rather than what *you* want for the child. And make it a fairly immediate wish; few children wish fervently *now* for something that is to happen next summer or in an indefinite future.

The Wish Fulfillment plot pattern is one of the most popular and most easily adapted to stories in which an animal or inanimate object is the main character, as you will see when you reach the chapter dealing with these stories. But for the present, as with the other plot patterns, you will do more for your own growth as a writer by limiting your first efforts in writing this type of story to the here-and-now story.

POINTS TO REMEMBER

1. The Wish Fulfillment story, when properly planned and written, satisfies a deep human desire that the good shall be happy.

2. The wish may be fulfilled because of a special character quality in the main character, or as a result of his natural tendency toward just and right action.

3. The wish must not be fulfilled until the end of the story, and it must not be fulfilled because of any action of the main character *directed toward getting the wish* but must be the *natural and logical* outcome of his action.

4. The wish must be a valid and immediate one for the main character.

5. The main character must be likable, and the reader must be made to feel strongly about him and his wish.

QUESTIONS AND EXERCISES

In the young people's publications you have collected, find at least three Wish Fulfillment stories. State each as a story-in-one-sentence, and note whether the main character made some effort or no effort at all to get his wish. Note also whether the main character got his wish as a result of what he is or of what he does.

2. Write a synopsis of one of these stories in terms of situation, problem, and solution.

3. Analyze the plotting of each of these stories. Is the wish clearly established early in the story? Is it valid? What effort, if any, does the main character make to get his wish? Does the reader really feel that there is no chance that the main character may get the wish? Is there any "fish peddling" in the story? Is the fulfilling of the wish a logical outgrowth of what the main character is or does?

4. Analyze the characterization. How has the author created reader sympathy for the main character?

5. Plan a Wish Fulfillment story for children 8 to 12 in which the main character is sure in the beginning that he cannot get his wish. Write the story-in-one-sentence, and then synopsize it in less than 250 words in terms of situation, problem, and solution.

6. Write this story in not more than 1,200 words.

7. Plan a Wish Fulfillment story for readers over 12 in which the main character makes some effort to get the wish but soon gives up. Write the story-in-one-sentence and synopsis as in Exercise 5.

8. Write this story in not more than 1,800 words.

NOTE: These stories, too, are for practice. You are building a good inventory that will be much more valuable to you than you can appreciate at present. So write these stories as well as you can, and then go on to the next chapter.

7

The Story of Misunderstanding, Discovery, and Reversal

One of the most marketable of the plot patterns is the story of Misunderstanding, Discovery, and Reversal. Its universal appeal is easily explained: We all *misunderstand* people, situations, motives, ourselves; we often *discover* our mistake and *reverse* our erroneous thinking and course of action. This simple sequence is the basis of our fourth plot pattern, though the story based on it may be quite complex, especially if written for teenage readers.

Editors like this plot because it offers opportunities to expose and deal in a realistic way with problems that young people meet trying to adjust to the world around them—a world they face without much experience or knowledge. For example, adjusting to a new stepparent is a fairly common problem among young people of all ages today. In a story dealing with this problem, perhaps the main character's mother has recently remarried. The boy, feeling insecure and displaced anyway, misunderstands what he sees as his stepfather's efforts to exploit him by asking him to caddie at the golf club. The story concerns the dramatic events that lead to his discovery that his stepfather simply wants to introduce him to a pleasant and rewarding activity. He then reverses his attitude and behavior toward his stepfather.

There is no limit to the mistaken ideas that young children entertain. Many have groundless fears of new environments or experiences that really present no fearful aspects and may even be quite pleasant: trying new foods or entering into a new game or activity such as talking on the telephone; the dark, thunder, or water; the dentist, barber, or policeman; an unfamiliar but harmless animal or insect; a make-believe character such as a lion in the backyard. They accept erroneous beliefs: that refusing to share some possession is pleasanter than sharing; that being "best friends" with a playmate precludes including a third friend in some happy occasion; that some other child's home, possessions, or way of life is better than their own.

A story for the youngest age group based on the last of these might go something like this:

Story-in-one-sentence: Seeing the casual habits of Crissie's family, Laurel, who feels burdened by duties, rebels, but discovers when Mother lets her chores go too, and Daddy has no time to play, and even Crissie is critical, that a mess is no fun, and so cleans up her room.

Now the synopsis:

Situation: Seven-year-old Laurel enjoys visiting at Crissie's house, where Mother's away at work and nobody cares whether beds are made or toys picked up. Crissie shares a room with her older sister, and like her sister and brother, eats when and what she likes, watches TV whenever she pleases, and goes to bed when she's ready. Laurel's life is scheduled, with definite duties that include making her bed, keeping her clothes and room orderly.

Problem: How can Laurel live the carefree life that Crissie does?

Solution: Laurel rebels. She tells Mother she's tired of work, of picking up clothes and toys. To her surprise, Mother says she need not do these things any more. The first day, Laurel finds her freedom beautiful; at bedtime her pajamas are on the bed where she left them. She drops soiled clothes on the floor and enjoys getting into the unmade bed with her toys strewn about. The next day things go rather well, too. But the third morning Laurel notices that her breakfast juice is in an old cracked mug. Mother says she too is tired of chores and has decided not to wash dishes or clothes or clean the house any more.

That evening Laurel asks Daddy to play checkers, but he explains that the shirt he needs for tomorrow is dirty, since Mother has stopped washing, so he must wash it. Between thinking about these things and her now really rumpled bed, Laurel doesn't fall asleep right away, and the next morning she's nearly late to school because she can't find her sweater.

After school Crissie comes home with Laurel to play. But when she sees Laurel's room, Crissie says, *"Laurel—* what happened to your room!" She says she liked coming here to play because Laurel's room was so pretty, unlike her own, which her sister will never help to clean. Says she's going home, and she does. Laurel has had enough. Eagerly she pitches into cleaning up. In the kitchen she finds sparkling dishes put out and Mother getting a good meal. As Laurel voluntarily sets the table, she says to Mother, "A mess is no fun."

The plot pattern is equally effective for older readers. Misunderstanding, Discovery, and Reversal stories in teen-age publications have dealt with the natural fears that one won't be accepted unless he has a car or other material possession or unless he follows a certain style or behaves in a certain way. Some deal with the popularly held beliefs that a new environment offers no opportunity for interest or happiness, or for pursuit of a cherished goal. Or that another environment—almost *any* other—would be preferable to the present one. One was based on the belief that dishonesty isn't too bad if one doesn't get caught; another on the belief that behavior standards set by parents were unreasonable. The possibilities are endless. You need only pick up any current newspaper or magazine to find a dozen viable ideas for good stories of Misunderstanding, Discovery, and Reversal.

Structurally, the beginning of this type of story introduces the main character, who has accepted an erroneous idea of some kind. It must be a genuine misunderstanding, something he could not be *talked* out of; it must be something about which his mind can be changed only through his own *experiences*. He initiates some kind of action based on this erroneous idea.

The middle, then, consists of the dramatic events that lead to his discovery of his error. It is important that the dramatic events be directly responsible for the discovery; otherwise, the story will lack interest and suspense. A dull, slow way of making the discovery—such as overhearing what someone else says or simply having someone explain matters to him, or even by nothing more than thinking about the situation—will not do. Others—his friends or a parent, for example—may *try* to show him his error, but this only results in his greater conviction that he is right and they are wrong. This conviction should be strongest immediately before the discovery that he is mistaken; this is the Black Moment.

The discovery should come suddenly, and as near the end of the story as possible; the discovery and reversal *are* the ending of the story. The reversal should be a definitive *act* by the main character that shows that he truly has seen his mistake and changed his attitude and thinking.

This final act is extremely important; without it, the story becomes a "come-to-realize" story, in which the main character simply comes to the realization of his error or of some universal and eternal truth; such a story lacks drama, and is almost never salable. The remedy for this weakness is usually quite simple; it is to have the main character *do* something as a result of his realization. The realization, instead of being the climax of the story, should be the crisis: Now that the main character has seen his mistake, will he continue in the path he has been walking, or will he make the needed change in attitude and take the right path? The act, then, becomes the climax, the answer to the crisis question. He changes his thinking and takes this specific action to rectify his mistake and *show* that he has changed. The ideal ending for the Misunderstanding, Discovery, and Reversal story is to have the discovery stated and the reversal shown by action, all in the last paragraph or two. This is not always possible, but skillful writers try to do it and often succeed.

All of us, children and adults alike, come to conclusions, make decisions, form attitudes, act on the basis of our beliefs; we live by what we believe. So it is vitally important that children and young people build right and constructive beliefs, a correct understanding of motives, behavior, themselves, and the world around them. Often a child who has accepted a wrong belief hides it so that no one is aware that he is confused or has a problem. It can be reassuring to such a child to discover through reading a story about a child with a similar problem that he is not alone in his error—and that it can be corrected.

Or he may realize that he is wrong, but seems unable to change. Perhaps he has been criticized and ridiculed for his attitude and actions. A Misunderstanding, Discovery, and Reversal story that deals with a similar problem can help him to think his way out of the situation by identifying with the main character and vicariously living this character's experience so that he too is healed of his wrong belief.

The story must never, however, become a mere vehicle for the message or moral. Always remember that you, the writer, are in the business of creating entertainment. Regardless of the age group or the publication for which you are writing, or the plot pattern you choose, the main purpose of fiction is to entertain; if it fails in this purpose, it fails utterly. You may have other purposes as well, but unless the story is first of all entertaining, you will not achieve any of your other objectives through it. You may wish to inform the reader, instruct him, inspire him with ethical and philosophical ideas. But if you do not entertain him and give him an emotional experience that he likes, all your labor has gone for nothing. This is the alpha and omega of *all* dramatic writing, whether you are writing the simplest Incident story for a preschool child or a best-selling novel for adults.

POINTS TO REMEMBER

1. The Misunderstanding, Discovery, and Reversal story is based on the many common mistaken ideas that readers of all ages have about people, situations, motives, themselves.

2. Structurally it follows the simple pattern of a main character who, on the basis of an erroneous belief, is about to act in some way that cannot bring him lasting satisfaction; his discovery of his error through dramatic events; and the reversal of his attitude and behavior as a result of his discovery.

3. The main purpose of the story, as with any other story, must be to entertain; any moral or message must be so well concealed in a good *story* that the reader who does not wish to see the message will still be entertained.

QUESTIONS AND EXERCISES

1. In the young people's publications you have collected, find at least one Misunderstanding, Discovery, and Reversal story for each age group. State each as a story-in-one-sentence.

2. Write a synopsis of one of these stories in terms of situation, problem, and solution.

3. Make a list of at least ten common erroneous concepts that children and young people are likely to have. Be as specific as you can, and try to include some for each age group.

4. Using one of these ideas, plan a Misunderstanding, Discovery, and Reversal story for any age group you wish. Write the story-in-one-sentence and then synopsize it in less than 250 words in terms of situation, problem, and solution.

5. Write this story, using a word length appropriate for the age group you have chosen—less than 1,000 words for children under 8, 1,200 words at most for readers 8 to 12, 1,800 to 3,000 words for readers over 12.

6. Repeat Exercises 4 and 5 for a different age group.

NOTE: Patience! You have just one more plot pattern to learn about, and by now you should be gaining some excellent discrimination in recognizing the different patterns and applying the principles yourself. Plotting will become easier with practice.

8

The Story of Decision

The story of Decision is particularly appropriate for teen-age readers. These young adults face many new experiences, freedoms, and capacities that sometimes involve difficult and even life-determining choices and decisions. They are consid-ering career options, thinking about whether to go on to higher education or technical school or to get a job, looking into different life-styles, religions, and values. Because read-ers under 13 or 14 have not yet come up against such really momentous decisions and have not yet had enough experi-ence with life to weigh one course of action against another, it is hard to write a satisfying story of Decision for younger readers. But there are a few, sometimes very good ones.

The plot pattern is simple. In the beginning the main character is introduced, his problem clearly established, and the obstacles to an easy solution made plain. The problem is always an immediate need to make a decision between two courses of action, one of them morally right, the other morally wrong; the right course may be apparent, or the main character—and the reader—may have honest doubts, at least temporarily, as to which is right. A better story usually results from the latter situation. Either way, the main character believes that making the morally right choice will bring him trouble, but making the morally wrong choice will bring immediate gain and satisfaction. Reader sympathy for the main character must be strong, so that the reader will care vitally and want him to make the right decision.

The middle of the story usually develops in 3 to 5 dramatic

scenes, in each of which the main character wavers between the two decisions, trying to determine which is right *for him, in this particular circumstance,* leaning more strongly toward the wrong decision. The individualization of the particular set of circumstances is all-important. Suspense depends, as in other stories, on the writer's building toward both the actual ending and the alternate one, the right decision being the actual ending and the wrong decision the alternate ending. Here the writer must carefully plant all of the factors that will make the ending believable and logical. These plants have to do with a wide variety of sources or roots from which the main character's decision springs: his heritage, conditions of his early environment, remembered conversations with and actions of parents or others who have strongly influenced him, what he had heard, observed, and read, his own past experiences, and so forth. The planting must be done naturally and unobtrusively, sometimes with misdirection, so that it does not tip off the reader to the ending; if the planting is not done adroitly, the story is likely to be returned by an editor with the notation "Too predictable."

In the ending something happens that causes the main character to reach the right decision as a logical result of all that has gone before. The story reaches its crisis when the decision can be put off no longer—the main character must reveal his decision by *acting* on the basis of his choice; the climax is his resultant action. In most cases, little if any explanation should follow the revelation of the main character's decision; this is what the reader has been waiting for, and if the planting has been well done, he can usually project in his own thinking the result of the decision. However, the story often ends with a brief, dramatic scene *showing* that the main character does not suffer the penalties he feared might come through choosing the right course, but instead has gained the respect of his comrades and is held in higher esteem than if he had chosen the wrong course.

One of my stories built on this pattern, "Uncle Henry's Nephew," sold to two noncompeting markets the year it was written, and two other magazines later bought reprint rights. The story-in-one-sentence went like this:

Faced with the decision of whether to go along with a plan to steal an examination or refuse, with the probable result of being depledged, incurring his uncle's displeasure, and having to quit school, Phil Marsh longs to talk with his father, but on hearing his father's voice on the phone knows what to do and refuses to participate, thus winning the admiration of his fraternity brothers and establishing himself with them in his own right.

The synopsis for a story of Decision, like all other types except the Incident story, can be stated in terms of situation, problem, and solution. Here's the synopsis of "Uncle Henry's Nephew":

Situation: Phil Marsh, Zeta Gamma pledge at State, is alone in the upstairs dorm, missing dinner with the others, trying to decide where loyalty to his own ideals ends and loyalty to the fraternity begins. In one hour he's to slip through the chemistry professor's office window and take a copy of the final exam. He's the only one small enough to do it.

Phil admits he could use the test himself, but it's mainly for others—specifically star athlete Frank Noland—that the fraternity brothers have planned the theft. Phil has no status in the fraternity. He is there only because his uncle was a member and is now a big supporter—and Uncle Henry is footing Phil's college expenses.

Problem: Should Phil carry out the theft, or should he refuse and risk being depledged, incurring Uncle Henry's displeasure, possibly having to quit school?

Solution: Wishing desperately that he could talk with his

semi-invalid father, to whom he's always been close, Phil has tried unsuccessfully to reach him by phone. Dinner is over; the time for the expedition has nearly arrived. Phil thinks of his friends, how much he wants to go on enjoying campus life. The phone rings; it's Phil's dad, anxious about why Phil called. Phil can't tell him—the fellows are listening. The father asks, "Is everything all right?" And suddenly for Phil it is; just hearing his dad's voice has restored his sense of values. He reassures his father, hangs up, and faces his fraternity brothers, telling them firmly that he's not going to participate in the theft. After a moment of stunned silence, Noland approaches Phil, embraces him warmly, says he doesn't like cheating either, and suggests that they study together for the exam. Phil knows he's now a Zeta Gamma in his own right.

The strongest story of Decision usually involves an intrinsically serious and important choice and resultant act. But it may be based on a relatively unimportant decision and course of action, provided something the reader feels *is* important is at stake. In this case, the writer must show clearly that the decision of the main character is of considerable importance, both actually and emotionally, to some minor character. Interesting and marketable stories have been written on such bases.

For example, we might write a story about a main character who must decide whether or not to lend his new and much-treasured sleeping bag to a less fortunate friend who has no sleeping bag and cannot afford to buy one. The lack will cause the friend to forgo a weekend trip where he would experience for the first time the joy of snow sports. The main character's decision, then, is of considerable importance to the friend. In the end, the main character wins his fight against selfishness and achieves a degree of character growth by lending his sleeping bag. Suspense would depend on making the reader feel great sympathy for the friend and stressing the narrative question: Will the main character decide to lend the sleeping bag?

In addition to the human needs we all have throughout life, the teenager is faced with four specific and immediate needs:

1. To establish himself with his peers—to find and adjust to a social position which he can accept and live with in a heterosexual society.

2. To choose, plan, and prepare for a career—to find a job.

3. To establish his independence from his parents—socially, emotionally, personally, and ultimately, financially.

4. To form his own standard of values.

Stories for young adults are very likely to involve one or another of these needs. The story of Decision provides an excellent pattern.

Stories of Decision for younger readers may be based on such problems as whether or not to keep money or something of value that one finds, whether or not to confess something one has done that is unlikely to be found out but that could bring harm or injury to others, whether or not to participate in shoplifting or vandalism required to be admitted to a club, whether or not to cheat in a game or on an examination, and so on. Even quite young children today are exposed to all sorts of proposals and temptations that were not such a common part of growing up a few years ago. Often they are reluctant to discuss these problems with parents or other adults, and reading a story in which the main character makes a responsible decision with good results can reinforce their own decision and behavior.

The story of Decision is always one of character growth. The clash, therefore, always takes place in the mind of the main character; and although this is the real battleground, the writer must externalize the conflict by translating it into *interesting action,* in good, dramatic scenes. Otherwise the story will deteriorate into a dull "think piece" that draws the editorial comment "Too mental." Suspense depends on making the seeming reward for the wrong decision great—something the reader himself would very much want—and the apparent penalty for making the right decision severe—something the reader would want to avoid at all costs. Above all, the story of Decision must be not only believable but, taking all factors into consideration, inevitable. When such a story is well written, it is readily salable.

POINTS TO REMEMBER

1. In the story of Decision, the main character is faced immediately with deciding between two courses of action: one morally right, which he believes will lead to trouble for him; the other morally wrong, which promises immediate benefits. The body of the story consists of his struggle to decide, based on his own experience and other factors of his past. As a logical result, he makes the right choice, and instead of incurring the expected penalty, wins approbation.

2. To keep the struggle from being too mental or too predictable, it must be translated into interesting, dramatic action. The main character leans more to the wrong decision at the end of each scene.

3. The story usually involves an intrinsically serious and important decision and resultant act, but may be based on a relatively unimportant decision and course of action if something the reader feels is important is at stake for a minor character, and this is dependent on the decision made by the main character.

4. The story of Decision is always one of character growth, and is therefore essentially mental. Suspense depends on the importance of the decision—its rewards and penalties. The decision and outcome must be made to seem inevitable.

QUESTIONS AND EXERCISES

1. In the publications with which you have been working, find at least one story of Decision. For what age reader is it? What decision

must the main character make? Is it intrinsically important, or relatively unimportant? If the latter, what *is* important enough to hold the reader's interest? List the factors that lend strength to each possible decision, and study the ways in which the author has used them. Is there really an "illusion of the alternate ending," so that the reader feels the main character is likely to make the wrong decision? How is the ending dramatized?

2. Assemble as many teenage publications as you can, both general and those published by churches or similar organizations. Compare the contents of these, noting the differences between those that carry advertising and those that do not.

3. Write a story of Decision for teenage readers. State your story-in-one-sentence and write a synopsis of the story. Then write the story. Keep it between 1,800 and 2,400 words.

4. Write a story of Decision for readers 10 to 12. State your story-in-one-sentence first, and keep the length below 1,200 words.

NOTE: You should now have a good inventory of your own stories as a basis for some questions in assignments in the next chapters. Do not be impatient to start marketing; you are going to improve these stories as you acquire new skills, and make them more salable.

III

Skill with the Tools

9

Story Ideas—The Raw Materials

You are now acquainted with all of the basic plot patterns that you will be using, whether your story is five hundred words or book length. Proficiency in recognizing and using them will come with practice and experience.

But of course no one *sets out* to write an "Incident story" or a "story of Purpose Achieved." A writer writes because he has something to say, a story he wishes to tell. He wants to write about a singular bond between a boy and his dog. Or he wants to dramatize the joy to be found in real, subsurface realization of the brotherhood of man. Or maybe he just wants to write something that's so much fun to read for its humor or whimsy that even the "nonreader" will find it irresistible. The plot patterns are not ends in themselves, but part of the writer's equipment; he studies his material, thinks about the story he wants to tell, and then selects the plot pattern that will best serve his need.

You will find stories in both secular and religious publications that were written purely for entertainment. But basically most stories are not merely about whether Sandy finds a suitable present for her father or how Henry leads the team to victory. Beneath this surface and immediate story is something deeper and more permanent. Because of what happens to her in her search for the present, Sandy *grows*. She discovers that the present itself is less important than the thought behind it; or maybe she finds that her father is not the hard-to-know person she had thought, but is warmhearted, even sentimental. Henry, perhaps, discovers that it takes humility as well as courage to be a leader—or that victory is hollow if the game ends with ill feeling from the opponents.

Somehow, in some degree, the main character—and therefore the reader—is wiser, kinder, gentler, braver, more tolerant or thoughtful, *more mature,* at the end of the story than he or she was at the beginning. The main character has acted to change the situation and is in turn changed by it. This is the second-level story. It is not a moral tacked on to "teach a lesson," but a natural and integrated part of the whole, giving depth and added dimension all the way through. It is the thesis, theme, or premise of the story; it is what the story *says.*

The surface story is the one in which the action occurs, the one where the suspense is, the one that keeps the reader reading to find out what happens. The second-level story is the one in which universal truth is revealed and character develops and changes. And it is what often distinguishes the salable story from one that fails.

Oliver Dibbs and the Dinosaur Cause, a book for 8 to 12-year-olds by Barbara Steiner, is about a boy with good ideas who now has one he considers great. High school students found stegosaurus remains in Colorado; why can't Oliver and his fifth grade class, studying dinosaurs, work to get stegosaurus named the official state fossil?

It takes a lot of work to introduce the bill in the state senate and house, then to help get it passed into law. In addition to Ollie and his friends, the whole school becomes involved—except for Lester Philpott, the class bully, whose jealousy of Ollie nearly ruins Ollie's great idea.

Two second-level themes run side by side in this book. One is the political science detail of how a bill has to have a sponsor from the Senate or the House of Representatives. Then many people have to work and campaign hard to get it passed.

A second theme is Oliver's handling of the bully, Lester. It's difficult for anyone to deal with a malicious troublemaker. In one scene where Oliver feels helpless, he discovers the technique of disarming an enemy by imagining him in funny or embarrassing situations.

At the end the two themes and the first-level story climax with Oliver's kind, unselfish decision to let Lester have the lead role in the campaign, that of wearing the stegotaurus costume when they testify at the state senate. The reader understands, along with Ollie, that Lester is lonely and needs attention. He *needs* to be Steggy. Oliver learns that feeling good about making someone else happy comes in second to being famous himself.

The second-level story is the real "meat" of most stories, for it deals with eternal and universal values. Children in every culture need to belong, to feel secure, to love and be loved, to achieve; they need change and aesthetic satisfaction. These are the raw materials out of which stories are made. Very often it is the second-level story that a writer really wishes to tell. He may want to tell it more than once, or to different age groups, and he does this by improvising different first-level stories to provide the necessary action, interest, and suspense—stories to keep the reader reading.

Because the basic values *are* eternal and universal, there is a technique that can provide you with an unlimited and immediate supply of new story ideas. It's called "reducing the story to its basic essentials," and it utilizes the habit you have already formed of stating your story in one sentence.

To reduce a story—one of your own or someone else's—to its basic essentials, first do the very best job you can of stating the story-in-one-sentence. Then go through this sentence, one word at a time, and change every concrete and specific term to an abstract and general term, thus:

Story-in-one-sentence: Feeling sorry for a three-legged

toad he finds, Jim takes it home, puts it in a cage, catches insects for it, and neglects his own activities—until it escapes and he discovers when he finds it later that both he and the toad are better off without his protection and that all of God's creatures need their independence, and so lets it stay free. This was the original story, "Hoppy's Independence Day," by Bessie Lou Gruen.

Plot pattern: Misunderstanding, Discovery, and Reversal.

Reduced to its basic essentials: Wishing to protect disadvantaged Actor B, Actor A succeeds only in wasting his/her own energies and making Actor B weak and unhappy—until he/she discovers that Actor B is better off on his/her own and helps Actor B enjoy the needed freedom.

This is the skeleton of the story, the bone structure from which the second-level story is made. By constructing different bodies on this skeleton, you can develop an infinite number of equally good stories. Let's try a few, based on the example we've just used:

1. Feeling that their new stepmother expects too much of her little brother Arnold, eight-year-old Patty tries to do his chores as well as hers—until one day he cleans up his room all by himself and is very proud of himself, when Patty happily joins the stepmother in praising Arnold.

2. Feeling compassion for Billy, a deaf child in her class, ten-year-old Marilyn gets behind in her studies because she's busy helping Billy find the right page, do his spelling, and get into the lunch line—until she discovers he's better at math than she is, and so releases him from her protectiveness and asks *him* to help *her.*

3. Hoping to find better equipment for Rodney, whose family is poor and who has only an old pair of too short skis for a day on the slopes, Brad misses his own first run, but returns to find Rodney happily demonstrating ski techniques to some admiring beginners, and quietly rejoins his

own group, realizing there's more than one way to enjoy skiing.

4. Wanting to help Tom in her English class because Tom is German—and also to interest Tom in her—Karyn neglects her girl friends and takes over tutoring Tom—until Tom's asking another girl he feels is less bossy to the basketball game, causes Karyn to change her attitude and behavior by asking Tom to help her with physics, which she's let slip to help him with English literature.

5. And just for fun, let's make the last one an animal story: Because of a cat's motherly instinct, Tabby continues to "mother" the family's dachshund, Fritz, even after he's bigger than she is—until Fritz drives a burglar away and Tabby has to admit that he no longer needs mothering and takes up a quieter role of mothering a child's stuffed rabbit.

Once you have established the basic essentials of any story at all, your imagination is immediately free to build up a completely new and original story on this framework, which you *know* is sound. If the main character in the first story was a twelve-year-old Indian boy, choose a teenage girl for a main character and a new story will develop, since a teenage girl's problem will necessarily be different in its specifics from that of an Indian boy. Or select a preschool child as your main character, and the resulting story will bear no resemblance whatever to either of the other two except in its skeleton, which is completely hidden by different flesh. Or try a story about a dog, a dump truck, or a fantasy adult.

These basic essentials, or story skeletons, belong to no one. They are used over and over by all writers, and each writer's story is an original creation, a product of his or her unique personality, character, experience, memories, values, and emotional responses. There is nothing illegal or even remotely reprehensible or subject to criticism in doing this. You may feel just as free to take any story you find in a magazine as you would one of your own, state the story-in-one-sentence, reduce it to its basic essentials, and then build your own story on this skeleton. Because there is no other individual exactly like *you* in the world, your story will be original, unique.

There is, however, one caution, and this is another reason for working with basic essentials. Always ask yourself, What does my story teach by implication? Inexperienced writers frequently write stories that could not possibly sell, no matter how well written or even how well plotted, because they say something that the writer had not meant to say at all.

For example, one might write a seemingly innocuous story about a young rabbit whose mother had told him never to eat anything from Mr. McGillicuddhy's garden because Mr. McGillicuddhy sprays his vegetables with poison. But Ronald Rabbit very much wants a fresh cabbage. He thinks this all over and reasons that *people* will eventually eat the cabbages, so he watches closely and sees that Mr. McGillicuddhy always washes the cabbages after he picks them. Sure he has found the secret, Ronald takes a cabbage one night, rolls it to the stream and washes it, and eats it with no ill effects. Then he shows his family what he has done and wins their praise.

What's wrong with the story? The main character has solved his problem through ingenuity. But what does it teach by implication? That disobedience to parental rules leads to reward and recognition.

The story can easily be rescued if, instead of having Ronald's mother warn him not to eat the cabbage, we have *her* concerned about finding a solution to the problem. Ronald makes his observations, tells her what he has observed and what he thinks, and together the family make a project of testing the idea.

If you are careful about stating your story-in-one-sentence and reducing it to its basic essentials, this often turns a glaring spotlight on something the story says that you did not intend at all, and you are then in a position to change it and make it acceptable.

One of the most common and at the same time baffling problems of the inexperienced writer is how to get story ideas. This difficulty does not indicate lack of talent or of creative ability—or even of imagination. It indicates only a lack of experience in *using* talent, creative ability, and imagination. After a writer has learned how to recognize story ideas and knows how to tap some of the many inexhaustible sources, it will no longer be a question of What shall I write about? but Which story shall I develop first?

Story ideas come from so many sources that we can only mention a few briefly here. The plot patterns themselves serve as springboards, especially when combined with the story-in-one-sentence and basic-essentials techniques. Plot germs often come from *characters;* you know a child or teenager who so captures your imagination that you think, *He'd be good in a story.* But *how* will you use him? Take the six questions on page 50 and put your imagination to work. The story may be labored, corny. Don't let that stop you; your imagination is just a little flabby, needs exercise. Next time you'll do better.

Or a story may be suggested by a *setting*—a spooky house, a wrecked ship, a shopping center. What might *happen* here? Who could carry on this activity? Keep pushing your imagination with questions.

Situations—either real life or imagined—provide endless raw materials for stories. Do you know a young person who wants something badly but there seems to be no way to get it? A dog? A friend? A chance to go away to school? A home where parents don't quarrel? Do you know someone who is having trouble of some kind with parents, teachers, friends, the law? What could this person *do* about the situation? Maybe you know a child or young person whose life seems to be without problems. Suppose she's going away to camp for the first time, or suppose her parents were to separate. Would this cause a problem?

Sometimes an obscure bit of *knowledge* suggests a story. A plant that blooms only once in seven years. An oddity of chemistry or physics. Some little-known fact about dogs, horses, fish—anything.

Keep your eyes open and *observe* children—on the bus, going to and from school, at play, at the library, in the supermarket. Often their actions and behavior suggest stories, and their conversations tell you not only their ideas but the way they express these ideas. You don't have to be snoopy; most of their conversations are for anyone within earshot to hear if he cares to listen. They'll even talk to *you;* an interested adult who will talk with them about *their* interests is something all young people want to find!

And read. Read, *read,* READ! Not only the best young people's publications from cover to cover, including the advertisements, but everything you find about children and teenagers, schools and education, in newspapers and adult publications. Many schools publish "guides for parents" and "guides for students." Read the writers' magazines *(The Writer* and *Writer's Digest)* and *The Horn Book Magazine.* Keep files of articles, notes from your reading.

You *must keep up* on what's going on in the world of young people—what is being said, thought, and done. This book has tried to avoid everything that can go out of date or become invalid; the plot patterns and other principles it presents are timeless. But the way you use them will change constantly, just as styles in clothing change. You need to know not only what is *being* published, but what is *going to be* published. Look ahead, anticipate, be ready; young people live for *today*—if you're going to keep ahead of them, you have to live in *tomorrow.*

POINTS TO REMEMBER

1. The surface story is where the action takes place; the second-level story is where the character growth takes place, and it contains the theme or thesis of the story.

2. Because the values contained in the second-level story are universal and eternal, it is often this story that contains the "meat" of what the author wishes to say, the basic essentials.

3. By reducing any story to its basic essentials, a writer can easily and immediately provide a basis from which to write innumerable other stories, all different and original.

4. The writer must always be alert to what his story may teach by implication, and see that this is acceptable.

5. Story ideas may grow from character, setting, situation, knowledge, or action, as well as from many other sources.

6. A writer must keep up with the world of young people through reading and observation.

QUESTIONS AND EXERCISES

1. Reread several of the published stories you have collected. Can you identify the second-level story in each? Are there some that have no second-level story? Would they have been better if they had?

2. Reread the stories you have written since beginning your study of this book. Is there a second-level story in each? Can you strengthen it if there is one? If there is not, can you weave one in?

3. Taking the stories-in-one-sentence you have written for some of the published stories you have studied and for some of the stories you have written, reduce each of these to its basic essentials. Then build at least one new story-in-one-sentence for a new story based on the same basic essentials, as we did on pages 82 and 83.

4. Write at least one of these stories for a completely different age group from the story out of which it grew. The word length will be determined by the age group for which you are writing.

5. For exercise, try to plan a story from each of the sources mentioned on pages 85 and 86. Write a story-in-one-sentence for each and identify the plot pattern.

6. Start a file for clippings and notes from your reading. Find in current magazines and newspapers at least six items for your file.

10

Characters That Come Alive

One of the strangest quirks of the human mind is its capacity for being moved to tears, laughter, anger, anxiety, joy by a "person" who exists nowhere except in imagination! The explanation is "identity." Because we are all made of basically the same stuff, the reader identifies with the imaginary individual invented by the author—in effect *becomes* that person, seeing what he sees, hearing what he hears, experiencing what he experiences, hoping what he hopes. But what is the magic by which the writer provides this imaginary individual with name, body, personality, family, a place of residence, habits, desires, and fears that make him "come alive" in the minds of readers?

First you must know him intimately—better than you've ever known a next-door neighbor or your niece or nephew. You must *live with* this story person, so that you know everything about him, inside and out—not only how he looks, but what kind of house he lives in, what his family does, who his friends are, how he feels about school, work, play, himself.

Only a fraction of this information will be used in the story, but oddly, by some strange alchemy, if *you* know your character thoroughly, even though you use only a few details about him in your story, the reader will reconstruct in *his* mind the same live, warm, three-dimensional individual you had conceived in yours. But if you don't know your story character thoroughly, he will be fuzzy and indistinct, wooden and flat—a mere prototype—in the mind of your reader.

Since children under eight or nine judge both peers and adults on the basis of what they can *observe* and have little awareness of or interest in the subtle characteristics that differentiate one individual from another, they accept story characters on the same basis. The secrets of characterization for this age group are simplicity and vividness. Make your physical descriptions vivid, but keep them simple. A name and an appropriate and visible distinguishing characteristic or two suffice as characterization in stories for very young children. But you, the author, need to know more about the story character than this; be sure you know him as an *individual* before you start to write.

As you write for older children—and as you work with longer stories and books—you will use more and more characterization. For teenagers, your characters should be as fully developed as when you write for adults, though the characterization may be less subtle and the characters themselves simpler.

Authors have various ways of arriving at a thorough understanding of their story characters. Some find it helpful to write out a brief biography—two or three pages—that includes the three dimensions necessary for good characterization: physical, environmental, and mental and emotional. The character chart on page 91 will help you to think fully about your story people and to develop skill in characterization.

Do not use the chart to *build* a character. Your character should have come alive for you sufficiently before you try to chart him so that you already know him well enough merely to fill out the blanks—much as you might for your own child or someone you know very well. Filling out a chart of this kind for your main character takes only a few moments and is time well spent. Improvement in characterization, more than any other one thing once your plot is right, invariably means more consistent sales and to better markets.

Character Chart

Story: _____ Main character: _____

Physical

Sex: _____ Age: _____ Height: _____ Posture and build: _____

Race: _____ Hair color, texture, & style: _____ Eyes: _____

Dress & grooming: _____ Health: _____

Special physical abilities or inabilities: _____

Environmental

Home: _____ Own room: _____

Family: _____ Monetary class: _____

  Parent(s) or Guardian(s): _____ Occupation(s): _____

  Siblings & their ages: _____

  Others: _____ Pets: _____

Neighborhood & culture: _____

School, camp: _____

Organizations or clubs: _____ Religious affiliation or activities: _____

_____ _____

Reputation among peers: _____

Mental and Emotional

Thought processes: Quick: ___ Plodding: ___ Creative: ___ Original: ___

  Conventional: ___ Special abilities, aptitudes, talents: _____

Education:

  History of schooling: _____

  Favorite subjects: _____ Grades: _____

  Hard or disliked subjects: _____ Grades: _____

  Extracurricular activities: _____

Work experience: _____ Special skills: _____

Interests and hobbies: _____

General outlook on life: _____

Attitudes toward:

  Parents: _____ Home and family: _____

  Adults other than parents: _____

  Peers: _____

  School and education: _____

  Moral standards and law: _____

  Sports & leisuretime activities: _____

  Work: _____ Money: _____

  The future: _____

  Himself: _____

What is his core quality? _____

Now that you really *know* your character, how do you make him live for your reader? Just knowing him as well as you do will help a great deal. Often a character will come to life so vividly and insistently that he takes over your story and tries to write it *his* way!

We have said that story ideas may come from characters— persons one observes in real life. But story characters differ in important ways from real-life individuals. The fiction character is simple, whereas the real-life character is complex. The fiction character is built around a single "core quality," and he is always consistent; neither of these things is true of real-life individuals. A fiction character's core quality may be honesty, hot temper, thoughtfulness, shyness, or anything else. Whatever it is, he can be counted on to display it and be guided and motivated by it in every circumstance, and every other characteristic he has must derive from or support this single quality.

This does not mean that your character should be either predictable or all "black" or "white" with no interesting shades of gray. A main character's core quality might be courage, for example, but courage can take many forms, from daredevil bravado to intelligent appraisal of the situation and preparation to go on in spite of danger. Or suppose the core quality is somewhat negative, such as shyness; the main character may be aware of this deficiency and try hard to overcome it. In fact, this is one of the surest ways to build all-important reader sympathy for the main character.

We've also pointed out that character growth of the main character should take place, providing a second-level story. This means that the writer must plan a logical, step-by-step change, with *reasons* for the change. Suppose, for example, that at the beginning of the story the main character has been cocky, boastful. We can count on him to be this way in whatever situation he encounters. At the beginning of the story he may appear to be attractive, a leader. But as the story progresses, his show-off attitude and actions embarrass his friends, and they begin to drop away. He ridicules them, taunts them, but, just the same, inside he hurts. Once too often he's cocky, and a bigger boy puts him in his place. His former friends are pleased—except for one, the one he has most abused. Because this boy knows how it feels to be put down, he befriends the cocky boy. The cocky boy sees his mistake, but cannot overcome it in a moment. Next time he's with the group, he starts to make a smart remark, but stops himself. The others see that he's making an effort and accept him again.

Be *sure* you include the step-by-step progression of any basic change in character, and that the change comes about as a result of what *happens* in the story and not merely to fulfill the necessities of the plot or to suit the author's whim. The character, to be realistic, must be motivated from within, and not a mere puppet moved through the plot by the author.

Skill in characterization will come with practice and experience. The one basic principle is to *show* your character through his action, speech, attitudes, and thoughts, instead of *telling about* him. Suppose a girl is adventurous. She will express this trait in her way of speaking, her selection of words, her manner, her gait, her gestures, her facial expression, her clothing perhaps.

The secret of showing rather than telling about your character is to adopt the rule, *Never pass judgment on your story character.* If you say, "Sally was naughty," that is the author's judgment; if you say, "Sally stamped her foot and shook her head," you have given the facts, and the facts let the *reader* make the judgment about her behavior.

An inexperienced writer might write: "Sam liked to argue. He never lost a chance to oppose others or try to get what he wanted. His classmates disliked him and showed it. . . ." Certainly this characterizes Sam, but it is dull because the writer is *talking about* Sam, making all kinds of judgments about him, stating generalities, failing to create any pictures, and arousing no emotion.

A more skillful writer would say:

> Sam picked up the sample sweatshirt Jack had brought. "This looks grungey," he said. "Let's have real jackets. Blue and orange."
>
> "The team voted for blue and white," Paul reminded him quietly. "And Coach said to choose something every boy on the team can afford."
>
> "So—" Sam began.
>
> "I think the sweatshirts are fine," said Howard. "We're not wearing them to a tea party, you know."
>
> "Yeah," Randy added, "I vote for the sweatshirts."
>
> "But we'll look like a bunch of slobs," Sam grumbled, dropping the sweatshirt in a heap on the dusty table.
>
> "I'd rather look like a slob than be one," Jack said pointedly.
>
> "Yeah," said Randy. "Why do you always have to argue, Sam? Why don't you think about the other guys once in a while?"

This characterization of Sam takes a few more words, but it also does several things for the story besides just characterizing Sam. It helps to characterize others in the story and moves the plot forward. Because it has action and conflict, it holds reader interest; and because the boys themselves feel emotion, so does the reader. The passage uses some of the commonest and most effective methods of characterization—the speech and actions of the main character tell the reader what he is like, and so do the comments of his friends.

The thoughts and feelings of the main character—who is also usually the viewpoint character—can also tell the reader what kind of person he is: "So I haven't got what it takes to win, Dale told himself. I can at least *try*. A good sport would have to try. . . ." Or, "Marcia looked at her plain, no-color hair and freckled nose in the mirror. If I were Tom, she thought, would I rather ask me to the prom than Saralee? Why?"

And of course the thoughts and feelings of the viewpoint character can also characterize others in the story: "Tom is different, she thought. Not like the others in his crowd. He may do what they do, but it's because he's decided for himself, and not just because eveyone else does it."

Straight narration by the author can characterize effectively, provided it does not pass judgment on the character and provided it keeps the story moving. When the author says, "Dave muttered" or "Angie giggled" when writing dialogue, this is characterization. So are passages that give background about the character: "Eric had lived in the big brown house at the edge of town almost as long as he could remember—ever since Dad had gone away and Mom brought Eric and Linda to live with her folks."

In choosing names for your characters, avoid names that are too unusual or difficult to pronounce, but don't immediately seize the commonest names or the first that come to mind. Try to choose an *appropriate* name, one that helps to individualize and identify. Avoid names that look alike or that sound alike within the same story. Andy and Louise rather than Andy and Amy. Don and Jerry rather than Don and Ron—unless, possibly, you're writing about twins.

Study published stories in the best publications to understand how the author has characterized and individualized the story people. You'll probably be surprised to find what a large portion of the story is either direct or indirect characterization. *Practice* the techniques you observe. This will help you develop the smooth professionalism that comes only with much practice.

POINTS TO REMEMBER

1. You must *know* your story character thoroughly to make him come alive for the reader.

2. For readers under 8 or 9, very little characterization is necessary.

3. For readers over 12, or when writing a book, check your understanding of your character by filling out a character chart.

4. A fiction character has a single core quality, and everything he does is consistent with this quality.

5. Character growth must come from within the character as a result of what happens to him, never from the necessities of the plot.

6. *Show* your character rather than *telling about* him; never pass judgment on your character.

7. Reveal character through action, dialogue, thoughts and feelings of the viewpoint character, and narration.

8. Choose appropriate character names that do not look or sound alike.

QUESTIONS AND EXERCISES

1. Find a published teenage story in which you think the characterization has been well handled. Read it through carefully, underlining everything that in any way characterizes the main character. Then with colored pens or pencils, do the same for minor characters, using a different color for each one. What proportion of the story have you underlined?

2. Find a story for children under 8 in which you think the main character is truly an individual. Underline everything that in any way characterizes the main character. Study these passages to understand what the author has done. What is the character's core quality?

3. Do the same with a story for 8 to 12s.

4. Select one of your own stories that you have written for readers over 12. Write out a complete character chart for the main character.

5. Study your story. Is the character *shown,* or merely *talked about?* Revise this story and see how much you can improve it by improving the characterization.

6. Write a new story, using any plot pattern except the Incident, for readers over 12. Before you start to write, identify the plot pattern, state your story-in-one-sentence, and write out a character chart for the main character. The story should be between 1,500 and 3,000 words, depending on the age group for which you write.

11

Viewpoint, Story Opening, and Title

Important as plotting and characterization are, they are still just the raw materials. The story must be told smoothly, interestingly, effectively, professionally. Many factors must be coordinated to make a salable story. In this and the next chapter we discuss the most common problems of presentation.

VIEWPOINT

The technique that causes the most difficulty and is most often bungled by beginning writers—and more advanced writers too—is handling viewpoint. Yet viewpoint need not be difficult.

With so few exceptions that they are hardly worth mentioning, stories for young readers are told from the single viewpoint—either first person or third person. This means simply that the writer will go into the mind and feelings of only one character—almost always the main character; the writer *becomes* the viewpoint character, seeing and hearing what that character sees and hears, thinking as he thinks, feeling as he feels, experiencing the events just as the viewpoint character lives and experiences them.

The advantages of this technique are so strong that any deviation from it—into multiple viewpoint or omniscient author viewpoint, which are found in a few adult short stories and most adult novels—will almost certainly weaken a story so that it will fail. Very rarely, there is a story that really can't be told from the single viewpoint; if ever you find such a story published, save it and study it, for it must be a very good story indeed, unusually strong in other respects, to have succeeded in spite of the viewpoint weakness.

The most important advantage of the single viewpoint is that it establishes immediately and then sustains a sense of reader identity. Because the *writer* has identified with the viewpoint character, the reader also identifies with the character, living the events of the story with him, feeling the same suspense, excitement, fear, relief, triumph that the viewpoint character feels. The reader experiences the events as they unfold, never for a moment feeling that he is simply himself, separate from the story, being *told* a story *about* the viewpoint character—which may have happened some-time in the past—by still a third person, the author.

The single viewpoint is both natural and realistic. In real life, one person cannot know what another thinks or feels, cannot know how something looks or tastes or smells to someone else, cannot know what is going on or being said in some place where he is not present. So the reader, once he identifies with the viewpoint character, is only annoyed or derailed if the subjective thoughts and feelings of some other character or of the author—things the main character could not possibly know—are introduced.

The same is true of scenes in which the main character is not present, though of course the main character, and the reader along with him, may *speculate* about these things, just as we all do in real life.

Once they understand the principle, most writers do not find the single viewpoint difficult, and are immediately aware of any deviation from it in their own or published stories.

Should you choose first- or third-person viewpoint for your story? Some writers find one easier, others the other; actually it's mostly a matter of practice, and you should learn both. Readers under 12 or 13 generally prefer third-person stories, whereas older readers often enjoy the intimacy and informality, the close identity with the subjective thoughts and feelings of a first-person character. But you will find both viewpoints for readers of all ages.

Both have advantages and limitations. It's almost impossible to write about a first-person "hero," for whatever he tells of his exploits and ingenuity seems like bragging. A similar limitation becomes apparent when he tries to describe himself or his possessions. On the other hand, if the main character is in some way inept, a blunderer, or in a position of disadvantage through no fault of his own, the choice of first-person viewpoint can often help to create reader sympathy whereas a third-person viewpoint might make him seem pathetic. If a character honestly recognizes his deficiencies and can accept them with grace and humor, showing good sportsmanship in spite of difficulty and defeat, he can become a most appealing first-person main character.

Another situation for which first-person treatment is effective is one in which the viewpoint character tells an entertaining, usually humorous account of another character who is really the main character. In such a story, usually the viewpoint character's goal is to help the main character solve *his* problem or reach *his* goal. For example, a story of a school election might be about Joan's campaign, told in the first person by her campaign manager, Frank. Frank's problem is to help Joan solve her problem, which is to be elected.

A few comments about the common errors made in working with third-person viewpoint should help you to use it with finesse: First, remember that you cannot go into the thinking or subjective feelings of anyone but the viewpoint character. You must not say, for example, "The boys' hearts were hammering against their ribs." Instead, say, "Rob's heart hammered against his ribs. He looked at Marty and knew he was scared too."

The viewpoint character may *surmise* what someone else thinks or feels. You might write, "Tim had tried all day to get up enough courage to ask, 'May—may I go with you on the elk hunt this year?' 'You might help the burro carry our gear,' Uncle Hank said, laughing. Uncle Hank thought he was joking."

"Uncle Hank thought he was joking" does not really go into Uncle Hank's thoughts; it is simply the conclusion Tim draws from what his uncle says and does.

Second, you cannot have a scene in which the viewpoint character is not present. You cannot say, "After Jack had gone to bed, Mother and Daddy sat up late talking." And conversely, you should not withhold from the reader anything known to the viewpoint character; you should not say, "Suddenly Lisa had a wonderful idea. 'I know it will work,' she said aloud, and ran to her room. . . . That evening, when the family gathered for dinner . . ." Usually you should let the reader in on what she has planned, so that the reader can enjoy the anticipation with her. Similarly, if the viewpoint character has been working to solve a mystery, you would not write, "Sammy looked down at his feet, and there it was, lying right in the dust before him— the one clue that might help. He stooped, picked it up quickly, and dropped it in his pocket." If Sammy knows what it is, the reader should be told, too.

Third, be very careful about describing the appearance of your viewpoint character, especially the facial expression and the eyes. If you say, "Emily's smile faded and her eyes grew sad," obviously you are not in Emily's viewpoint, but in the viewpoint of someone looking *at* her; Emily is not aware of this change in her facial expression, and would not thus describe herself if she were. Instead, stay "inside" Emily: "Suddenly Emily felt all alone again, and tears were close to the surface." Similarly, if you say, "Emily was a picture of grace as she danced in the blue taffeta dress," you are outside Emily's viewpoint. Instead, you might say, "Emily caught a glimpse of her reflection in the glass of the French doors as they danced past. The blue taffeta is just right, she thought happily." Or you could use dialogue: " 'That dress is perfect for you, Em,' Myrna said. 'It just matches your eyes and makes your hair even more golden.' "

If you are ever in doubt about these points, simply transpose momentarily into first person, and you will see immediately whether you're at fault. You would never say, "I was furious—my eyes became pinpoints of anger." If it's absurd in first person, it is equally absurd to assign it to a third-person-viewpoint character.

Fourth, avoid author intrusion; think of your story as a play on a stage, where everything must be conveyed by the action and dialogue of the characters, and you, the author, can tell nothing. This will keep you from ever being tempted to say something like "This was the naughtiest thing she had ever done." There simply isn't anybody on stage to make such a remark. It will also keep you from getting ahead of your story: "Little did they know when they left home that before nightfall . . ." It will keep you from saying, "Paul was so busy tacking up the decorations that he didn't see Andy and Myrna come into the gym," or, "Jan was so miserable that she didn't notice the bright sun." What your viewpoint character fails to see or hear or notice will have to be left out.

Finally, avoid ever addressing the reader as "you": "Marie ran to the back porch to feed Muff, and what do you think she found?" This is another form of author intrusion that immediately destroys reader identity, reminding the reader that he's simply reading *about* the character. And avoid epithets to refer to the characters, especially to the viewpoint character. To the writer, it seems as if he is repeating a character's name endlessly, and trying to avoid this, the beginning writer will refer to the character as "the older boy," "the young cowboy," "the redhead," and so on. Actually, such epithets draw attention to themselves far more than even a great deal of repetition of the name, because the name is natural and the epithet is not; the characters in the story—especially the main character—do not think of themselves or one another as "the older boy" or "the young cowboy." So use only the character's name or a pronoun to refer to him.

Study viewpoint techniques in the best published stories. Note really fresh and clever devices authors have used to handle difficult problems. E. L. Konigsburg found an ingenious way to use a double viewpoint legitimately in her Newbery Award–winning book *From the Mixed-Up Files of Mrs. Basil E. Frankweiler.* The whole book is a letter, written by Mrs. Frankweiler to her attorney, in which she tells of the children's adventure; she has had both Claudia and Jamie tape-record their account of their activities, so she has the subjective account of each, and quite naturally relates both in her letter. If you understand what you are doing and why, viewpoint will not give you any trouble.

STORY OPENING

Even seasoned writers often wonder why story openings have to be so troublesome. There aren't any real "rules" to help with openings, and often one simply has to try several different approaches before finding the best one; sometimes it's well to wait until the story is all written before making a final decision.

The first problem is deciding *where* to begin. Since all stories for children and all but a very few for teenage readers are told chronologically without flashback or retrospect such as is used in many adult stories, the decision is simplified somewhat: you begin at the beginning. But novice writers tend to start *before* the story begins, with explanations of who the character is and how he happens to be in this situation. For example, if Mary is spending the summer with Uncle Ben on his farm, the inexperienced writer will start with Mary packing her bag, going to the airport, saying good-by to Mother, being met by Uncle Ben, and so on. The story isn't even started yet and half the allowable word-age is gone. The story should start with Mary at the farm facing her problem, whatever it is.

The all-important aim of the opening is to "hook" readers immediately and hold their attention. The best way to do this is to introduce the main character and his situation and problem as promptly as possible. The author should also indicate why the problem will be difficult to solve and why the solution is important to the main character. At the same time, the writer should make the reader like the main character and care what happens to him.

To do all this in the first few sentences demands that the story open with the main character doing something interesting. His action should characterize him a bit and at least hint at the story problem; it can be developed more fully as the story progresses. Of course the action must happen in some setting, so that the reader sees the character "on stage"—in the living room, walking along the street, on the playground, or wherever he is.

The character may be alone or with others. Having others present makes dialogue possible, which always adds interest. But the writer must be sure to make clear the relationship of those present and show clearly which is the main character and from whose viewpoint the story will unfold. The main character should be the first one mentioned, and is usually the first to speak.

Right from the start, the main character should feel some

emotion, and the reader should understand clearly what the emotion is and identify with it. The beginning should arouse curiosity and promise dramatic action. Remember that the reader isn't interested in description and information. He wants a story, an emotional experience; he wants to feel excitement, suspense about what will happen next. So avoid static, explanatory details in the opening; any *necessary* explanatory details can wait until later, where they can be woven in unobtrusively with action and dialogue.

Study the openings of stories in current young people's magazines. Stop at the end of fifty or sixty words and ask yourself, What makes the reader want to go on reading? If you find openings you think are weak, study them to understand why; see if you could improve on them. This practice will help you greatly in writing good openings for your own stories.

TITLE

Sometimes a title comes easily, sometimes hard. Often the title is the last thing about a story to be decided—after it's all written, perhaps. And then after all your struggle to come up with a good title, an editor may decide something else would be better!

But try to think of at least a working title when you first start to write, for this helps you to crystallize your story, your theme; it helps you to shake down your story material and decide exactly what story you wish to tell.

Your title, together with the opening sentences of your story, should say, Pay attention; here's something you want to know about. Try to find a title that arouses curiosity and that's fresh and provocative. "Billie's Bad Day," "Susan Learns a Lesson," "A Present for Mother," and so on have been worn threadbare.

Think of your title apart from the story, as it would appear in a table of contents. Would it make a reader want to turn immediately to the story to see what it's about? Refer to your list of "magic words" to help with titles, and don't be too easily satisfied. The "brainstorming" technique of writing quite rapidly a dozen or more possible titles—even those you know aren't right but may lead to something that *is* right—often produces something good. Alliterative titles can be appealing: "Lucy's Lucky Lollipop" or "The Serendipity Social." A phrase from the story may suggest or provide a good title.

Be sure your title doesn't telegraph your punch by giving away the outcome of the story. "Andy's Home Run" or "A Scholarship for Josey" lets the reader know in advance just how the story will end.

Editors do sometimes change a title if it's too similar to another in the same issue of the magazine or to the title of another story they've recently published—or in the case of a book, if it's too similar to a title recently used by another publisher. Or sometimes an editor wants to give a story a slightly different emphasis. For this reason, if you've been able to think of more than one good title, you may wish to let the editor know; it's quite appropriate to type, immediately under the word count in the upper right part of page 1, "Alternate Title(s)" and then list one or two other possible titles. *(See model manuscript in Appendix B.)*

A good title helps to sell a story, so give it the thought it deserves.

You will find in published stories plenty of examples of exceptions to and violations of all the principles outlined in this and the following chapter. This does not mean the principles are invalid; it means only that the stories succeeded *in spite of* these aberrations, not because of them. Either the story had something the editor liked well enough to buy in spite of the weaknesses, or she took it because she *needed* a Valentine story—or a baseball story or a summer camp story—and nothing better came in. But *you* want to be a real craftsman; your aim is to do things right, not to see what you can get away with. So don't be influenced by examples of technical flaws you find in published material into thinking it's really all right to do these things. Set your standards high, and don't be satisfied with anything less than meeting them.

POINTS TO REMEMBER

1. Stories for young readers are told from the single viewpoint, either first person or third person. One must *master* the technique of the single viewpoint to write professionally.

2. The story opening must hook the reader by introducing the main character and his problem through some kind of interesting activity; reader identity with and sympathy for the main character must be established in the first few sentences.

3. A truly fresh and appropriate title rouses reader curiosity and makes him want to read the story.

QUESTIONS AND EXERCISES

1. Reread the stories in Appendix A, giving special attention to the viewpoint in each. Try to understand why the author chose the viewpoint he did, and note any particular skillful ways in which the author conveyed necessary information without violating the viewpoint.

2. Do the same with the published stories you've been working with. See if you can find examples of the viewpoint violations mentioned in this chapter; if you do, rewrite these passages and see if you can correct the violation.

3. Go back over at least half a dozen of your own stories—selecting those you think are best—giving close attention to your handling of viewpoint. Correct any violations you may find.

4. Study the opening 50 to 100 words in the stories in Appendix A and the published stories with which you've been working. Analyze each to see why the author began where he did, how he introduced the main character and his problem, what makes the reader want to go on reading. What details of setting or other descriptive details are included? How are these woven in with the action? How is the reader made to care what happens to the main character?

5. Reread the openings of your own stories. Did you always choose the best place to begin? Can you improve on what you've written? Try rewriting the three that seem poorest to you.

6. Study the table of contents of the publications you have collected, and list half a dozen titles you think are best. List the ones you think are poor. Can you think of better titles for these stories?

7. Look at your own titles. Can you improve on them? Supply an alternate title for at least three of your own stories.

8. Write a new story of between 1,200 and 1,800 words for teenage readers, using first-person viewpoint. Give special attention to the opening and title. Use the plot pattern of your choice, first stating your story-in-one-sentence and writing a synopsis of not more than 250 words.

12

Dialogue, Scene Building, and Transitions

By now you have begun to develop some real professionalism—and to appreciate the value of learning your craft before trying to market your product. You are strengthening mental muscles you didn't know you had, and learning skills that will help you all the rest of your writing life, whether you confine your efforts to writing for young people or branch out to write for adults as well. Ready for the next round?

DIALOGUE

Well-written dialogue is an indispensable part of practically every story, and of many articles, too. It creates realism and adds interest to the page; readers are instantly drawn to a page with lots of "white space," where the print is broken into short paragraphs with irregular-length lines and quotation marks. Most of your skill in writing smooth, realistic dialogue will come from observation and practice, but a few guidelines will help.

"Story talk" is like real-life talk in that it uses the spoken language: short, common words and simple sentences, rather than the more "literary" words and complex sentence structure of the written language. Legitimate contractions such as *can't, won't, haven't,* and so on are entirely in order, though careful writers avoid such contractions as *gonna, runnin', s'pose,* and the like, and such barbarisms as *aint* or *caint.* The main character should never use them.

There should be no profanity, and very little slang for readers under teen age, though most editors allow an occasional "golly" or other mild expletive. Slang for any age group presents a problem, in that it is so ephemeral that it dates a story, and is sometimes so regional that readers in another part of the country may not get it. One way to get around this problem is to invent your own slang; make up an expression that your character might make up—it can add freshness and originality that brightens the story.

Your main character should use standard English, though a few colloquialisms typical of his time and culture may not be objectionable. Generally it's best to give these colloquialisms, dialects, and speech mannerisms to minor characters, however; and even then they should be used sparingly.

Fragmentary sentences are occasionally acceptable in dialogue, and sometimes interruptions are realistic and can help to pace a passage faster or add to conflict:

> "Is Skeeter going to try for the team?" Dan asked.
> "Not that I know of."
> "Did he tell you whether—"
> "He didn't tell me a thing," Hank said impatiently. "We didn't even talk bout it."

Although dialogue is like real-life talk in these ways, if you were to tape-record and then transcribe conversation, you would immediately see that it could not be put into a story at all. In real life, people use many more words than necessary, they digress, they repeat themselves, they trust facial expression, voice modulation, and gestures to convey their meaning. In a story there is no room for "small talk"; every word of written dialogue must be necessary to the story—it must move the story forward, and at the same time it should help to characterize the speakers.

Speeches in written dialogue are much shorter than in real-life talk. Often there is just one sentence—sometimes just a word or two—in each interchange, especially when the story is for young children. This is partly because the writer must tell not only *what* is said, but must keep the reader aware of the total scene, letting him know *how* something is said, how the speaker looks or gestures when he says it, and how it is received by the others present. Even in writing for teenagers or adults, the writer should not let a speech run more than three or four lines; speeches as long as this are rare. When they grow longer, it's best to break them up with gestures, "stage business," or even a "he said" tucked into the middle.

This brings us to the matter of using *he said* with finesse. As you begin writing dialogue, it will seem that you are writing *he said* and *she said* every other word. Don't let it bother you; it's so unobtrusive that the *reader* doesn't even notice it, any more than he notices many repetitions of the words *the* or *a*. Trying to avoid this repetition, many novice writers try to think up all sorts of substitutes, so that the character *says* one thing, *proclaims* the next, *reminisces* another, and so on. Actually this does draw attention to itself and becomes annoying.

Some substitutes are appropriate, and when they are exactly right, use them: " 'Look,' she whispered, 'do you see what I see?' " " 'Get out!' he shouted. 'Get out and stay out!' " Be sure, though, that a substitute really is a legitimate substitute. People can *say* things—they can *snarl, stammer, murmur, call,* and possibly even *laugh* or *giggle* things. But they cannot *smile* anything, or *grin* it or *nod* it. Instead of writing, " 'I like it,' she smiled," write, " 'I like it.' She smiled," or " 'I like it,' she said, smiling."

As you gain skill, you will often use gestures and stage business in place of *he said* to add effectiveness and help the reader to see the speakers as well as hear them. Suppose two girls are getting lunch:

> "I think Tom is the nicest boy in Jefferson High." Linda took two plates from the cupboard.
> "You don't *know* all the boys in Jefferson High yet," Ann reminded her, spreading thick peanut butter to the very edges of the bread. "Maybe you'll meet someone you like better."
> Linda stirred the pitcher of lemonade dreamily. "I don't think so. Tom's the nicest boy I ever, ever knew."

The object is to create the illusion of naturalness, at the same time weighing every sentence, every phrase, every word, to be sure it carries its load in the story. Writing smooth, realistic dialogue is a skill that comes with practice.

SCENE BUILDING

Whether your story is a 300-word Incident for preschoolers or a teenage novel, it will be told in a series of scenes; and learning to think of a story in terms of scenes will help you plan and write good stories. Each time there is a change in setting or time, or a major personnel change, the scene changes. Each scene is like a miniature story, complete with its own problem, crisis, and climax. The main character enters the scene with a purpose, makes some effort to achieve it, and is either successful or defeated. Thus each scene moves the plot forward and adds to the suspense, with the main character sometimes gaining a bit on his ultimate goal, sometimes being thrust back.

The scene breakdown for "The Mystery of the Fourth-Floor Cat," one of my own stories, goes like this:

Scene I: Nine-year-old Shelly's Christmas, two days away, looks bleak. She should be happy about the new bunk beds already delivered and set up; but Smudge, her cat, has been missing for five days. She's asked every one of their fourth-floor neighbors, but no one has seen Smudge. Defeat.

Scene II: Shelly sees Mike, a neighbor, enter through the stairs door, and when she realizes people use this door all the time, she thinks Smudge could be far away. Defeat. But Mike tells her about the radio pet patrol and suggests Shelly call there for help. Hope.

Scene III: Shelly's mother is sure the cat got out into the hall and has been stolen, but reluctantly agrees to call the pet patrol when Shelly pleads. Shelly writes the radio announcement, and Mother phones it to the patrol. Success.

Scene IV: Shelly hears the announcement read, the next morning. Hope.

Scene V: Shelly is wrapping presents on Christmas Eve, the last a catnip mouse. Still no word of Smudge. Defeat. Black Moment.

Scene VI: The delivery man who brought the beds comes with Smudge. He explains he's had the cat for nearly a week, after finding it in his van, but had no idea where it came from until he heard the radio announcement. Smudge had crept into one of the mattress cartons. Shelly knows it's the best Christmas ever. Success.

Breaking the story down this way into scenes gives you smaller pieces to work with—something you can handle—instead of trying to shape and mold the whole unwieldy mass of the story. It helps you hew to your story line. Most stories, especially those by beginning writers, tend to grow too long, both for the market and for the story they tell. Outlining your story in scenes, either before you write it or when revising and polishing, will often show you where to cut. Perhaps you can start it at a later point, with some of what you now have in the beginning worked into dialogue later on. Often you'll find you can cut out an entire scene, combining what it achieves from a plot standpoint with what happens in another scene.

Cutting, shaping, tightening invariably results in a better, more compact, faster-moving story. It ensures your story against sagging because of scenes that don't build toward the climax. There should never be a single scene or episode that is not essential to the working out of the plot.

When you write your scene—and when you revise and polish it—concentrate on the action. Use only what information and description are necessary, and weave these in with the action and dialogue. Two or three well-presented details usually provide enough for the reader to go on and fill in other details for himself.

Think about the time span covered by your story. To achieve unity, coherence, and suspense, it should be as short as the story material permits. Keep scenes compact, time lapses between scenes as short as possible. A short story rarely covers more than a week or so. Many cover only a day or two, and some of the best take place in an hour or two.

In most respects the scenes in a story are very similar to the scenes of a play, and thinking in terms of scenes will help you to write both. Make it a general rule to give the opening and closing lines of each scene to your main character; be *sure* to give the opening and closing lines of the *story* to the main character. Give him the spotlight with every important entrance and exit he makes.

TRANSITIONS

How do you move smoothly from one scene to the next? The secret of making adroit transitions is to find or provide a common denominator between the scene you are completing and the one you are about to start. For example, one scene may end with Myra saying to her friend, "We'll meet at my house after dinner." And the next scene might open:

"Myra had cleared the table and laid out the poster materials when the doorbell rang."

Another device is to end one scene with a question and start the next with the answer to the question: "And even if he did manage to talk Dad into letting him use the station wagon, how was he going to get nine boys and their instruments, including Bill's drums, into it?" The next scene, which might be a day later, could open: "Steve and Bill had rearranged the instrument cases six different ways and were unloading for a seventh try when Larry drove up in his brother's VW."

Sometimes you can cover elapsed time with a quick montage: "Two Cokes and an ice-cream soda later, Louella was still sitting there in the booth trying to compose an acceptable letter."

By giving attention to skillful scene transitions in published stories in the best magazines and analyzing how the author achieved them, you will find ways to adapt these methods to your own writing. Work to develop a variety of devices and methods, so that readers will not become conscious of a repetition of just a few devices used over and over.

POINTS TO REMEMBER

1. Although written dialogue is like real-life talk in its use of the spoken language, it is unlike real-life talk because speeches are much shorter and every word contributes to the development of the story.

2. Observation and practice are essential to learning to write smooth dialogue. "Finger exercises"—writing detached bits of dialogue simply for practice—will build facility.

3. Thinking of a story in scenes helps one plan and write efficiently and build a story that will be structurally strong.

4. Scenes should be compact, and the total time covered by the story should be as short as the story material will permit.

5. Smooth transitions help to keep the reader oriented; learning to use a variety of transition devices with finesse adds to professionalism.

QUESTIONS AND EXERCISES

1. Reread some of the published stories with which you have been working, giving special attention to the dialogue. Note what proportion of the story is dialogue, what the dialogue achieves in moving the plot forward and in characterization. How long are the speeches? Do you *see* the setting and characters as they speak? How has the author made the characters come alive through their speeches? Note any violations of the "he said" principles presented in this text.

2. Mark each scene change in these stories. Outline briefly the scenes in at least one of the stories, as was done in this chapter, noting whether each scene ends in failure or success. How is the transition made from one scene to the next?

3. Go back over the stories you have written, giving special attention to the dialogue. Select the one you think you can improve the most by reworking the dialogue, perhaps telling more of the story in dialogue, and revise it.

4. Select another of your stories and outline it briefly in scenes, noting whether each ends in success or failure for the main character. Have you given opening and closing lines to the main character? Are your transitions clear and smooth? Could you tighten the story, give it better unity and coherence by combining scenes, shortening the time span? Revise this story to the best of your ability.

5. Write a new story, for any age group and using the plot pattern of your choice, working very consciously from the standpoint of scene building and applying the ideas you have gained from this chapter. Use the appropriate length for the age group you choose.

NOTE: You have now been introduced to the basic techniques of writing for young people. If you have as many as six stories you feel are marketable, you may want to turn to Chapter 23, on marketing. Otherwise, you will do better to wait until you have studied some of the intervening chapters.

IV

Expanding the Field

13

Fantasy and Science Fiction

Almost everyone who attends the first class of a course in writing for children wants to begin with a fantasy. He has a story he's sure is the most irresistible make-believe and just can't wait to write it—or more likely, he's already written it. So when the instructor says quite firmly, "No. *No fantasy* for a *long time* yet," he feels dismayed and frustrated.

Why not begin with a fantasy? Fantasy is so *easy* to write! *Poor* fantasy *is* easy to write; *good* fantasy is the most difficult of all fiction forms. And until one has mastered the basic techniques by writing the here-and-now story, he can't tell whether his fantasy *is* good or bad. By the time he's disciplined himself to adhere to the plot patterns, draw live, three-dimensional characters, hew to his story line, build well-structured scenes, and so on—and has a dozen or so of his own really well-conceived and well-written here-and-now stories in his file, or even sold—he may begin to think about writing a fantasy. By this time, however, he has probably abandoned the story he was bursting to tell, having seen that it doesn't fit any plot pattern, is far too long, and instead of being the fresh, irresistible story he had thought, is probably something that's been tried a hundred times before but was never published because it wasn't any good anyway.

Perhaps the reason fantasy *seems* easy is that freed from the limitations of a material, three-dimensional world with its rigid demands of time and space, one also feels free from the demands of logic and the rules of writing. The fact is that the demands of logic are, if anything, even stronger in a fantasy—at least they are harder to follow because one must keep *reminding* himself to be logical, whereas in real life, logic is "second nature." A doodlebug pin that's lost in the grass can no more climb a rock to find its bearings in a fantasy than it can in real life. A spaceship on a collision course with a comet will not "miraculously" be steered away from it.

Furthermore, instead of being relieved of the writing rules, one must follow them even more carefully in writing fantasy so that the fantasy will have an illusion of reality. The story must fit one of the basic plot patterns, and the writer must observe all the techniques of characterization, viewpoint, scene building, and so on just as much when writing about a monkey in the zoo or an imaginary woozle or tajar as when writing about the boy or girl next door. On top of all this, he must have a truly original idea and present it superbly.

Good fantasy and science fiction are enormously popular with readers of all ages, including adults. Television and movies, with their animated cartoons and puppets, their almost unlimited potential for making realistic pictures of things that don't exist, have stimulated interest in the world of make-believe. Disenchantment with materialism, a growing idealism and appreciation of intangibles, and a new awareness of and interest in mental and spiritual forces have attracted both writers and readers to serious exploration of realms beyond the three-dimensional world. And with today's travel into outer space, genetics that could create entirely new species, and plans for whole cities on man-made islands or enclosed under a plastic bubble, who is to say what "can never be"?

Children *need* fantasy. They all love to pretend, and they need this stretching of their imagination, this reaching out from the practical, sometimes drab and meaningless world around them to the world of "what if?" Some of the most treasured books of all time are fantasies—which is to be expected, since a fantasy often has a timelessness that a here-and-now story cannot achieve. *Charlotte's Web* and *Stuart Little*, by E. B. White; *The Wind in the Willows*, by Kenneth Grahame, and other old favorites continue a steady sale year after year. Some, such as C. S. Lewis' *The Lion, the Witch, and the Wardrobe*, have been made into movies or TV shows.

Fantasy may be just for fun, or it may be deeply philosophical. It may be "high" fantasy in which the author creates a setting that exists nowhere in reality and characters that are totally imaginary, like Tolkien's Hobbit. Or the story may be "light" fantasy, in which everything in the story is normal and commonplace except for one object or character. Light fantasy is generally more marketable than high fantasy because it presents familiar settings and activities and a main character with whom the reader readily identifies. The young people's librarian at your local library can help you to find the best in today's fantasy and science fiction.

Traditional or "classic" fantasy, dealing with giants and elves, princesses and fairy godmothers, glass mountains and enchanted forests, is almost impossible to sell. Hans Christian Andersen and the Brothers Grimm have already supplied the need for such stories. Children still love *scary* stories, however. Ghosts, monsters, and dinosaurs—sometimes gentle and fun, and sometimes scary—are very popular. For a fantasy to succeed, it must be totally new, different from both the traditional and everyone else's modern fantasy.

There are several kinds of fantasy that all except a few editors will buy if a story is truly original and measures up to all the standards set for conventional stories. Perhaps the most common is the picture book or magazine story featuring one or more personified animals. The animals may be pretty much living their own normal lives, talking little, and then only to other animals; or they may be practically human beings, dressing in ordinary clothes, living in houses, cooking on stoves, going to market and school, and having human problems. The problems must be ones that children readily understand and appreciate, often problems they themselves have, such as those involving obedience, getting along with others, learning to accept new situations, and so on. Sometimes the problems are simply humorous ones that a child would find amusing, such as the raccoon's problem in Rosemary Wells's *Benjamin and Tulip*. Every time Benjamin passes Tulip's house, she beats him up. But Benjamin's parents, who know Tulip only as a sweet little girl raccoon, hold her up as a good example to Benjamin and criticize *his* behavior.

Most of these stories are for children under 8; so it is generally best to use animals or birds that are familiar to children, either through seeing them alive or on television, or reading about them. A story should not introduce more than one or two unfamiliar animals—perhaps with some others that are well known.

Another type of fantasy is the story of an imaginary animal or animals. Dr. Seuss, with his star-bellied Sneetches and Nutches, his Whos living on a speck of dust, and other phantasmagorical creatures, is the best-known and most successful writer of this type of fantasy. This is an extremely limited field that requires real creativity and ingenuity, and a rare talent for writing nonsense in a very serious and sober way.

Less limited is the story for the youngest age group that uses what appears at first to be an adult main character, thus seeming to break the rule against featuring adults in children's stories. A closer examination will show that these characters are not really adults at all, but "made-up" characters with problems that interest children. These characters have fantastic and amusing names: Mr. Twinkleberry, Mrs. McQuickly, Mr. Pennyfeather.

There are also a *very* few stories in which the main character is an inanimate object. Enough books and magazine stories of this kind are published—and enjoy a comfortable sale—so that one cannot arbitrarily rule them out. *The Little Engine That Could* has been a standby for generations. Editors say, "Please, please not a story in which toys come to life." And yet who could ever forget Winnie the Pooh and his companions? They are so alive, so real, that the reader is perhaps a little startled to realize that they *are* toys.

Such stories must be fresh and original, sparkling in every facet, if they are to succeed. There is no place for the hackneyed story of the little cloud who was sad because he could not carry enough water to refresh the forest, or the house that wished for someone to come and live in it, or toys that come to life while everyone is asleep.

As has been said elsewhere, the story that is a dream virtually never succeeds because nothing really happens in it; it cheats the reader. But the story that is an imaginative experience should not be overlooked by the writer who wishes to try modern fantasy. It relates experiences that the child or children in the story *imagine* they have. Though similar in some ways to the story that is a dream, it has important differences. For one thing, the reader is not deceived; he knows from the beginning that the story is being created in the imagination of the child character. Children often daydream, tell themselves stories of imaginary experiences of which they are the hero. So they go right along with the story taking place in the imagination of the main character, enjoy the action, and do not feel cheated or let down at the end.

Science fiction is closely related to fantasy but is different in important ways. Fantasy typically includes magic or supernatural forces, bizarre cause and effect. Science fiction, on the other hand, projects into the unknown on the basis of what *is* known scientifically. Fantasy is set in the past or present, science fiction in the future. The "fantasy" of today's science fiction may be the "reality" of tomorrow.

Fantasy has traditionally been mainly girl oriented, with girl main characters and events that appeal to girls. Science fiction used to be an almost totally male-dominated genre, with many technical details that presumably did not interest girls, and derring-do by heroes who met and overcame great physical dangers, often related to war. The trend today seems to be for the two to blend. Sylvia Engdahl's *Enchantress from the Stars*, for example, opens with a space ship but has a girl main character. It combines magic and the supernatural with science, and is read by boys as well as girls.

Writing such a story demands, in addition to outstanding creativity and a keen but disciplined imagination, a firm grounding in the natural and physical sciences. It also takes superb storytelling talent and unerring mastery of the fiction skills. A little pure genius also helps!

Actually, if your heart is set on writing fantasy or science fiction, the surest and shortest way to having it accepted is to establish yourself as a children's author by selling at least half a dozen here-and-now stories first. When an editor has come to know you and is convinced that you really do understand your craft and have mastered it—then she may be willing to look at a fantasy you've written.

POINTS TO REMEMBER

1. Although good fantasy is hard to write, if it succeeds at all it is likely to succeed very well and live long.

2. To succeed, fantasy and science fiction must be entirely new and

original, and must follow all the technical rules and principles that govern other kinds of stories.

3. Although there is little market for traditional fantasy, both book and magazine editors use well-conceived and well-written stories about personified animals, imaginary animals, "made up" adult characters, imagined experiences of children, and science fiction.

4. One should demonstrate mastery of the basic techniques by selling several here-and-now stories before venturing into fantasy or science fiction.

QUESTIONS AND EXERCISES

1. In the young people's publications you've been working with, find examples of the kinds of fantasy discussed in this chapter. Study these to discover why they were purchased. Identify the plot pattern in each, and state the story-in-one-sentence. Collect a few good examples of fantasy and science fiction for your permanent notebook.

2. Talk with your local librarian about fantasy and science fiction, and ask to be shown the best recent examples. Try to get at least one book for older readers. Take these home and study them carefully, analyzing their appeal and value. Identify the plot pattern in each, and write out a synopsis, in not more than 250 words, of one of them, in terms of situation, problem, and solution.

3. Write a fantasy or science fiction story of any type, for children under 8, of not more than 1,000 words. Use any plot pattern you wish, and state your story-in-one-sentence before you start to write.

4. Plan a fantasy or science fiction story for older readers, using any plot pattern you wish. State the story-in-one-sentence, and then write a synopsis of not more than 250 words, in terms of situation, problem, and solution. If the story interests you and you think you really want to pursue this kind of fiction, go on and write it.

14

Picture Books

Specialists in early childhood education know that a child's exposure to books during the preschool years is vital to his success in school and in life. Some state that the child who has not had regular experience with books between the ages of 2 and 6 starts school with a disadvantage that is nearly impossible to overcome. Programs to introduce many more children to books and reading at earlier ages have increased the demand for good picture books.

Whether you think you are interested in writing picture books or not, you will find it a worthwhile exercise to try at least one or two; for this will help you learn to think visually—to *see* your story characters, settings, and actions. And this kind of thinking will make you a better writer no matter what kind of writing you do. If you're thinking of writing plays or film or television scripts, you *must* develop the ability to think visually.

Picture books have a picture on every page or every other page, with the text interspersed. Most are for children from 4 or 5 to about 9 years old, though there are some for younger children and also "picture-story books" for slightly older readers. A picture book is not just an illustrated story, but must be planned from the beginning with careful consideration for the pictures. The pictures are part of the story, complementing the text, so that both text and pictures are essential to the full sense of the story.

This does not mean you're expected to be both artist and writer, or even to find someone to illustrate your story.

Unless you are a professional illustrator—or unless you *know* you can produce truly professional illustrations—editors prefer to arrange for the artwork themselves. You will find some very fine picture books written and illustrated by the same individual, but you'll find many more illustrated by someone the writer had probably never heard of at the time he wrote the story.

If you are thinking of illustrating your own book, unless you are so dedicated to your own artwork that this is principally what you wish an editor to accept, you should negotiate this part of your sale separately from the text. Send a sample or two of your artwork along with the script, but make it clear in a cover letter that the script is submitted for consideration with or without your artwork.

One caution: Often two friends, one a hopeful writer and the other an artist or hopeful artist, have a wonderful idea that they will do a picture book together. Only rarely does this plan work. The first difficulty is that some very fine *artists* are not good *illustrators.* They may not have the necessary understanding of the problems and processes of reproducing various media in print, and the style and medium in which they work may not be the most effective and appropriate for the particular book in question. Knowing outstanding artists of many different specialties is an important part of a picture book editor's business; most prefer to work with those whose work they know—often those near enough at hand so that across-the-desk conferences are possible.

The second pitfall in collaborating with an artist friend is that the project may move along smoothly until the completed work is submitted; but then suppose that after three or four rejections, a letter comes from an editor accepting the story but rejecting the pictures. The author is elated; he's sold a book! But the artist says, "What about *me?* Let's try somewhere else."

The only way to avoid this unhappy possibility, if one

feels he *must* try such a collaboration, is for the writer and artist to make a *written contract, before the project ever begins*, stating as one of its terms that the completed work will be submitted for acceptance with or without illustrations, and that each has the independent option of accepting any offer of purchase.

Your effort in writing a picture book should go to producing the best text you can, in the best style you're capable of, while giving the necessary *thought* to the picture possibilities. The story—if your picture book is to be a story, and not a piece of nonfiction—will follow one of the established plot patterns but will differ sharply from a magazine story. To achieve unity and coherence, the magazine story deliberately reduces to a minimum the number of characters, settings, scenes. The picture book, by contrast, must provide lots of *variety* in the pictures; so the author deliberately plans many short scenes with different settings, and the cast of characters is often quite large, with new minor characters introduced throughout the story. Since the magazine story writer has no pictures to help him, he must use words to paint word pictures that his reader can "see." The picture book author, on the other hand, will leave many of the details of physical description to the pictures: if the house in the picture is white with green shutters, there's no need to mention this fact in the story. A good magazine story would almost never make a good picture book.

The best way to start writing a picture book is by reading; since at least half the story is told by pictures, nothing we can say here will take the place of your own careful analysis of recently published picture books. You should read a great many, and of different sizes and kinds, to get the "feel" of the style and to appreciate the wide variety in format and technique as well as in subject, length, and appeal. Take an hour or two in your local library to browse through the picture books; then select as many as you're allowed to take at one time for more thorough study at home. Choose those published within the last few years, especially "first" picture books by their authors; these reflect what editors are publishing today.

Your study will show you that all the rules for good writing that apply to magazine stories for children apply with equal force in writing picture books—and also that all the rules you've ever heard of about writing for children, including those in this book, can be broken, provided they are broken effectively! Note the action, suspense, fast tempo, freshness, enthusiasm. If the book is fiction, identify the plot pattern; you'll find the Incident pattern occurring more frequently than any other, especially for the youngest age group. It gives the writer an opportunity for a series of exciting episodes, the introduction of one or more new characters in each episode, and a variety of picturable action.

Look at the subjects. Some are fiction, some nonfiction. There are books about numbers, letters, words; "help" books about tying shoes or telling time. Here-and-now stories, fantasies, absurd or nonsense stories, funny stories. There are books with an almost breathless pace of physical activity, and quiet, introspective books that widen a child's understanding of the mental and spiritual world in which he lives.

Note the variety of characters. Most, by far, are children or personified animals. You may find a sprinkling of fantasy adults and possibly an inanimate object, but these are rare and must be truly irresistible to succeed. The great majority of child characters are present-day American children of various ethnic backgrounds.

Study the length—both the total length and the amount and distribution of wordage per page. Picture books vary from about 100 to 1200 words, with most about 500 to 800 words. There are usually 24 or 32 pages; the first four are "front matter"—title, copyright, et cetera. So the text begins on page 5, a right-hand page. Editors look for "page turns," something interesting enough at the end of each right-hand page to make the child want to turn the page.

Observe the style and presentation. Some picture books are told from first-person viewpoint, others from third person; you will even find a very few that address the reader as "you." Some stories are told almost entirely in dialogue, others have none or very little.

When you have made a study of picture books in general, select two or three that seem similar to the one you wish to write and reread them several times. You will find it helpful to type out the script from one to two of these, so that you can see how the story looks, separated from the pictures, in the form it had before it became a book. It will give you an idea of how the word count varies from page to page, a sense of proportion, and a new perspective from which to think about picture books.

Now, what will you write about? Give this some real thought; it's certainly true that some slight and trivial picture books are published, but such books are not the aim of either writers or editors. Good picture books are enduring. The picture-book crowd are not satisfied simply to read a book and be done with it; they demand that it be read over and over and over. A picture book should be as much fun for the reader as for the listener.

Try to find a subject simple enough to appeal to very young children, yet significant or entertaining enough to warrant repeated readings. Of course it must be something within the limits of the child's comprehension and experience. A picture book in which an octopus makes his own ink for writing a letter, for example, is an intriguing idea, but a difficult subject to handle, since the octopus itself is unfamiliar to the average child under eight, and octopus ink is a totally unknown phenomenon.

But do try to find a fresh subject; editors plead with

new writers to avoid the old, threadbare subjects: the "Peter Rabbit" plot of the animal who disobeys his mother and learns better through unhappy experiences, the "journey" story in which the main character goes from place to place or from one minor character to another trying to find the answer to some question, the story of the rejected animal or toy that is unhappy because of its rejection until it discovers that it is now or had really always been beautiful or useful, and the dream story. Don't think about the books that have already been written when you are looking for subject matter; to imitate is to fail. There are plenty of fresh, new, vital subjects without imitating.

Freshness and sparkle are also the keys to successful presentation. Today's world is full of arresting sights and sounds and experiences that attract a child's attention. There is no place for a dull, plodding, lusterless book. Or for the book that talks down to the child, telling him things he already knows, or doesn't care to know, in a boring, lifeless way. Or for the patronizing, moralizing tale; most editors demand "value" of some kind, but if the story has a moral, it should be such a natural part of the story that it does not stick out. Show the moral by action rather than talking about it, unless you or your story character can do it without becoming preachy.

The beginning of your story is vitally important; something *picturable* must happen at the very outset. Arouse reader interest and curiosity at once, and then keep the action moving the story forward fast. Don't stop for long explanations, thoughts, or static talk. If you can devise something that keeps the child interested—a question or some other suspense device that makes him want to turn each page—this often adds to the value and marketability of the book; but don't distort a good story just to include a gimmick. Whether you use such a device or not, the basic way to keep the child interested is to keep the story moving, suspenseful, exciting, building toward a climax.

In writing for the youngest age group, every paragraph—almost every sentence—should provide material for a picture. One of the easiest and most effective ways to achieve the needed variety for pictures is to include plenty of varied physical activity. Use action verbs, generously. Sentences should be short, words simple. Visual details can be left largely to the pictures, leaving room for more attention to other sensory details—smell, taste, feel, and sound. Sound, repetition, and rhythm can be used effectively to add interest and to fill out the story, or to slow the action when it becomes too fast.

Almost everyone has run across picture books that make him think, Well, surely I can do better than *that!* But it takes a special skill to write for a small child at *his* level without "writing down." The secret lies in taking both the reader and the subject seriously. This doesn't mean that the *book* must be serious; lightness and humor are much in demand. But one can say something serious and significant in a humorous way. The writer must respect the child's intelligence, which is every bit as keen as an adult's. Remember, always, that a child can comprehend *anything,* provided it is said to him in words and terms he is familiar with. He often has a keen sense of humor, but resents "silliness" as much as an adult does. Some editors also warn against "cuteness" and "sweetness." One editor asks for books "written in language that a grown man would not be ashamed to use to a child he did not know very well."

When you have finished the first draft of your story, test it to see if it will break into reasonably well-balanced portions. Don't have so much story on one page that the child gets bored with the picture, and then so little story on the next page that he hardly has time to look at the picture. Some planned variation, of course, is good, and adds to the dramatic effect—especially a reduction in wordage at a critical or climactic point.

You will find it helpful to type a new draft of your story with extra space between sections to indicate the paging you suggest. Many picture book authors at this point make a "dummy" of their book for their own use, to help them *see* how the book will develop. There is no need to prepare a dummy for submission to editors. Your writing should be so visual that an editor or an illustrator will immediately "get the picture," and most editors very much prefer that you not even include a description of the pictures as you see them, but leave the matter of illustration entirely to the editor and artist.

Whichever way you do this draft, read through each part to see if it ends with a stimulus to turn the page. Think about the picture possibilities for it, considering each picture not only by itself but in relation to the preceding and following pictures, to be sure there's some continuity and good variety. Then reread your text in relation to the picture you've imagined, and see whether you've included details that might just as well be omitted or shown in the picture instead of told in words. Drop every descriptive detail that isn't essential to the story.

Work this draft over thoroughly before typing a final draft. Since it will be read aloud, read the story aloud over and over to test it. Think about every sentence, every word. Can you gain added suspense somewhere, better emotional appeal, a bit of humor? Keep polishing until the whole story is as bright and sparkling as you can make it.

Most picture book editors prefer to receive the script typed much as you would type any other script. Some like triple spacing, with extra-wide margins—at least two inches. It is sometimes helpful to leave extra space between lines where you expect page divisions, especially if you have used some device for page turns, though this is not necessary.

Since so many beginning writers inquire about the inexpensive books for very young children available in department stores, drugstores, and supermarkets, we shall mention them briefly. Strictly speaking, these are not picture books, but storybooks with illustrations. Publishers of these books add only a few new titles each year, and the free-lance market is very limited. Although you may wish to try writing for this market, in general you will do better to study as models the picture books in bookstores and your library.

Should you write your picture book in verse? Not unless you are especially adept in writing verse for children. Even then, your chances are very much better in simple prose. Even the outstanding successes like Dr. Seuss and Aileen Fisher, who have demonstrated their skill in one book of verse after another, have succeeded in the more difficult medium in spite of, rather than because of, their choice of verse over prose. It has been said that there is no such thing as bad verse—either it is verse or it's not. Verse for children must *sing;* it must scan perfectly and flow so smoothly that there is never a hitch. Inversions are unacceptable. If you have a compulsion to write verse and can meet the extremely high standards of the best in children's verse, go ahead, with the full knowledge that you have an additional hurdle to leap.

What about using a "controlled vocabulary"? A few publishing houses want their picture books written within the word lists appropriate for the grade level in school for which the book is written. Some require a very limited vocabulary—often two hundred words or fewer. Standard word lists are available through colleges of education, or any elementary-school teacher in your locality can help you to such a list. Some publishers specify that they do *not* accept stories written within a controlled vocabulary. Most publishers have a brochure stating their requirements. Since these vary considerably, you should write to half a dozen publishers who you think from your own research publish the kind of picture book you wish to write.

POINTS TO REMEMBER

1. Although both follow established plot patterns, picture-book stories differ from magazine stories in that the former usually have many more scenes, many more characters, more physical activity—things that provide for good variety in pictures.

2. Picture books should be "read-aloudable" and deal with subjects within the experience and understanding of the child but significant enough to justify repeated readings and fresh in both content and presentation.

3. The text should divide readily into reasonably balanced portions, each of which can be illustrated with an interesting picture. If possible, each should stimulate a page turn.

4. The text, as well as the pictures, must get the child's interest immediately and hold it; this means appealing to the child's basic intelligence and never "writing down."

QUESTIONS AND EXERCISES

1. At your local library collect at least 20 picture books—the more recently published, the better. Prepare a tabulation of these showing whether the book is fiction or nonfiction; first person, third person, or a "you" approach; number of characters in each; number of settings or scenes; who the main character (if any) is; length, both in words and in number of pages; and general category—humor, "concept," verse, and so on.

2. Choose three of these books most nearly like one you think you would like to write to take home for further study. Type out the text from two of these, leaving two-inch margins and extra space between lines to indicate page changes. Then reread these stories from your own typescript. Note all details of sensory appeal. Go back and look at the

pictures without the text, and see how much of the story is told simply by the pictures.

3. Using any plot pattern of your choice, write a picture book of not more than 1,200 words. State your story-in-one-sentence, divide it into portions you would use for each page, and describe very briefly for your own use the picture that would illustrate each portion.

4. Describe briefly a nonfiction picture book you might write, with a fresh idea.

15

Other Peoples, Other Places, Other Times

Young people of all races, nationalities, and cultures need and want to know and understand each other. Families from other countries come to the United States to live. American families visit or spend several years in foreign lands. Television brings the customs and life-styles of the whole world into our living rooms.

The last decade has shown an encouraging growth in stories and books that feature Jewish children, black children, American Indian children, children from Spanish-speaking or Oriental backgrounds. Stories that both readers from these groups and the mainstream of young Americans can enjoy are welcomed by most editors. Some have made extra efforts to attract and help writers who are themselves members of a minority ethnic group. The purpose of the Council on Interracial Books for Children, based in New York, is to encourage publication of such books and to help such authors find publishers for their work.

Any writer who hopes to work in this fertile field must meet two often difficult requirements: He must have such a thorough knowledge of the particular ethnic background that what he writes will ring true to members of the race or culture of which he writes, and he must have a realistic understanding of the intercultural situation itself. The black child and black home and way of life usually portrayed by a white writer, for example, are rarely realistic. It is very difficult for the white writer, even one who knows black people quite well, to *think* from the black standpoint; yet this is what he must do if his story is to ring true.

The first mistake most often made by the beginning writer attempting a story of this kind is that he acknowledges in the story that there is a problem of race prejudice. Young children, left to themselves, apparently have no prejudice that springs from race or color; they accept a child different from themselves as a pleasant companion until prejudice is instilled in their minds by adults—unless the child's own actions ostracize him. So for children up to 10 or 12 the story problems and plots should be those used for any other stories of children, and should ignore the race question completely. In Ezra Jack Keats's picture books *The Snowy Day* and *Whistle for Willie,* for example, the main character could just as well have been a white boy as a black boy; only the pictures tell us that he is black. Such stories help both black and white children understand that persons of different races are essentially the same in their hopes and pleasures, their fears and frustrations, their need for security and love.

Stories for older readers may come to grips with race prejudice, for the teenager is very conscious that it exists. But a better story is likely to result when the race problem is subordinated to, or a smaller part of, some other situation. Stories dealing just with the race problem are almost invariably bare-faced propaganda, and will draw a rejection slip from the better publications and most of the secondary ones as well as from book editors. As with any other kind of story, the message should be there, but it should be shown, not talked about.

The second common mistake is failure to see members of minority groups as individuals. The tendency is to think of a stereotype with all of the picturesque surroundings: the Mexican wearing a sombrero, leading a burro, living in a flat-roofed adobe house; hot sunshine, desert, cactus plants, and so on. Somehow it seems hard to think about a Mexican child separated from this total stereotyped environment and still keep him Mexican! Yet this is what the writer must do. He must discipline himself first to *see* it as it is, so that he can tell it as it is without either exaggeration or understatement—without making the picture either too rosy or too bleak. One has to *know* his story characters as *individuals* to do this.

The great need is for stories of children of minority groups in urban situations, but there is a good market for other types of intercultural stories, too. Children want to know about people of other cultures: the way they live, what they do best, what characteristic foods they eat, and so on. Stories about children of different racial and national backgrounds who are living in the United States offer opportunities to give readers accurate pictures of these groups.

Sometimes the stories show two or three children or a family all of one race or culture, with slight or no association with American children. In this case, emphasis is on interesting and pleasant customs characteristic of the heritage of these children.

More often, one or more children of another background will be shown in association with an American child or children. The story brings out the attractive qualities of the "foreign" child and shows that he or she does not differ materially from the American child. Understanding and mutual acceptance come at the end of the story, usually as the result of solving some problem that has little or nothing to do with their "differentness."

Other stories may be about foreign children living in their own lands. These are generally limited to the 8 to 12 age group—children old enough to know something about foreign countries. Magazine stories of this kind, and books too, for the most part, are often keyed to school curricula;

locales are those the reader has become familiar with in his studies. Curricula vary in different parts of the country, but not so much that a writer who checks with the school system of the nearest large city cannot gain an adequate idea of what is appropriate. Teachers and editors want writers to show the admirable and pleasing qualities of foreign peoples; they want American children to know and like them, to understand that we and they have much in common.

Coming closer to home, we have the *regional story,* a story set in the present time but so dependent on its locale that it could not happen anywhere else; it thus gives the reader information about a specific region that is different from all other regions. One such story was set in Florida, having as its background the sponge-fishing industry carried on there by persons of Greek extraction. Another used the mud geysers in Yellowstone Park as its background. Wherever one lives or travels, if he keeps his mind alert and receptive, he will find material for such stories.

The facts, information, and specific details must be correct. The chamber of commerce in the area one visits will gladly supply maps and leaflets, usually without charge. A camera is a great help, for it records a wealth of detail that cannot be remembered or even put into a notebook. And one who has some real skill with a camera may even come up with a picture that can be used to illustrate the story, or as a model for the artist who is to draw illustrations. The well-plotted story or book that presents a vivid, authentic picture of a region or industry made interesting to the age reader for which it is written is always in demand.

Closely related to stories of various cultures and regions, because they present some similar problems, are *period stories* and *historicals.* Just as children need to gain concepts of other peoples, they need also to appreciate their own heritage.

A *period story* is one that takes place during a time in the past, but concerns itself very little, if at all, with the history of that time. Many stories about the Pilgrims, the pioneers who crossed the plains, or the settlers who home-steaded in the West are of this type. They show a way of life characteristic of the period rather than specific historical events or famous personalities of the time.

Period stories are usually for readers over 10. They may be set in any time and place from ancient Greece or Rome to the American colonial period or World War II, in either the United States or Europe. Those related to subjects and times somewhat familiar to readers through their school work are most likely to succeed. The prime demand, how-ever, as in every other kind of fiction, is for a good *story;* old letters or diaries, nostalgic memories of a grandparent, may provide good authentic background material from which to develop a dramatic, suspenseful story; but the writer cannot depend on the romance or drama of the period alone to provide the needed interest. Bette Greene's book *Summer of My German Soldier,* which was made into a TV movie, tells of an American Jewish girl's efforts to help a young Nazi escape from a prison camp near her family's farm. Laurence Yep's *Dragonwings,* set in San Francisco at the time of the 1906 earthquake and fire, tells of a Chinese boy and his uncle whose dream is to build a flying machine—as well as life in the Chinese colony and the great disaster. Perusing a stack of young people's magazines and browsing in the public library will show the unlimited and exciting scope of this kind of story.

The drama, danger, excitement, and suspense inherent in the circumstances of life in times past make the period story fairly easy to write, provided the writer does enough research. The *facts* must be accurate in every detail, but the story itself may be completely imagination.

The true *historical story* takes place in a definite time

and features well-known events and people. The main character or characters are not necessarily famous persons of the past, though they may be, but such persons should definitely walk through the pages in person and their historic acts should affect the course of the story. Such a story might have as its main character a cabin boy aboard Columbus' flagship; he would have a definite story of his own, but one that is affected by the historical acts of Columbus during the voyage.

A quite different kind of historical is the *Bible story,* of which there are two kinds: those that simply retell the story as it is in the Bible, and those that fictionalize to the extent of using someone who might conceivably have been present when the biblical account took place—usually a child—as the viewpoint character. For example, the story of the loaves and fishes might be told from the viewpoint of the boy whose lunch was multiplied and served to the five thousand.

Most editors insist on strict adherence to what the Bible account actually contains, so that no confusion results in the child's mind about what is in the Bible and what is not. It is quite all right to clothe a character in a "blue robe" and to mention sandals, veils, and whatever else research reveals to have been typical clothing at that time; reference to flowers and trees known to have grown in the area at that time is fine, as is some description of the typical houses, villages, pathways, wells, and so on—whatever helps the story to come alive. But what the characters say and do should not deviate from the biblical account, though the wording may be made more modern and within the child's understanding. Retold Bible stories are for children under 12.

Along with these stories of remote times and places we've been discussing, we should consider *legends, folktales, fables,* and *parables,* some of which are very old and may be refurbished and retold to children.

A *legend* is a nonhistorical and unverifiable story handed down by tradition from earlier times and popularly accepted as historical. Most legends published for children conform only loosely to this definition, for often they are completely imaginary, pure fiction, though some are based on a real legend. Often they purport to give an account of firsts: the first use of fire by man, the first canoe, the first bridge across a stream, and so on. Others are stories that have grown up around actual historical figures such as St. Nicholas or George Washington. Many historians say that the story of Betsy Ross and the flag is totally or partially legendary. Nearly every community has local legends that may offer grist for a writer's mill.

Since the first qualification for a legend is that it is unverifiable, it concerns itself with a happening about which nothing is known; this leaves the writer's imagination the fullest freedom. For example, somewhere, sometime, someone must have made the first aboriginal bow and arrow, the first sewing needle, the first stringed instrument. But who knows who or where or when? Yet the inventor must have ranked among his own people as Edison or Burbank ranks with us today. What that long-ago individual did required original thinking and brought better living conditions to his tribe. Such a feat provides a good springboard for a legend for children.

Authentic legends, too, may be used, but most of these require considerable rewriting. They are usually too long and rambling, full of symbolism long since forgotten; often they show great cruelty and suffering, and evil is rarely punished. But a creative writer can find a way to condense and retain the spirit and essence of some of these stories and make them suitable for children.

The same is true of *mythological stories, folktales,* and *fables*—Greek, Roman, Japanese, Mayan, American Indian, and so forth. These stories, with their sense of wonder, magic, grandeur, and sometimes humor, hold a universal and undying fascination for children. The source material is practically inexhaustible; books of these old stories and parables are available in almost every library, and since the stories themselves are in the public domain, authors are free to use them as they wish. One may rewrite them into single stories for magazine use or picture books like *Stone Soup,* or collect several stories together for a book. When sending retold stories of these kinds to an editor, one should enclose a brief letter stating the source of the original material.

All of the stories discussed in this chapter have some common problems. First, as with all other stories, one must decide on a plot pattern and then tailor his material to fit it. Sometimes this is very easy, and sometimes it is difficult or even impossible. Making historical facts or the fragments of a biblical account fit neatly into a plot pattern can present insurmountable difficulties; in this case, it's best simply to handle the piece as nonfiction, but to write it in a dramatic, interesting, fictional style.

Second, the writer may feel that he cannot establish rapport or reader identity with a foreign child or child of ancient times. Yet this is not difficult if the writer will remember that although the outward forms of life vary, basic human desires and emotions are universal and remain the same. Only the expression of them changes, and this less than one might think. Persons of other times and cultures felt and feel fear, anger, joy, and love just as we do. The desire to "belong," to hold positions of importance and respect, to have loving and loyal friends and family, to possess the comforts and adornments or status symbols that associates possess, to have enough good food, warm clothing, security, social recognition—these things are basic to all peoples everywhere. If they are made plain in the story, the present-day American reader will quickly identify with the story character; the comfort an Eskimo child feels as he snuggles into his skins in his igloo is the same as that experienced by any child snuggling under a favorite quilt or an electric blanket.

It's important also to remember to present the unfamiliar in terms of the familiar, so that the child can understand. For instance, in describing the building of a sod house, one might say that the people cut large bricklike slabs of turf; because the reader is quite familiar with bricks, he immediately gets the picture.

The third sometimes troublesome problem is how to handle the dialogue in a story about characters who do not speak modern English. The basic principle is simple: Write it so that it gives the feel of the time and place and people, and at the same time keep it so simple that it is easy to read and does not distract the reader's attention from the story. Often the writer can create the illusion of another time and place and language by using a faintly formal or archaic type of speech; he avoids the common contractions, and his characters may use a very few words or oddities of speech typical of the time and culture. These must be clear to the reader from the context, and are purely for flavoring; a little bit of this kind of flavor goes a long way.

The same is true of the use of foreign words. A very few common words sprinkled lightly through the story add just the right flavor without being so noticeable that they attract attention to themselves. The meaning of a foreign word or term must always be clear from its context; one never "explains" the word or translates it crudely by putting the English equivalent in parentheses.

Many writers feel that incorrect grammar is a characteristic of the early settlers, particularly laborers, and that to portray these persons—as well as members of some minority groups—realistically they must have them speak incorrectly. This is not necessarily the case; many of these persons had or have a fine command of the language, though often they have colloquialisms peculiar to their time and culture. A few colorful and often very individual oddities of speech may be used for flavor; the point is to avoid stereotypes generally assigned to certain cultures or groups. One must be careful also to avoid slang, and even common and proper words, that are *not* appropriate to the time and culture. The word "roundup," for example, came into the language during the times of great open ranges for cattle on the western plains; it would be inappropraite in a story of colonial New England.

One must not discount the amount of research required to write well of other people, other places, other times. In addition to digging out needed facts, a writer should read widely and deeply to steep himself in the "feel" of the time and place and culture. He must be able to visualize the details of scenes and settings and know the people, both actual and imagined, so intimately that they seem real and alive to him. Anything less is too little. He must know without stopping to think about it what his characters would say and how they would say it under any conditions that may arise in the story. Maps, pictures, letters, diaries, and if at all possible, a visit to the locale, where one not only gets the "lay of the land" but may visit museums and unearth some firsthand material—all these things help to extend what a writer gets from a great deal of reading about his subject. Thorough research takes an enormous amount of time, patience, and often detective work. For this reason many writers find it best to specialize in a single period and place, learning everything they possibly can about it, and then using this knowledge for a number of books and stories.

Because so few persons are willing to do the research required, there is less competition in these areas than in some others. If you enjoy ferreting out facts and find different ways of life fascinating, you can make them fascinating for others also, and you have a wide-open market.

POINTS TO REMEMBER

1. Stories for young children should not deal with racial or cultural prejudice, though they may include and identify children of different races and cultures; stories for older readers may deal with race prejudice, but preferably as a problem subordinated to another specific problem that might involve *any* normal, typical boys and girls.

2. Stories of foreign children in their own lands, and period and historical stories are generally keyed to school curricula; they are written for readers over 10.

3. Regional stories and books have a good market if the writer matches the industry or activity he chooses as background with the interests of the age group for which he writes.

4. Facts in regional, period, historic, prehistoric, and Bible stories must be accurate; imagination may be used to fill in details and make the story come alive.

5. Old stories such as legends, myths, folktales, fables, and parables are in the public domain and can often be rewritten for children; a writer may also make up "original" legends.

6. All stories discussed in this chapter, like all the other stories, must follow one of the recognized plot patterns; when facts cannot be tailored to fit a pattern, the material should be handled as nonfiction.

7. If the writer portrays the basic hopes, fears, frustrations, pleasures, goals, and loves common to all mankind, readers will readily identify with a main character outwardly very different from themselves.

8. A slightly formal speech, sprinkled lightly with a few words and expressions appropriate to the culture of which one writes, results in realistic dialogue.

9. One must be a thorough researcher to write well of other peoples, places, and times; usually he will find it advantageous to specialize in one time and culture.

QUESTIONS AND EXERCISES

1. In the periodicals with which you have been working, find as many examples of the stories discussed in this chapter as you can. Analyze

these as to age group, plot pattern, general subject matter, story problem, and main character. Study the dialogue and discover what creates reader identity.

2. At your library, find some books of old legends, folktales, myths, or fables. Look through these to find one or more that might be rewritten for children. Try rewriting one, just for practice; be sure you have a definite plot pattern in mind and state your story-in-one-sentence before you start to write.

3. Think about the various types of stories mentioned in this chapter. Which kind would you like most to try? What background do you already have for writing this kind of story? What further research or preparation will be necessary? For what age group will you write? Go on and think through the whole project, and then write your story.

16

Five Special Kinds of Stories

When you branch out from the typical here-and-now story, you may want to try a mystery; or perhaps you like sports and want to write football or skiing stories. Or maybe you're a natural wit and humorous stories are your goal. This chapter will explore these and other possibilities. As you continue to read magazines and books for young people, keep alert for stories that are good examples of the kinds in this chapter. Study them and try to write some similar stories, if only for the practice and enlargement of your skill.

SPECIAL-DAY AND SEASONAL STORIES

Since magazines are issued at monthly intervals, editors try to make each issue fit the month or season. The need for fresh, well-plotted, special-day, and seasonal material is always greater than the supply. Some editors insist that writers believe the magazines fold up in summer, because they receive so few summertime stories. Others complain that they get too many of the obvious, too familiar plots built around Christmas and Thanksgiving and would like some fresh stories of these favorite holidays; they would also welcome stories with a background of less popular days such as Arbor Day, Columbus Day, or holidays of minority groups, and an alert writer can find ways to build stories around anniversaries of important events or discoveries.

But stories about even the commonest holidays are in constant demand. New Year's Day, the birthdays of our national heroes, Valentine's Day, Easter, April Fool's Day, May Day, Fourth of July, Mother's Day, Father's Day, Halloween, Thanksgiving, and Christmas are featured every year by most children's publications.

Seasonal stories may be written around appropriate sports and outdoor activities such as kite flying, raking leaves, sledding, planting or harvesting crops. And of course there are the many special weeks such as Book Week, Fire Prevention Week, Be Kind to Animals Week, and dozens of others. An almanac is a gold mine of ideas for special-day and seasonal stories.

The advantage in writing these stories is that the demand is great and few writers write them, but there are disadvantages too. Usually the best time for writing them is during the season in question, when one is in the mood; it's hard to generate enthusiasm for Halloween at Christmastime. But then, of course, the time for *marketing* the new story is not right, and the marketing period, when it does come, is limited. If a Halloween story doesn't sell between about January 10 and April 1, it must be shelved until the following January. And if an editor buys it but fails to publish it in October because he has overpurchased, then it will be another whole year before the story appears.

Special-day and seasonal books are also welcomed, and may be marketed any time of the year. Editors and librarians well know the appeal the loved holidays have for children regardless of the season; Christmas books, especially, circulate as actively in July as in December.

SPORTS STORIES

The demand for sports stories is also greater than the supply, though here, too, a fresh angle is important. Too many sports stories are simply variations of the routine plot in which the main character is hopeful of making the team or of his team's winning *the* game, discovers during the contest that he has a skill or stamina beyond what he thought he had, and emerges victorious. Although these ingredients may be in the plot, the author should have enough ingenuity to individualize them by adding unusual or unexpected complications and fresh solutions to problems. Attention to the second-level story can help to add freshness, as can better characterization that makes the main character a true individual instead of a prototype.

For readers 8 to 12, sports stories may be about Little League baseball, swimming, ice skating, bicycle rodeos, skateboarding, playground events. (Closely related to these are stories of a main character getting his or her pet ready for some show or competition; horse and dog training are popular subjects.)

Older readers like everything from Ping-Pong to car racing. Tennis, skiing, swimming, and the usual team sports at school are all popular. But less common sports, such as bowling, archery, lacrosse, and rock climbing, also have a strong following. The advent of competitive sports for girls, and admission of girls to formerly all-boy activities, has created a market for girls' stories about basketball, field hockey, tennis, swimming, track, gymnastics, and other sports.

There's a need for good, swift-moving sports stories for boys over twelve. This is an age when many boys tend to abandon reading, perhaps in favor of the sports themselves. The writer must show a command of the fine points of the sport, for *readers* know the fine points. The sports story should not only entertain, but give some new information and perhaps provide some pointers about the sport.

MYSTERIES AND SUSPENSE STORIES

Children from tots to teens are as avid devotees of mystery stories as are many adults. There are two main types: mysteries without detection and mysteries with detection.

Since children under 8 have little power of deduction, which involves assembling facts, analyzing them, and arriving at a conclusion, the mystery for the youngest age group is usually solved without detection. Yet the basic construction of these simplest mystery stories is exactly the same as that of the most complicated adult mystery novel: the beginning rouses the reader's curiosity about the answer to a specific narrative question; the middle makes him still more curious, more desirous of knowing the answer; the ending gives him the answer. Although the answer may not seem exciting to an adult, it should be one that is exciting to the child.

One such story was about a dog sitting in front of a candy store. He seemed to be waiting for someone. Who? The author builds a brief incident around each of several passersby, increasing curiosity as to whether *this* is what the dog is waiting for—a telephone repair man, a little girl, a fire engine, twin babies, a yellow cat, a bus. But the dog is not waiting for any of them. Then a boy comes out of the candy store carrying two ice cream cones. He gives one to the dog, and after eating it, the little dog follows his master down the street. This story, like almost all stories of this type, follows the Incident pattern; it was told in just 200 words.

These general narrative questions make good bases for mysteries without detection:

1. What is it?
2. What causes it?
3. What is he (or are they) doing?
4. What (or whom) is he looking for?
5. Who took it?
6. Who did it?
7. How did it get there?
8. Where did it come from?
9. Where did it go?
10. Where is it?
11. Why does he do it?
12. What is inside?

The story in which the mystery is solved by deduction or detection is necessarily built on the pattern of Purpose

Achieved by ingenuity, sometimes combined with special capacity or courage. The main character starts out to solve a mystery and does so by clever deduction, reasoning from cause to effect, sometimes helped by a special knowledge or ability, sometimes having to use courage to go into a frightening place or confront a person who may be hostile. These stories may be quite simple or quite complex, depending on the age for which they are written and the length of the story.

A good mystery requires considerable ingenuity, but a writer who has mastered the plot patterns sufficiently to succeed with other types of stories can learn to write mysteries too. He needs one added device—misdirection. The writer deliberately misleads the reader, inducing him with false clues to believe something that is not true. At the same time, the writer must be scrupulously honest with the reader, never stating in narration what is not true. This all goes back to the principle of building to the actual and alternate endings: the actual ending is the truth of the situation; the alternate ending is the illusion, what *seems* to be true. The writer builds toward both throughout the story, thus creating suspense.

The secret of honest misdirection lies in keeping strictly within the viewpoint of the main character. The main character may—and does—come to false conclusions honestly arrived at through wrong interpretation or because he does not yet have sufficient information. Or he may have been led astray by wrong information given him by other characters; story characters may declare as true something they believe to be true, though they too are honestly mistaken. The reader, then, who has identified with the main character, is also misled—and experiences the same satisfaction the main character experiences when at last he corrects his errors of judgment, deduces the situation correctly, and solves the mystery. The writer must be sure he does not withhold from the reader any clue known to the main character.

The suspense story has become even more popular than the conventional mystery. The distinction is that in the mystery the main character's problem is to unravel the mystery, whereas in the suspense story the main character—and therefore the reader as well—knows almost from the beginning, or is pretty sure, what the truth is. His problem is to prove and reveal this truth, which others in the story either don't know or don't accept. The suspense lies in efforts to expose the "villain" through fast and clever action before he either escapes or brings harm to the main character or other innocent persons. The principles for writing the suspense story are much the same as those for writing mysteries.

HUMOROUS STORIES

Whether or not one sets out to write funny stories, a little humor improves almost any story—or article. Editors ask, often wistfully, for humorous stories; yet the instant response of most writers is "Oh, I can't possibly be funny!" This is unfortunate, for almost any writer, once he understands the principles of humor, can make readers laugh. Here are a few of the basics, for readers of all ages:

1. *Incongruity* brings together people, character traits, objects, or ideas with little or no relationship. It's the "bull in the china shop" situation. A story for young teens was about a group of girls preparing an elaborate meal for their boyfriends. After several minor and humorous disasters with recipes beyond their skill, they wind up serving hot dogs and potato chips—exactly what the boys wanted—on Mother's best china, with a fine tablecloth, sterling silver, and linen napkins. The occasion is great fun and a complete success.

2. *Discomfiture* takes advantage of the almost universal

trait of human nature that enjoys seeing something mildly unpleasant happen to someone else. What happens should not be serious, for then it becomes cruel, and cruelty is not funny. The humor is often enhanced when the discomfiture comes to someone who is rather pompous, a bit of a "stuffed shirt." It is usually of the slapstick variety, shown in action rather than speech.

If you want to create sympathy for the character, instead of having him pompous and the butt of the humor, you can use a first-person approach; when the main character can laugh at himself, the reader laughs *with* him rather than *at* him. One such story was of a boy who is maneuvered into going on a skiing party with his friends, all good skiers, although he has never skied and has had "poor coordination" written under "Remarks" on his P.E. report card ever since third grade. He has especially wanted to impress a particular girl, and everything he does makes things worse. In the end, he's such a good sport—and entertains everyone so spontaneously at the after-ski party at the lodge—that he wins the friendship of the girl and everyone else.

3. *Reversal of roles* shows a character acting radically differently from the way the reader expects him to act, or from his natural behavior, often with amusing results. Incongruity is a part of this, but is subordinate to the reversal of roles. One such story was about an athlete who blunders into participating in a cake decorating contest, which, of course, he wins.

4. *Exaggeration* may take many forms, from the "tall tale" to the story in which the main character goes to great effort to achieve some trivial end, or an end that could be achieved quite easily. Such a story was built around a boy's "invention" of an elaborate machine to melt snow off the sidewalk so that he will not have to shovel it; the machine does work in the end, but is much more effort to operate—and takes much more time—than a snow shovel.

5. *Understatement* can be as effective as exaggeration. Throughout the story, a character makes casual remarks about highly important situations, objects, or actions, very much underplaying their qualities or significance. Suppose two boys have become marooned by a flash flood; they stand looking at the half-mile of muddy water that lies between them and their destination. One says, "We can't swim out—we forgot our bathing suits." This kind of dry humor woven into a story as a characteristic of one character always amuses and entertains.

6. *Gentle foibles or immature behavior of a character that makes the reader feel both superiority and compassion* is the kind of humor in *Winnie the Pooh*. Pooh's weakness for honey that gets him into so much trouble is a human failing that most readers readily identify with and yet laugh about.

Humor may be intrinsic in the situation or a matter of phraseology, or both. A little practice, plus the conviction that you *can* be funny, will help you write humorous stories—or at least to put some humor into the stories you write.

STORIES OF ANIMALS IN THEIR NATURAL HABITAT

Interest in ecology and in the preservation of endangered animal species has stimulated the market for books and stories about all kinds of animals, birds, and fish in their native habitat. TV programs showing wild creatures and the way they live have made children familiar with and eager to know more about them. Barbara Steiner, Lorle Harris, and others have written simple, yet well-researched, action-packed stories about wolves, whales, whooping cranes, and other species. The animal "biography" series published by Putnam's provides excellent examples.

The main characteristic of these stories is that the animals live normal lives as animals in their natural environment. They do not "think" in the usual sense of the word, but they do have feelings and instincts; they have urges, purposes, and desires that are, at a higher level, felt also by human beings—such as the desire for self-preservation, love of mate and offspring, attachment to home, love of play, and so on. These characteristics make the animal understandable to the reader and permit considerable reader identification.

This kind of animal story is told more objectively than most other stories; the reader is shown what the animal does and how and why he does it. The word "thought" is not used. Instead, the writer makes use of such words and phrases as "sensed," "felt," "knew," "circled in indecision," "became aware," "searching . . . she found. . . ." The animal is never shown as having human goals, values, ambitions, or reasoning power. It keeps its own animal nature throughout the story.

POINTS TO REMEMBER

1. Special-day and seasonal stories are important to magazine editors; marketing them presents some problems because of time limitations. Special-day books are popular.

2. Both book and magazine editors welcome sports stories for both sexes; they may be about either well-known or little-known sports, and must have a fresh, timely angle.

3. Mysteries are of two kinds: mysteries without detection for children under 8 and mysteries with detection for older readers. Suspense stories are also popular.

4. Humorous stories are not difficult to write if one learns the principles of humor; touches of humor improve almost any story.

5. Stories of animals in their natural habitat provide an opportunity for the nature lover to show the drama and secrets of nature to young

readers in interesting and unusual ways. One must learn their special technique to write them.

QUESTIONS AND EXERCISES

1. In the publications you have been working with, try to find examples of each of the kinds of stories discussed in this chapter. Identify the plot pattern of each, and state each as a story-in-one-sentence. Study the way in which each is developed, how special interest is provided by the holiday or season, by a particular sport, and so forth.

2. Carry your search further by hunting books in the library representating each of these kinds of story. Read the ones that interest you most.

3. Write a special-day story for children 8 to 12, using the plot pattern of your choice, in not more than 1,200 words. State your story-in-one-sentence before you begin to write.

4. Write a mystery story without detection for children under 8, using the Incident pattern and basing your story on one of the 12 questions given on page 152, in 850 words maximum.

5. Just for practice, write a humorous story for any age group, using the plot pattern of your choice; use one of the devices discussed as the basis for the humor.

V

The Nonfiction Skills

17

Articles for All Ages

Exposed by both print and audiovisual media to the vast world beyond their immediate experience, even very young children are eager for information about this world. The need for facts and their interpretation in language a child can understand is unlimited. There is also a strong and constant market for other kinds of nonfiction, from hobby and craft ideas to inspirational and self-development aids. Almost every publication that buys fiction for children and young adults also buys nonfiction.

Articles for young people are of four general types: How-To, Interesting Personality, Informational, and Self-Development. There is overlapping, of course; but a moment's consideration of the *purpose* the author had in writing the article will usually classify it in one of these four categories.

THE HOW-TO ARTICLE

Fresh and really helpful articles that give readers detailed, workable instruction on how to do anything from making a birthday present for Dad to getting better results from half an hour's piano practice are used by publications for all ages. If you have found a new way to use a normally discarded object, invented a better way of doing a routine task, or developed a set of personal guidelines that helped you or someone else to use money or time more efficiently— or if you know someone else who has done these things or hundreds of similar things—you have the raw material for a How-To article.

Some magazines favor craft and hobby ideas; a few use recipes for simple cooking projects for young children. Some teenage girls' publications buy fashion and beauty How-Tos, though for the large, popular magazines these are likely to be staff written. Teenage boys like sports and mechanics How-Tos. Both boys and girls want articles on money-making projects and career preparation, also human-relations How-Tos that help them get along better with peers and parents. Party ideas, complete with invitations, decorations, entertainment, prizes, and refreshments, are popular with all ages. Puzzles and games are also grouped with the How-Tos. A survey of publications in the age group for which you wish to write will show you what is wanted.

The procedure for writing a successful How-To article is simple. In the beginning tell what the project is and show its worth; make the reader *want* to do it and believe he *can* do it.

In the middle of a craft article tell clearly and specifically what materials and tools are needed, and follow this with the clear, step-by-step directions as to what is to be done. If there are pitfalls or if the reader is likely to make a fatal mistake by using a substitute material or doing the operation in a different way from that outlined, point this out and explain briefly why the right way is important. Craft projects for children should employ materials that are likely to be available in most households or easily and inexpensively obtained. If yours requires some unusual ingredient or material, tell where it may be obtained. The directions should be within the child's capability, though *some* help from an adult is usually acceptable.

End your article with a paragraph that shows the happy result and makes the reader eager to get at the project immediately.

The article may use the "cookbook" approach that addresses the reader directly: "Smooth the edges with sandpaper and glue the felt to the frame." Or it may use an impersonal, third-person approach: "After the plaster has set, the mold may be tapped lightly and lifted off." The first is usually better, as it involves the reader immediately; the main thing, however, is not to combine the two; if you use the "you" approach, use it throughout.

Some articles for very young readers use a fictional approach. "Billy needed a new house for his white mouse. He took a matchbox that Mother had just emptied and cut a door in one end. . . ."

The essentials for a How-To article are clarity, workability, and freshness. Directions must be complete and clear. To be *sure* that yours are, before you submit your article to an editor, try to find someone to help you. Ask someone in the age group for which you are writing, who has had no previous knowledge of the project, to take your directions and actually follow them through. Drawings or photographs can often be helpful; these are discussed in the next chapter.

Editors don't want projects that are not really workable and useful. A craft idea should be something the child himself can use—something for his room, a toy, something to wear, a fad perhaps—or something Mother or Dad will truly be pleased to have and use. A money-making idea must be really fresh and practical. A writer only damages his own reputation and the whole free-lance system by sending in material that is unsuitable.

THE INTERESTING PERSONALITY ARTICLE

People are always interested in other people, and almost all young people's publications except those for the youngest children use articles about both well-known and unknown adults and young people whose activities and achievements are interesting to young readers. Subjects include popular TV, movie, music, and other entertainment personalities; athletes and sports personalities; little-known or unknown persons who have unusual careers or who have started youth programs in their communities. Religious publications use articles about their own leaders and missionaries, and local leaders of youth groups or others whose activities are of interest to young people.

Also in demand are articles about teenagers or persons in their twenties who have won recognition as athletes or entertainers, as safe drivers, or as standouts in almost any field, including community, church, and school activities. Young persons who have developed a small business such as an earthworm farm or a teenage employment agency, or who have found or invented a money-making job for themselves are good subjects for Interesting Personality articles. So are teenagers who have done something unusual such as taking a cross-country bicycle trip or participating in an archaeological expedition.

The essentials for an Interesting Personality article are finding an angle that makes the subject interesting to a wide cross section of readers and then supplying a well-developed coverage of the activities. The more thorough and comprehensive the research, the more valuable the article. An interview with the subject can provide fresh, accurate, up-to-the-minute material, and should not be overlooked if at all possible. But secondary sources are also important, and the writer who is willing to dig for everything available on his subject can find such efforts well rewarded. Interviewing is discussed in more detail in the next chapter.

Must you have the subject's permission to write the article? If he or she is a public figure, the answer is no. If not, you should get permission; usually this is not difficult. In writing for young people, you will be writing only about personalities you want the reader to like and admire. Most persons are flattered to be written about in this way.

What does the author owe the subject of such an article? Nothing, except a thank you and a copy of the article when it is published. If the individual is willing to read the article before you send it in, it is usually a good idea to arrange for this. He can correct any errors; and if the piece pleases him, he is likely to supply some additional tidbits that add interest and color. His approval also adds to the value of the article.

THE INFORMATIONAL ARTICLE

Informational articles cover such a wide variety of subjects that even a partial listing is not practical. Most-wanted subjects include biographical sketches of historical or present-day persons; occupations, careers, and the world at work; science, nature, and natural history; fashion, fads, and popular music; sports and camping; places and travel; geography, social science, and social issues. Religious publications buy articles on church life and history, missions, religious case history, the Bible and Bible personalities.

The essentials in writing Informational articles are interest and understandable presentation, plus a wealth of facts. The material must be made interesting to the age group for which it is written, and it must be presented in language and terms the average reader in the age group can understand. The secret of doing both is to keep putting yourself in the place of the reader. Ask yourself, What angle on this subject will interest the average child of 12—or 16, as the case may be? Which of all the facts I have gathered will be meaningful to him? How can I present these facts in terms he will understand?

Presenting a complex and often abstract world to children

8 to 12 may seem like a formidable undertaking, but it need not be so if the writer does not feel obligated to tell the child more than is necessary. There is the well-known story of the child who, when asked by his grandmother how he liked the book she had given him for his birthday, replied, "Well, it was good, but it just tells more than I care to know about penguins."

The trouble with most articles for younger readers is that the writer tries to tell too much and fails to relate what he does tell to the present understanding and experience of the reader. To tell third- or fourth-graders that the flow of the Gulf Stream could generate 180 million kilowatt hours of power annually is futile. Tell them that ocean currents along our east coast might be used to produce all the electricity our whole nation could use. Remember that a child's intelligence is just like an adult's. He can comprehend anything at all, provided it is said to him in words he understands and is related to his own experience and interests. If you choose a subject that is itself interesting to young readers, and then limit your subject to what you can cover adequately in a single article for the age group for which you are writing, you are well on your way to a successful Informational article.

This kind of article for younger readers, like the How-To, is sometimes told more as a story than as an article; one such article tells of a boy finding a horned toad which he believes at first to be a baby dinosaur. Taking it to his father, an engineer who has recently moved with his family to the Southwest, the boy learns several interesting things about horned toads and their habits from a geologist who is talking with his father.

For older readers you must use more details. Teenagers are well informed on subjects that interest them and demand that an article tell them something *new* about a subject. Many of them read adult publications, and Informational articles for them should be on practically an adult level but slanted more specifically to their own interests.

THE SELF-DEVELOPMENT ARTICLE

Articles that help the reader to understand himself better, gain a clearer sense of his own identity, feel better about himself, and want to try harder are bought mostly by religious publications for young adults. Some teenage secular publications use such articles if they have real meat in them and will truly inspire without talking down or preaching. They must have strong teenage appeal and be well researched and up-to-date—up to the standard of the best adult articles, but slanted to the teenager's interests and written in his language. This does *not* mean using the teenager's current slang. A brief article on appreciation of parents in one of the poorer teen publications began: "Let's face it, chum. You and I have a good thing going for us." This was followed by a liberal sprinkling of such expressions as "How come we rate all this for free?" "Well, brace yourself for a real jolt, chum," and "Kinda shakes you up, eh?" Anyone who thinks he is reaching teenagers this way is mistaken.

The writer should be himself, using an easy, conversational style such as he might use in *talking* with a teenager he has never met before. Young people are embarrassed by a strange adult's effort to show he's "one of them" by using their private jargon. It's insincere—an affectation. If a writer wants a reader's respect, he must be respectable—and he must respect the reader's intelligence and ability to rise to *his* level of expression.

A bit of humor in a Self-Development article is often its saving grace, and sometimes a "we" approach makes the reader feel that the writer is *with* him, not talking *at* him. When one can say honestly, "When we're hurt or angry we want to strike back," this can help the reader feel that the writer understands and sympathizes with him—has felt this way himself—and this makes him willing to listen. Empathy—the ability to put yourself in the reader's position—and a light touch for serious subjects are the best qualifications for writing Self-Development articles.

PLANNING THE ARTICLE

It is not just hunger for facts and the need for children to learn about their world that accounts for the growing popularity of nonfiction. Articles for both children and adults are better written than they were a few years ago. Today's article writer uses every technique and device of the fiction writer except plot. He knows the necessity for gaining the reader's immediate interest and holding it, and he does this by using fictionally presented anecdotes and case histories in which setting, characters, and dialogue are realistic and alive; he creates curiosity and suspense, building to a true climax; he paints vivid word pictures and includes specific details that appeal to the physical senses; he exploits every opportunity for humor, oddities, human-interest items, and surprising facts, thus giving his piece emotional appeal. He makes the reader *care* what happens in the next sentence, the next paragraph, the whole article.

Whatever kind of article you write, the basic structure will be the same, and this brings us back to our now familiar principle of beginning, middle, and ending. In the beginning the writer must state his premise clearly and let the reader know what he proposes to tell or prove or demonstrate in the article. Here he must say everything he is going to say in the whole article; nothing new should be added after the end of the beginning zone.

The middle, then, is an expansion, exploration, elaboration, examination of what was said in the beginning. Here the writer uses facts, quotations of authorities, examples, anecdotes, analogies—any and all appropriate devices of exposition—to develop the premise he has set up in the beginning.

The ending is not a summary: rather it is a *conclusion*; it draws conclusions from what has been shown and stated in the middle. The ending is the answer to "So what?" It relates its conclusions to the reader's interest and shows him why they are of significance to him. It says, in effect, "Therefore, dear reader, as I said in the beginning . . ." and returns full circle to the initial premise.

Only a piece that is put together in this way will be well organized. A good paragraph has a "topic sentence" as its first or second sentence (there may be a transitional sentence first). The idea expressed in the topic sentence is developed in the body of the paragraph, and the paragraph will end with a "periodic sentence" that drives home the point or draws a conclusion leading to the next paragraph. This is not a rule thought up by editors or teachers of composition but is simply a natural law of communication that can no more be set aside than can the law of gravity. Fortunately, because it *is* a natural law, most of us follow it rather naturally without being conscious of it, just as we obey the law of gravity whether we know of it or not. But understanding the principle can often be a help when it comes to organizing material or to working the rough spots out of a paragraph or a whole article.

A provocative title and an immediate interest-getting opening are essential to the success of any article, just as they are to the success of a short story. The title is the writer's first opportunity to attract interest. Generally it should be short, although some editors like long titles; tailor yours to fit the publication when possible. It should always be accurate and exact.

Superlatives help a title because they are curiosity provok-
ing: "The Largest Bird in the World," "The Smallest Book
Ever Printed." Rhyming or alliterative titles are attractive:
"Dollars for Scholars," "Twinkling Twirlers." Labels sometimes work: "Smitty Schmoll, Rock King of Tucson." A
question or statement of direct address can make a title:
"Don't Sell Yourself Short," "Are You Ready for College?"
Bracketing incongruous ideas results in curiosity-rousing titles: "Dark Stars," "The Tree That Talked." As we suggested in discussing titles for short stories, if more than
one good title comes to mind, offer both by using your
own first choice as the title and mentioning alternate titles
immediately under the word count on your first page.

The opening sentence and paragraph provide the next
opportunity—and really the last—to hook reader interest.
One of the easiest and most effective ways to do this is
with a startling statement: "Some species of butterflies can
stand the bitterest Arctic cold." Again, a superlative can
be effective: "The world's largest artificial ice rink, in Tokyo,
Japan, covers an acre." The narrative question may make
a good opening: "What would happen if the temperature
of the earth were to rise just one degree?" Sometimes it's
a series of questions: "Who is Santa Claus really? Where
does he live? And why does he come down the chimney
when surely anyone would be glad to let him in at the
door?"

An opening sentence may address the reader directly:
"How would you like to take a trip around the world?"
or, "You don't *have* to be late everywhere you go." The
first sentence may state a common problem: "Nearly every
girl would like to have more clothes." Or an article may
start with a summary of the message, or with the conclusion:
"High-school students who love animals can find summer
jobs at stables, kennels, zoos, pet shops, humane agencies,
or veterinary hospitals." These opening sentences establish

what the article is about, and at the same time rouse curiosity. They promise interesting material to follow.

An article may open with an anecdote that makes it seem at first to be a story—and it may have other anecdotes sprinkled throughout. There is no excuse for dull articles; any subject that has interest for a child—or that can be given interest—can be presented interestingly if the writer knows his craft and will take the trouble to think about his material until he finds an arresting angle. All he has learned of fiction techniques will help him make the article suspenseful, readable, emotionally appealing. A good writer will take a subject that seems at first to have little interest and write an article about it that holds reader attention from start to finish. Another writer may take a fascinating subject and write an incredibly dull article about it. Actually, a writer with any imagination can make almost any subject interesting, for young people are naturally curious and eager for new ideas.

How long should an article be? Length will vary greatly, and is determined by the subject matter and treatment. As a general rule, any article should be as short as it can possibly be and still say what it has to say. Of course, it must meet the length requirement of the market to which it is submitted.

POINTS TO REMEMBER

1. Articles for young readers are of four types: How-To, Interesting Personality, Informational, and Self-Development.

2. Basic structure of all articles is the same; each has a beginning, a middle, and an ending, and each part has its specific functions.

3. Article titles and opening sentences provide opportunities to attract attention and hook interest.

4. A good writer can make almost any subject interest young readers.

QUESTIONS AND EXERCISES

1. In the young people's publications with which you have been working, find at least one example of each of the four basic types of articles; the exercise will be more valuable to you if you find several of each type, each for a different age group. Look also for different kinds within each type. For example, find a How-To that tells how to make some article, and another that tells how to gain value from an intangible, such as study or getting along with people.

2. Reread all of these articles to discover the beginning, middle, and ending of each. You may find some that are not built on this basic structure. Give special attention to such an article, trying to understand its weakness—for it will be weak. See if you can improve it.

3. In your publications for the younger age groups, find at least one article that is presented fictionally. Study it to see how the writer made the subject interesting by fictionalizing it. Find its beginning, middle, and ending.

4. Study the titles of articles you have collected. See if you can supply another title for each that you think is as good as or better than the one used. Try writing out at least one title of each kind mentioned in the text.

5. Study the opening sentence and paragraph of each of the articles you are using. What is there in them that makes the reader want to go on reading? Try writing a dozen opening sentences just as "finger exercises," with no special thought of the article to follow.

6. List at least 10 subjects about which you might write articles. Be as specific and as realistic as you can.

7. Write a How-To article for any age group. The length will depend on the age group and the subject; it should be as concise as possible.

8. Write an informational article for young children, using a fictional approach. This should not be more than 900 words.

18

Some Technicalities
of Article Writing

The approach to article writing and marketing is often different from that of fiction writing and marketing. It's true that some articles are written purely "off the top of one's head," from the writer's own ideas and knowledge, and that some articles would be just as acceptable one month or season as another. It's also true that some fiction stories require extensive research or may be so timely that they must be published soon or never. But more often the reverse is true. One has an idea for an article and some of the needed factual material. But then to fill out the article he usually needs to go out and find more material—often much more than he's going to use, so that what he does use will be firmly based. And often his subject is of such timely interest that it would be out-of-date in six months or a year.

The research may take hours of digging in the library; correspondence with government agencies, chambers of commerce, organizations and individuals who can supply needed information; visits to locations to observe firsthand a process or an event; and interviews with persons who can furnish information or who are to be the subject of an Interesting Personality article. The actual writing of a really worthwhile article may be almost insignificant compared to the time and effort required to obtain the needed material.

For this reason you should do some careful planning before embarking on an article. You should think realistically about what material you will need, where you can get it, how much time and work and expense will be involved—and where you can sell the article after you have collected the material and put it together. If getting the material will take 30 or 40 hours of research, plus a trip that will cost $50, and the article would have only one or two possible markets, either of which would pay a maximum of $75, writing the article is obviously a losing proposition. If an article may become outdated before it finds a market as it makes the rounds of several magazines, this is too great a risk to take.

QUERY LETTER

The answer to these problems is the query letter. Many publications that buy nonfiction include in their market information the request "Please query." What does it mean, and how do you query?

It means simply that the editor would like to know what you have in mind and to discuss your idea with you, if it interests him, before you write the article—or at least before you write the final draft. Articles are often the "meat" of a magazine. An editor plans and balances the contents of the issue around a variety of up-to-the-minute articles. Since he must work six months or more ahead of publication dates, it's important for him to know what will be coming in. And when he has query letters from numbers of writers, he is in a position to plan his future issues and help his writers by letting them know just what he can use and often how he would like to have an article handled. Similarly, the query letter helps the writer by letting him know quickly if his idea is not acceptable to one market, so that he may try another before his idea is out-of-date.

What should you say in a query letter? As clearly and concisely and interestingly as you know how, tell the editor what you plan to do, how you plan to do it, why you believe this particular article will be appropriate for his publication, and what your qualifications are for writing it. You may include the opening fifty words or so of the proposed article and a brief outline of the remainder, though this is rarely necessary in the initial contact letter. If the publication uses pictures, you should state what pictures or other illustrations are available or could be supplied. You should ask for any specific suggestions he may have, and indicate your willingness to submit the article without obligation to the magazine; a favorable response to a query letter does not promise that the editor will buy the finished product.

The query letter should be reasonably brief—less than a page if possible, never more than a page and a half. You should enclose a stamped, self-addressed envelope for the editor's reply. The following sample gives a general idea of what a query should include:

Dear Ms. Blank:

    Twelve sophomores at our Centennial High School have written, acted in, and produced a thirty-minute film titled *Monterey Fugitives* about the history and points of interest in our area. Their social studies teacher, who makes educational films in his spare time, provided the equipment and technical guidance. To raise money for the project, the group solicited donations from Chamber of Commerce members and held a rummage sale. Admissions from the premiere and donations from service clubs and civic groups that have borrowed the film have netted $370, which the group has contributed to the school's fund for new band uniforms. The students learned a great deal, not only about making a motion picture, but about teamwork, fund raising, and local history.

    I should like to write an article on this project for you, probably with the slant that any enterprising group of students from a reasonably large high school could carry out a similar project. My son was one of the actors, so I have plenty of firsthand details about the many surprising and humorous incidents that happened during the filming. I also have five good black-and-white pictures of the group making the film.

I have had articles in *High School Focus* and *Team Topics*, and I'm sure I can write an entertaining article that will also provide a basis for a similar project that your readers might like to plan. If this idea interests you, please tell me how many words you can use and suggest any special emphasis you would like. The article will be submitted on speculation, of course.

Yours truly,

The query letter is probably most effective when used by a writer who has sold a few articles of a similar nature to similar publications, or who has had at least some previous contact with the editor to whom the query is sent. When a writer and his work become known to an editor, the correspondence between the two can be considerably more significant to both, and they will discuss projects quite specifically, to the benefit of both. It is not unusual for an editor to suggest an article to a writer whose work he has come to know and trust.

There are some instances when a query is not only futile but a waste of time for both writer and editor. If the article is very short, it takes little more time to write or read it than the query would require, so it's better just to send the article along. Or suppose a writer has a humorous article on selling peanuts at a football game. He knows the editor he has in mind uses sports articles and likes humor. What can he say in a query except that he'd like to submit the article, and what can the editor say except that he can't tell whether he wants it until he sees it? The same is often true of a purely inspirational article. As a general rule, if the article will be bought for its factual or informational contents—because of *what* it says—query. If the *expression* is more important, it's often just as well to send it "cold." Common sense and experience will tell you when to query. It is probably best for a writer to work gradually into the article field, starting with some of the smaller publications that do not ask for a query. With a few sales to such markets to his credit, a writer is in a better position to approach larger, more competitive markets.

You will, of course, query only one editor at a time for any one article, waiting for a reply before querying another. If your material is extremely timely, and you have no response within two weeks, you may feel free to query another editor.

RESEARCH

The need for accuracy in all nonfiction is so obvious and fundamental that it hardly seems necessary to mention it. Historian Bernard De Voto's cardinal rule was "The writer's first obligation is to be right." It is an embarrassment for an editor and a strike against his publication to receive letters from teenagers—or ten-year-olds—pointing out an error in his magazine. And the writer may be sure that the editor's discomfort will be passed on to him in the form of a good long look, if he looks at all, at the next piece the writer submits. A reputation for accuracy and reliability is one of the most valuable assets a writer can have.

A discussion of research procedures is outside the scope of this text; every writer should have on his ready-reference shelf a good, recent college handbook of English, and this will include valuable help on research methods. Research should be systematic and thorough. The article chock full of interesting facts, examples, and details like the goodies in a rich fruit cake is what every editor is looking for. If an article is worth doing at all, it is worth doing to the very best of the writer's ability, and there should be no vagueness or padding.

Your research techniques will improve with experience and will be rewarded with more sales, better sales, and a by-product of more good ideas for other articles than you could write in a lifetime. For inevitably as you dig out information for one article, you will run across all kinds of fascinating material from which to plan other articles. Be alert to these possibilities; jot them down, together with a notation of where the source material is. But don't get carried away from the project at hand.

The important thing is to keep a very accurate record of your sources, and to *save this record until at least three months after your article is published.* An editor may accept your article, pay you for it, and put it in his file. Four or five months later, when he rereads it in preparation for use, he sees something that he questions. Or maybe the article is published, and a reader writes to the editor challenging something you've said. The editor passes the letter on to you. And you'd better *know* and know immediately, where you can check the information, and direct the editor to book, chapter, and verse. When you clip a newspaper or magazine article as resource material and put it in your file, attach to it a note of the name of the publication, date of the issue, and page of the item—and *save* such items until all possible need for them has passed.

Be *sure* you have a reliable source for every fact you include. Sources can be wrong. The longer you write, the more amazed you will become at some of the inaccuracies and contradictions that find their way into print. When sources disagree, or when something doesn't seem to jibe with the rest of the information you've collected, check the fact carefully before including it in your article.

Becoming a fact sleuth and running down details that

seem impossible to find is real adventure. Sometimes you have to dig through mountains of worthless material to find a little high-grade ore, but you may find a nugget of pure gold.

DOCUMENTATION

Most editors insist on documentation of all facts except those of general knowledge. There's no need to supply documentation for the fact that Sacramento is the capital of California, or that dates of leap years are evenly divisible by four. Editorial offices have their own reference libraries where widely known facts can be quickly checked if there is doubt. But if an article states little-known biographical information about a celebrity, or facts about a new scientific discovery, or statistics on the numbers of teenagers employed in Yellowstone Park, the author should supply the sources for such statements.

Documentation need not be formally footnoted on the page where the fact occurs, but may be listed simply and briefly on a separate page at the end of the article, in the order in which the facts occur. Such entries might read:

P. 3 The facts about metals used in sheath knives are from *The Knife Makers Who Went West*, a book by Harvey Platts, published in 1978 by Long's Peak Press, Longmont, Colorado.

P. 5 The information on the effects of very cold temperatures on metals is from an interview with Dr. Harry Zimmerman, of the Cryogenics Laboratory, National Bureau of Standards.

If an editor feels he needs more specific information about a particular reference, he will ask for it.

INTERVIEWS

There are two kinds of interviews you are likely to be conducting. One is with persons you visit to get firsthand information on a subject you are writing about; the article may or may not mention the person, but it is not *about* him, though you may quote him in your article (be sure to ask if you may). This kind of interview is generally easy.

The other kind may be a little more difficult in that the interviewee is expected to talk about *himself,* and many persons, especially teenagers, who can hardly be stopped from talking about themselves in casual conversation, become tongue-tied when *asked* to talk about themselves, particularly to a stranger.

Your library has books on interviewing that can be helpful after you've had a little experience in article writing and decided you want to go further. Most of these are about interviewing celebrities, busy executives, or persons in public office, and assume some reluctance or even hostility on the part of the interviewee. But most of the persons you will be interviewing for articles for young people's publications—at least until you have gained considerable experience—will not be celebrities, and will be reluctant only because being interviewed is a new experience for them that makes them self-conscious. A few guidelines may help:

1. Find out as much as you possibly can about both the interviewee and your subject *before* you ask for an interview. Then you will know what to say and can show him from the start that you have a genuine, intelligent interest in him and his subject.

2. Forget the word *interview;* it frightens people. Whether you write or phone for an appointment—the latter is less formal—just say something like "I've heard from [someone he knows] about the telescope you've built. It sounds very interesting, and I'd like to see it and talk with you about it. I think it might make a good subject for a teenage magazine, don't you?" (Be sure to identify yourself and your purpose.)

3. Write out your questions and take the list with you,

but don't bring it out immediately. Don't confront him at once with pencil and paper. After you've talked awhile and the ice is broken, you can find a natural point to say, "I'd like to write that down—do you mind?" Keep note taking to a bare minimum, unless, of course, you're talking with someone who *wants* you to take notes to be sure you get his information right.

4. Be natural, informal, at ease; if *you* are at ease, your subject will be at ease too.

5. Keep the subject's mind off himself by getting him to talk about what he *does.* This is what you are going to write about, and when he talks about what he does, he'll tell you about himself, too, without realizing it.

6. Be a good listener, a good observer. If you gain the person's confidence, he will tell you more. If your subject is a teenager, remember that there's nothing a young person loves more than an adult who really is interested in *his* ideas and will discuss them with him. Don't criticize or offer advice. Question just enough to keep him talking and on the track.

7. Think of your readers. Keep asking yourself, What would my readers like to know about this person, this subject? Look for human-interest tidbits you could use, as well as information.

Begin interviewing with someone you know slightly—a teacher, pastor, or young person in your community—to gain some practice. Don't try to start out with someone of whom you stand in awe! In time, you'll become an expert.

SLANTING

Interviews and careful, thorough research take a great deal of time and effort; and if research is going to justify itself, it should serve for more than a single article. Few writers get the mileage from their research that they should—and *could* if they would learn better how to slant their material. Slanting not only improves the quality of the article at hand by making it hew more specifically to its line, but suggests other ways in which the same material can be used for several different articles.

Suppose, for example, that the writer's original idea was to write an Interesting Personality article about a teenage girl in his community who is earning money for college by training dogs for local residents. The only planned research is an interview with the girl. But during the interview the writer learns many interesting facts about how dogs learn, and finds that among the dogs the girl has trained is one that won a medal for saving a child from drowning in an irrigation ditch. All of this is colorful material for an article, and will be included in it. But the writer should not stop there. How about a How-To article for children 8 to 12 on training a dog to obey? And how about a short, simple article on the dog that saved the child, for 6–8-year-olds? Some dogs "flunk" their course, the young trainer explains, and their masters are terribly embarrassed. Is there an angle for an article here? Perhaps. Maybe some library research on dog training will turn something up, and it just might supply some data that will add depth and richness to the article originally planned, too. There will have to be pictures, of course—and while the writer is at it, maybe he can work out a picture story on dog training for another publication.

PHOTOGRAPHS AND ILLUSTRATIONS

Pictures often enhance the value of an article, and the availability of pictures can make the difference between a sale and no sale. Some articles require no pictures, and in some cases the publication furnishes illustrations—either photographs or drawings by a staff artist. But with readers becoming increasingly picture oriented, and with steadily improving reproduction methods that require little expense, the demand for photographs keeps growing.

Where can a writer get needed pictures? There are several possibilities. First, he can learn to take his own pictures, and many writers do. It can simplify things considerably— no need to set up appointments with photographers and subjects, no need to draft a contract with the photographer for a percentage of the price paid for the pictures, no need to split the income. But unless the writer really is interested in becoming a photographer and is prepared to invest in reasonably good equipment, this is not wise, at least to begin with. The pictures, like the article, must be of truly professional quality.

One alternate possibility is to work with a photographer on a percentage or an outright-purchase basis. Another is to try to find suitable pictures in "stock"—that is, from agencies that have many pictures of various kinds and charge a fee for their use. Newspapers and libraries often have large collections of pictures that can be used on the same basis, usually at a much lower fee. So have museums, state publicity offices, chambers of commerce and tourist bureaus, and various government agencies.

Another good possibility is to try the public relations departments of various industrial concerns. If one is writing a biographical sketch of Charles Steinmetz, for example, he could write to the General Electric Corporation, where Mr. Steinmetz served for many years. A manufacturer of sporting goods would have pictures of persons playing basketball, tennis, and so on. These pictures are often supplied free, or for a nominal charge for the cost of the print and mailing, usually with the request that the firm be credited unless this is against the publisher's policy. One advantage of this source is that the pictures will be of excellent quality, and they will be absolutely correct.

Whatever the source, black-and-white photographs must be glossy prints at least five by seven inches. More and more young people's publications use color slides, which must be of top quality.

Locate your photograph sources, but don't put out money for pictures or send pictures to an editor until he asks you to; your query letter will have mentioned what is available. Before you send a photograph, type a notation on paper the same width as the photograph, telling what the picture illustrates and the credit line if this is to be included. Paste the top of this to the back of the picture, along the bottom edge, so that the typing appears below the picture. If you leave a long enough flap, you can fold the notation up over the front of the picture to protect it. On another slip of paper type your name and address, and paste this on the back of the picture. Pictures, of course, require special packaging, with protective stiffening, for mailing. They should go first class, and the outside of the envelope should be marked "Photographs." If you're sending slides, each should bear your name and an identifying number. A separate sheet keyed to the numbers can carry captions to explain each picture. Sleeves of clear, tough plastic with pockets for individual slides protect from possible scratches or other damage and travel well when packaged properly.

Sometimes you will want to illustrate a How-To article with drawings or diagrams. You don't have to be an artist; a staff artist of the publication can work from your rough drawings. Put each on a separate page, the size of regular typing paper, and make the drawing as large as you can on the page, showing as clearly as possible what you wish to illustrate.

Don't let the technicalities of article writing scare you out! You don't have to face them all at once. Begin with the simpler article projects, meeting whatever technical problems are involved, and work up gradually to the more complicated techniques.

POINTS TO REMEMBER

1. A good query letter shows an editor that you have a professional attitude toward writing and is the businesslike approach to article writing.

2. Be systematic and thorough in your research, and save all research material and records until at least three months after the article is published.

3. Document all little-known or newly established facts in your article on a separate page at the end.

4. Prepare carefully for interviews and conduct them skillfully. Your skill will grow with practice.

5. Use ingenuity in finding ways to make your research serve for more than one article by slanting your material to various noncompeting publications.

6. Use ingenuity in locating pictures to illustrate your article if an editor expects you to furnish pictures.

QUESTIONS AND EXERCISES

1. Select from the articles you have been studying a fairly long Informational or Interesting Personality article. Pretending this is an article *you* had planned to write, write a query letter to the editor of the publication.

2. Draft a query letter to an editor of a teenage publication for an article you think you would like to write. Assume that you have made previous article sales to other publications.

3. Using a newspaper item as the germ of an article, plan your research. List every possible source of information you can think of. Then study the chapter on researching and writing a term paper in a college English handbook, and carry out your planned research.

4. Using the publications you have been working with as a guide

to subject matter, research and write an Informational or Interesting Personality article for the age group of your choice, and a publication that does not require a query letter. Length will be determined by the subject and requirements of the market. Supply the necessary documentation for this article.

5. Make an appointment for an interview with someone you know only slightly or not at all who can give you authoritative information on a subject about which you wish to write. Plan the interview and carry it out.

6. Do the same with an individual about whom you wish to write an article.

7. Reread some of the articles you have been studying. Can you think of any ways this material might be used for other articles for other publications? Study your own research notes from Exercises 3 and 4, and plan at least two other possible articles based on the same research.

8. Choose one of the original articles you have been planning or writing, and consider the picture possibilities for it. What facilities in your community might supply pictures, or what arrangements could you make with a friend or professional photographer to take needed pictures?

9. Giving attention to all you have learned in the last two chapters, plan a thoroughly researched article for any age group on any subject, carry out the research, including any appropriate interviews, and write the article. Try to write at least two other articles from the same research.

VI

Looking to the Future

19

Fiction and Nonfiction Books

Sooner or later most writers want to try a book. Some choose to serve an apprenticeship writing magazine material; others plunge directly into the more ambitious project. Which approach *you* take depends largely on how you feel about writing a book. If this is the area in which you wish to work and magazines simply do not interest you, if you don't mind waiting longer to see your work in print and to receive payment for your product, if you're willing to gamble a longer time and considerably more work before you find out whether you are producing marketable material—then you may want to start out with a book. You may have to do more rewriting than does the writer who begins with shorter material, but you will be working in the field of your ultimate goal, getting acquainted with people and practices in the world of young people's books, and that is important.

In any case, almost everything we've discussed so far is as applicable to writing books as to writing for the magazines. The basic plot patterns are exactly the same. The techniques of characterization, viewpoint, dialogue, suspense, and emotional appeal are the same; like a short story, a fiction book is made up of a series of scenes put together with smooth transitions. All the basics of article writing are the same in writing a nonfiction book.

Still, a book is not simply an expanded short story or article; and the planning, writing, and marketing are quite different in important ways. The larger canvas will require more material to cover it; there can perhaps be less perfection in minute details, but perspective, unity, and depth become more important—or at least more demanding.

One's attitude is different. A book requires a sustained and dedicated effort—a much larger effort. In many cases there will be a great deal of deep, serious, and time-consuming research. The author must become steeped in the time and place and way of life with which his book deals. He must live with his characters day in and day out, talk with them, work with them, play with them, eat with them, move about with them in their everyday activities. They may easily become more real to him than members of his own household!

The subject matter and the author's thought about it are different. Magazines are like newspapers in their timeliness. Their material, in the main, is of immediate but transitory interest, planned for relatively quick publication to fit the current scene, important for the moment but rarely of lasting interest. Except for a very few magazines for children under 12, magazines are planned to be read and discarded; books are written to be read and saved. An author needs to ask himself, Is my idea important and *enduring* enough for a book? A book is the whole show—not just part of something that contains work by other authors, editors, and staff.

A book has a more selective audience. Magazines are distributed on a continuing basis to a general audience; the subscriber is paying for a product to be delivered in the future, sight unseen; even the editor hasn't seen the final issues covered by a year's subscription, since many of the stories and articles have not yet been written. But a book will be bought by the consumer after examination or screening by critics.

For this reason, and because the author has more room in which to explore his subject fully, a book may deal with a subject that most magazine editors would hesitate to handle; it may include episodes and situations that a writer could never get away with in a magazine story, such as Jamie's not only playing cards for money, but cheating at it in *From the Mixed-Up Files of Mrs. Basil E. Frankweiler.* The language may be more frank, the choice of words more explicit. Controversial subjects or a position that might be objectionable to a substantial number of subscribers in a particular location or culture group are avoided by most magazine editors, whereas such a consideration is less important to book editors, who do not have a presale obligation to please subscribers.

On the other hand, after publication a book must sell on its own merit; and the remuneration, instead of coming immediately and in a total lump sum on acceptance, is spread out over the years on a royalty basis and is unpredictable, depending on the number of copies sold. This is explained fully in Chapter 23. Because the publisher's return on investment also depends on copies sold, the company will take reasonable steps to promote the sale; some publishers are financially better equipped for promotion than others. Critics and reviewers will turn merciless spotlights on the book, and their reports may be enthusiastic or devastating—or both. Although favorable reviews are pleasant and undoubtedly help the book's acceptance and sale in some quarters, an author should not be crushed by unfavorable reviews. It's an axiom among authors that the nicest thing that can happen to a book is a good review, the next best thing is a bad review, and the worst that can happen is no review at all!

Finally, there is generally a greater stature and prestige attached to books and their authors than to magazine material and magazine writers. The book author is a soloist, the magazine writer just one member of an orchestra. Although the two media have many things in common, they are in some ways two separate worlds. A writer should look seriously at both; perhaps he will decide to work in both, at least for a time. Each has its rewards and limitations. Each has its place and fills a need.

So let's assume that you've taken all these things into consideration and have oriented yourself to writing a book. How do you begin? First, with a great deal of planning. Presumably you already have some idea of what you want to write about, whether the book will be fiction or nonfiction, the age reader you have in mind. Perhaps you have several ideas; usually it's best to explore more than one possibility before making a decision.

A trip to the library is in order. You need to find out what else of a similar nature has been published recently, what prospects your book may have. If you're planning a personal-problem novel for young teens, or an adventure story for readers 8 to 12, ask the librarian for some recent titles and authors of such books. Ask to see publishers' catalogs; thumbnail reviews of a firm's books will give you an idea of how many of what kinds of books it buys. Round up a dozen or so books of the kind you wish to write, and select four or five to take home for careful reading.

The idea is not to find something to imitate, but to know what's going on. If you were a fashion designer, you'd have to get out to fashion shows, read the fashion magazines, learn what people are buying, what your competition is doing. The same is true for writers. If there's been a tide of historical books in the last year or two, probably the market for such a book will be weak for a few years. Look ahead; if the Olympics are coming up in a couple of years, a good competitive sport book might be promising.

Once you've decided on your subject and know the age of your audience, you're ready for more specific planning. If your book is fiction, will the main character be a boy or a girl? Think carefully about the age and sex of your audience before deciding. The same considerations we have discussed earlier apply.

Selection of a plot pattern must come early in your planning. As we've said before, the two plot patterns best suited to books other than picture books are the Purpose Achieved and Wish Fulfillment patterns. Often these are combined in the same book. The main character will have a purpose that he or she achieves in the end, and also a wish that comes true. But one or the other of the story lines is dominant, and the two are always very closely interwoven; frequently the surface story will follow the Purpose Achieved pattern and the second-level story the Wish Fulfillment pattern.

This brings us to the matter of thesis or theme. The writer must know exactly what he wants the book to *say* over and above the mere telling of the story. This, of course, is the basis of the second-level story, which is even more important in a book than in a short story. For a book must have this basic substance and enduring value if it is to succeed. Write out your theme as accurately and specifically as you can in a single sentence; work on it until it says exactly what you want it to say.

How long should your book be? Few editors specify word limits, but rough guidelines can be helpful. "Chapter books" for children who have outgrown picture books and begun to read for themselves are from about 15,000 to 20,000 words. For readers 8-12, books 25,000 to about 45,000 words are within a marketable range; and books for readers over 12 are usually 40,000 to as much as 60,000 words. You will find longer and shorter books in all categories.

When you have your story worked out in your mind, you should write it in one sentence. Yes, it can be done, if you have a sound, unified story with a simple central story line. It's just this central story line, shorn of all subplots and even the second-level story, that your sentence will cover. Then write out the synopsis, again in terms of situation, problem, and solution, in not more than 250 words. Practice writing the story-in-one-sentence and synopsis of half a dozen published books, and you will find that it is not too difficult, that it will help enormously with your own planning.

The next step is a running outline, presented in narration and using the present tense, and simply telling what happens; it will be between 1,500 and 3,000 words long. Writing it will help you weed out irrelevant material, strengthen dramatic crises, and become better acquainted with your characters and your story. It will show you where you need to do more research. And while you're working on your outline, you should sketch any maps, house plans, or other diagrams you will need for orientation as you write.

When you are satisfied with this shaping of your story, you can go over the outline and break it into chapters. In some books it's appropriate to try to end each chapter with a cliff-hanger that will make the reader want to go on. For younger children it's often well to end a chapter with a lull, a good place to stop bedtime reading. The chapter breaks are tentative at this point; you'll almost certainly want to change some of them as you write.

How many chapters should you have? This varies greatly; most books have from 10 to 25. Generally chapters should not run over about 2,000 words; long chapters discourge young readers. Chapters need not be the same length, though one should try to make them roughly so. Interesting, curiosity-rousing chapter titles help induce children to read the book; with teenagers this is less important, and chapters may or may not have titles.

The first chapter is almost always the hardest to write. You may rewrite it many times—almost every writer does, even seasoned professionals. A great deal has to be done quickly, interestingly, and in a few words. Setting and mood must be established, the main characters introduced, the situation and problem made clear—all without giving any false leads that will cause the reader later to have to go back and correct wrong impressions he has formed. Ideally the story should open with a crisis for the main character, in which neither he nor the reader knows what is going to happen next. The opening should show the main character worried, uncertain, or in some kind of trouble. Trouble seems necessary for drama, emotion, and reader interest.

Remember that your book must have a beginning, middle, and ending. The beginning may require as much as two or three chapters, or it may be concluded at the end of the first chapter. The important thing is not the length, but that it perform all the functions of a beginning.

The middle chapters will develop the problem; it becomes more important and more difficult to solve. Each chapter must have plot significance; each incident, which will have its own minor crisis and climax, in some way moves the main character closer to his goal or thrusts him further from it.

The last chapter is usually the second most difficult to write. The climax must be sharp and vivid, truly the highest dramatic point in the whole book. The final pages must tie up loose ends of all story threads, including those of the second-level story, without slowing the action, which must be very swift. In the last chapter the author artfully reminds the reader, through action and dialogue, of all that has happened and shows the results of these happenings. Ideally the climaxes of the first and second-level stories coincide, to give the ending all the drama possible.

If you're planning a nonfiction book, your initial research is one of the most vital parts of the project. Talk with your librarian about the idea you have in mind. It's a librarian's business to know the field, and perhaps he or she can tell you of other books on your subject recently published or about to be released. Study the publishers' catalogs thoroughly. If you find that there are already three or four current How-To books on skiing, your chances with still another are slim. If you find that someone else has written a teenagers' biography of the person you expected to write about, you'll want to do some rethinking—either change to another subject or perhaps use the same subject but for 8 to 12's. Could the individual be made interesting to readers this age?

Notice *who* has written books in the field that interests you; would you be competing with a well-known, well-established author—or one who is a recognized authority on the subject? Find out, too, what resource material is available. There may be a great deal, even sources not generally available in other libraries or localities, or there may be so little that it would be difficult or impossible to do the project you have in mind. Keep looking, asking; maybe you can uncover some primary resources, such as someone whose work in the field is well known. Maybe you can find access to the person whose biography you wish to write, or to persons who knew or worked with him or her. Ferreting out possible sources of information is an important part of a nonfiction writer's work.

Of course you have no way of knowing what is about to be published, what a publisher may already have contracted for; but this is a risk you have to take. After you've had a book or two accepted, *you* can be in the happy position of being able to plan ahead with your editor and having your book already virtually accepted before it's written.

This brings us again to the matter of a query letter about your project. With nonfiction books especially, editors often want to see a query before looking at the whole manuscript. Some editors want a query even on fiction books, but you should have your novel completed before you write to an editor about it. Sometimes it's appropriate to send two or three chapters and an outline of the rest of the book along with the query letter. The market books, with which you have by this time become quite familiar, will tell you what procedure each editor prefers. The query letter is similar to that for an article. It states succinctly what you expect to do—or have done—in your book, the age of your intended audience, your own writing credits and qualifications for writing the book, and any other pertinent facts. The letter should be about a page long, never more than a page and a half.

Writing a nonfiction book involves exactly the same skills and principles as writing a magazine article. Making information interesting to young readers requires skill in all the techniques you've been learning for fiction except plotting. Because the unifying and compelling force of a plot is missing in nonfiction, one must achieve unity, coherence, and suspense in other ways. The basic pattern of beginning, middle, and ending, each with its special functions, applies not only to the book as a whole but to each chapter in the book. The book must have rising interest that builds to a climax and a satisfying ending.

A good craftsman will find a way to unify loosely related material, or incidents that cover a long time span. Often the solution lies in finding one common factor, such as a person, an object, or a setting, that can be used as a unifying force. Sometimes this is easy; the subject of a biography is its unifying force. Other subjects require more ingenuity. As you survey the field before writing your book, note the ways in which authors have made their books so compelling that the reader cannot lay the book aside until he has finished it. Although you will not want to imitate these devices, they will give you ideas as to how you may give your book unity, rising suspense, and significance.

A whole volume could easily be written on writing books

for children and teenagers—and such books have been written. We do not mean to slight the subject by devoting only one chapter exclusively to books. Writing a book—*any* book—is a very large undertaking. We might think of it as a backpacking trip alone into a wilderness area—as opposed to the pleasant afternoon hike up a nearby hill that a short story might represent. The backpacking trip takes a *lot* of planning, preparation, conditioning—both physical and mental. Short hikes—writing magazine material—can be a significant part of the conditioning but not all of it. One needs to accumulate equipment and supplies, test them, get maps of the territory and study them, talk to people who have made similar trips. No amount of magazine writing can substitute for these preparations.

A book is a different project, a bigger project. Not only does it take more time and thought and effort, but the time lapse between completion and publication of a book is usually much longer. The marketing is likely to move much more slowly, and it will usually be a year or longer after it is finally bought by a publisher before it is released. A writer should understand fully what he is entering upon in writing a book, and thus prepare himself mentally and practically for this major project. If he prepares well and has gained command of the basic writing skills, he can succeed. The competition is somewhat less in the book field, and the rewards can be satisyfing. Planning and writing a book is a unique and unforgettable experience—and so is every book that follows it.

POINTS TO REMEMBER

1. Although basic skills and requirements are the same, writing a book is different from writing magazine material. The writer should understand and appreciate these differences.

2. Time and thought given to *planning* either a fiction or nonfiction book are well spent and can save much wheel-spinning in the writing.

3. Books, like all other forms of written communication, must have a beginning, a middle, and an ending; it is the function, rather than the length, of each part that is important.

4. Whereas plot provides unity and suspense for a fiction book, the nonfiction book must depend upon other devices for these vital qualities. The author must see that his nonfiction book builds to a climax and that its contents have interest and significance for the reader.

5. Review of all the techniques of plotting and presentation given in this book will help a writer prepare to write a successful book. None can be overlooked.

QUESTIONS AND EXERCISES

1. From your library borrow half a dozen fiction books for different age groups and of different lengths. Analyze them in the light of points covered in this chapter. Note the number of chapters, length, chapter titles if any. Identify the beginning, middle, and ending of each book. Write the story-in-one-sentence for each, and a synopsis of at least 3. Write a running outline of one of the books in 1,500 to 3,000 words.

2. Make a similar analysis of half a dozen nonfiction books. Note especially the ways in which the authors provide unity and suspense. What keeps the reader reading? Could the author have done better in this respect? How?

3. Follow through the steps outlined in this chapter for writing a fiction book, through the writing of the running outline. Write the first chapter.

4. Follow through the steps outlined in this chapter for writing a nonfiction book. Write the first chapter.

20

Schoolbooks and Educational Materials

Anyone who considers the quantities of textbooks, workbooks, and supplementary reference materials used in classrooms from kindergarten through high school must realize that this is an enormous, ongoing market—and a very lucrative one. Add to these print media the hundreds of films and filmstrips, records and sound tapes, flip charts and flash cards, study prints and slide shows, transparencies and overlays—plus programmed instruction (PI) materials, tests, home study courses, "special education" materials, occupational briefs and career guidance materials—and the possibilities are truly unlimited.

The education field does not provide a direct market immediately open to the unproven free-lance writer, however. One must have some recognized standing in his field, usually as a teacher, to have a textbook or education program even considered for publication. But this does not mean that there is no place for a free-lance writer in the education field. There are, in fact, many rewarding opportunities for writers who search them out and qualify themselves by gaining a working understanding of what is wanted. Writers of educational materials must know children, the school curricula, and state education codes, as well as how to write for young readers. Teachers or published writers who have some background in teaching have an advantage. But many writers who have no formal background in education have made a place for themselves in this huge and relatively uncrowded area.

How do you get a toe in the door? The most likely way is first to be published in several of the best magazines for young people, or to have a children's book to your credit. Often a writer becomes conscious of the education market when a large textbook publisher asks to buy book rights to one of his stories that appeared in a magazine. The magazine paid perhaps $35 to $50 for the story, and the publisher, who is compiling a supplementary reader for grades 5 and 6, offers $100 for the "nonexclusive book rights." Nonexclusive means that other book publishers may also buy the story, for another $100 or so. This practice is not uncommon, and such requests may continue for the next ten years—if the story is not dated.

Tantalizing as these prospects are, negotiation for book rights to a magazine story nearly always begins with the book publisher rather than the author. Authors should not send unsolicited story manuscripts or their published stories to education publishers, who have no staff or facilities to handle such submissions. The large publishers of textbooks or other schoolbooks are not even listed as such in the popular market sources, although they are listed in *Literary Market Place,* an annual directory published by R. R. Bowker Co., of New York, and available in your public library. But there are other interesting possibilities.

Many large education programs, such as a reading or social studies series that extends from kindergarten through elementary school (K to 6) or even high school (K to 12), involve years of development and testing. Usually they result from a joint effort of one or more university professors, the publisher's staff, and classroom teachers who test the program with their students. Such a project is generally well financed, with the expectation that it will continue and grow over many years.

Very often such a program needs the services of one or more writers who have specialized in writing for children. Publishers who produce supplementary "reading enrichment" readers, for instance, sometimes request specific kinds of stories from authors whose work they have come to know, as well as stories they select from magazines. A natural science program employed several authors whose books for children had shown knowledge of wild animals, fish, insects, and so on, to write books to fit the publisher's format. And a large economics series, used nationwide, includes simple fiction stories as part of each unit at every grade level, to illustrate the economics principle discussed in the unit. These were written by several authors selected by the professor who headed the program.

There is a constant need for "high-interest, low-reading-skill" fiction and nonfiction at all grade levels. These are stories, articles, and books with subject matter interesting and suspenseful enough to lure the reluctant reader of junior high school age, for instance, who reads at only a third- or fourth-grade level; they are shorter than stories and books generally read by this age group, and written with simple vocabulary and sentence structure. There is also a limited need for books and articles of this kind in areas such as practical mathematics, government, health and nutrition, and other subjects that one needs to know just to get along in the workaday world.

Material of this kind is often written by teachers with some training and experience as reading specialists, simply because they understand the need and are best prepared to produce what is needed and what will work. But the market is by no means limited to these experts, and any writer who gains the necessary understanding can enter this field. He may, in fact, have certain advantages if he has mastered the fundamentals of *writing* for young readers— the plot patterns, characterization, dialogue, scene building, suspense, and so on—skills the teacher-writer is not likely to have learned.

Audiovisual media offer another very big field to writers who find out what is wanted and master the necessary techniques. Practically all school systems and public libraries have extensive audiovisual departments, and what used to be the school library is now more often known as the "media center." Films, filmstrips, videotapes, records, sound tapes, and cassettes are as common as books to pupils from kindergarten through high school. The students operate movie and television cameras, projectors, and sophisticated sound equipment as naturally and easily as they toss a baseball or ride a bicycle, and one is likely to find even elementary-school children making their own videotapes and slide shows.

Producers of audiovisual materials may be looking for anything from a simple script for a set of study prints for kindergarteners to a series of twenty-minute motion pictures for junior high or high school students. Many publishers and producers of audiovisual materials are listed in market sources such as *Writer's Market,* and studying such a list helps a writer gain an idea of what is wanted. Most of them will send a catalog of their materials and a brochure outlining their policies, needs, and format to qualified prospective writers.

Ordinarily such a company, in cooperation with some education specialist or group of specialists, develops its own basic format and complete "package." Typically this is a coordinated "multimedia" social studies program for grades K–6. The package may include sets of study prints or transparencies and overlays, accompanying cassettes, student work sheets, and a teacher's guide, for each grade level. Or a company's package may consist of a book and a coordinated filmstrip and record or cassette for each unit of a program. Some companies produce only silent films or filmstrips, sometimes with a script to be read by the teacher or a student as the filmstrip is shown. Others produce just records, sound tapes, or cassettes.

Another specialty is programmed instruction (PI) materials. These are self-instruction materials, sometimes for use with a "teaching machine," but often just a series of pages that ask the student a question or direct him to perform certain tasks as he progresses a step at a time, getting instruction for each new step from the program as he completes the previous step.

Where the writer fits into these programs depends on the individual company or even the individual program and the personnel already involved. He may work on various details of the entire package, or he may be needed only to write script for the sound tapes, from resource material supplied by the producer. The package planners may have people to take care of everything but scripts for the filmstrips that are to be part of the package. The more versatile a writer is, and the better he understands the whole concept of multimedia presentations, the more useful he can be to planners and producers of these materials and the wider his opportunities will be.

Several publishers produce only career guidance materials and assign to free-lance writers the job of researching and preparing comprehensive, up-to-date occupational briefs for use by junior high and high school students and their counselors. Some big business and industrial firms also employ free-lance writers to write this kind of material, often as a public service or sometimes to present a favorable image of their company to young people while at the same time introducing them to the kind of work performed there.

Some insurance companies, business organizations, and large industrial corporations produce science, economics, or health-related materials for classroom and reference use. Both national and local organizations, such as animal humane agencies and medical organizations, employ free-lance writers to prepare materials for their education program in the schools. Most religious denominations have extensive education programs, and many have their own publishing facilities. A writer who has earned a few credits in writing for children is in a good position to approach the education department and explore possible writing assignments.

Payment for writing educational materials varies but is generally comparable to that for other kinds of writing. The sale may have the advantage of being somewhat more certain than free-lancing in the magazine or book fields, in that one is generally not competing with other writers on any given project and is often writing under contract— though of course what one produces must be acceptable to those issuing the contract. Payment may be on a royalty or outright purchase basis. Although royalty *percentages* are generally smaller than those paid by trade publishers, often only 5 to 7 percent instead of the usual 10 to 12 percent paid by trade publishers, the great *volume* of sales of a successful education program, often over a period of ten years or longer, more than compensates for the lower percentage rate.

If you think you might like to become involved in writing some kind of educational materials, the best place to begin looking into possibilities is right where you are. Get to know teachers and school librarians. Become familiar with books and educational series or programs used in your local schools. If any of the terms used in this chapter are unfamiliar to you, ask about them; observe some of the audiovisual equipment, such as transparencies and overlays being used with an overhead projector, or a child studying in a bilingual program by listening to a cassette tape and following along, perhaps with a set of study prints.

Teachers in elementary schools are often hard pressed to find suitable material for a unit on the local community or region; an enterprising writer may look into what is being done in this direction in his own locale, find out who is responsible for compiling material and putting the unit together, and then possibly arranging with these teachers for writing a program: for example, a history of the community directed specifically to the grade level (usually third or fourth grade) where this unit is taught. A writer without credits or experience in education writing may have to do such a project on a purely volunteer basis, receiving no payment. But if it is successful, he has an important credit to show to other prospective clients, who *can* pay.

If there is a college of education in or near your community, or if the educational department of a local university is developing a program for schools in, say, mathematics or science or ecology, this could provide a good contact. You may be able to get some sort of job—collecting materials, typing manuscript, copy editing, or proofreading, either paid or as a volunteer. Anything you do will provide valuable experience in learning how such a project grows, the many details involved. The more you can learn about the whole process, the better you can see where your own writing skills may fit in. And you'll be there when the need for a writer emerges.

As you learn your way around, gain a little experience, and demonstrate your capabilities by having a project or two to your credit, you can reach further afield. New technology in electronics communication media continually makes possible new kinds of education devices. You may want to try writing educational or entertainment films or filmstrips, or programs for children's television (all discussed in the next chapter). When you are ready for these steps, send a résumé and sample of your writing to education publishers or filmmakers who are producing the sort of material you are prepared to write and ask for any guides they have for writers. Your inquiries may lead into some very appealing areas where you'll find an opportunity for expression of your creative talents and abilities.

POINTS TO REMEMBER

1. Although the education market is virtually closed to beginning writers, it offers a wide variety of attractive possibilities to writers who first prove themselves in other areas.

2. Teachers and writers with some background in teaching have an advantage, but others who have learned the principles of writing for children also have an advantage and can learn what they need to know about education, curricula, and other specific demands.

3. There are many kinds of educational materials, including books to supplement and enrich the regular curriculum, books and shorter material for bilingual programs and for pupils who read below their grade level, audiovisual and multimedia materials, and occupational briefs and career guidance helps.

4. In addition to the education publishers, large business and industrial corporations, public agencies, and religious organizations produce educational materials.

QUESTIONS AND EXERCISES

1. If you have sold a few stories or articles to the better publications for children and would like to explore possibilities in the education field, make an appointment with a teacher in your local schools to discuss possibilities. Find out as much as you can about regular and supplementary books and series of educational materials used at the grade levels that most interest you. Ask to see catalogs of other such materials.

2. Do the same with someone in the education department of a local church or synagogue. Find out about education programs of other religious groups in your area.

3. Study market lists of education publishers and producers of audiovisual materials in *Literary Market Place* and *Writer's Market,* to find out which produce material that your experience may fit. Then compose a letter to education publishers requesting information about their programs and expressing your wish to participate. Prepare a résumé of your experience, qualifications, and writing credits that you may send with the letter.

21

Poetry

Boys and girls of all ages enjoy poetry—although some don't like to admit that they do. Poetry is usually an infant's first experience with literature as mothers and fathers sing songs or recite poems to entertain or comfort little ones; often these childhood pieces are ones they learned themselves as children. As a child learns words and speech, he soon begins to memorize the familiar lines; and nearly every adult still finds pleasure and sometimes wisdom in poems he learned as a child.

Most magazines for young people publish some verse in each issue. A poem may be used as a filler but occasionally is given a full page with an attractive illustration.

Writing poetry is a very specialized field, one you should not attempt for any audience without first learning the craft. Editors quickly reject verse that is merely cute or "sing-songy," or worst of all, "poetic." And no amount of studying methods of writing poetry can guarantee that you can produce salable verse.

What is a poem? The classic definition, by William Wordsworth, says that poetry is "emotion recollected in tranquillity." Other efforts at definition include George Meredith's calling it "walking on tiptoe" and Maxwell Bodenheim's saying it's "the impish attempt to paint the wind." Perhaps defining poetry is as difficult as writing it.

Let's look at some questions you can ask yourself to see whether you might succeed in this field. Do you enjoy words, their sounds and rhythms? Do you delight in arranging them, rearranging, so the result is pleasing to your ear? Do you have a finely tuned ear and eye for detail in the world around you? Do you have creative imagination? Are you willing to work very hard, polish to perfection, expend the energy and thought it takes to make a poem? If you answered yes, give it a try.

Gather around you the needed tools: a good dictionary, a rhyming dictionary, and a thesaurus. You may receive one line, a rhyme, a perception of some object, an emotion. Make a note of these to build on later. A poem rarely comes whole, but in pieces. These pieces fit with other pieces. So we might say that a poem is built rather than written, built around a nucleus that teases your imagination.

Since the goal of a poem is to link the imagination of the poet to that of the reader, a child, we need to consider the subjects that do this best. As in writing plays, the key to a piece of verse that will have child appeal is simplicity.

Children wonder about everything, but especially the natural world around them. Probably half the poems for children are about trees, flowers, insects, animals, the sky, the earth. How did the stars get up there? How does a seed know when to grow? How do birds know how to find their way cross country and when to migrate? Why can't I fly?

WINGS

I like to lie down in the grass
    And watch the bumblebees fly past.
A beetle landed by my nose—
    His landing strip, a garden hose.

A diving bomber dragonfly
    Came buzzing close, then swooped on by.
The world is full of flying things;
    Sometimes I wish that I had wings.

—Barbara Steiner

SEED MAGIC

If I were inside a seed looking out,
How would I know when it's time to sprout?
Would Someone say to me, Little Seed, grow?
Would Someone whisper so that I would know?

—Barbara Steiner

A child's world is especially linked to sensory image. Good poems tap into these images. You are putting pictures into children's minds to delight them, and often this picturing comes through simile and metaphor. Emily Dickinson uses metaphor to say, "The Lightning is a yellow Fork from Tables in the sky." Humbert Wolfe calls snowdrops "a little gasp of white astonishment." This concept is too esoteric for young children, but your aim is to make the child say, "I never thought of that," or "I never saw it that way, but yes, it is." Using a simile to say the harvest moon is like a pumpkin or that a squirrel looks like a tea pot, his tail the handle, paints a picture for children that will cause them to laugh and agree.

As with any good writing, the poet must give attention to sound, smell, touch, and taste as well as sight. A good poem paints a vivid word picture that can go on and on expanding in a child's mind. Children are very much aware of shape and color.

MORNING

A birdie with a yellow bill
    Hopped upon my window sill,
Cocked his shiny eye and said,
    "Ain't you 'shamed, you sleepy head?"

—Robert Louis Stevenson

Close your eyes and think about familiar sounds, smells, tastes—the lullabye of the ocean at night, "hush, hush, time to sleep." Or the "Boom, Boom, Boom of the big brass drum." Think of the smell of mother's kitchen when she's baking bread. A strawberry, first taste of spring. The feel of grandmother's hand in yours. How cozy your bed is, especially when rain is falling. Remember sensory images from your childhood. List your favorite things to see, smell, hear, taste, and touch. Be specific: a cat's eyelashes, the fuzz on a peach's rosy cheek.

Poems about holidays are always in demand. Editors ask for poems about all the holidays, not just Christmas and Halloween. And poems about people in the child's world are popular—mother, father, siblings, grandparents.

While you're thinking about holidays and people, you may wish to consider the possibiities of expanding into the very active greeting card market, where editors welcome short, fresh verse suitable for valentines, birthday cards, Easter, Thanksgiving Day, Christmas and Chanuka, and New Year's Day. This is a very large though specialized market. The slant is a little different from that in magazines. Greeting card verse must have an intimate "from me to you" message—something a parent or grandparent, aunt or uncle, or adult friend might wish to say to a specific child. Or that a child might wish to say to a sister, brother, or friend. The message may be serious or funny. If you browse in the "child" section of the greeting card display at the supermarket, card shop, or book store, you'll probably be amazed to discover how many different kinds of cards there are in the juvenile field, and you may get really excited about the possibilities.

Greeting cards for children are not limited to holidays, but include congratulations, get well, and just "hello—I'm thinking of you" messages. And of course not all messages are poems; some are simple, pithy prose. Some are popups, games, or puzzles. It's a field worth looking into.

Feelings, emotions are sources of good subject matter for poems. Tap into stored emotions from when you were a child. A surprise that pleased you. The death of a pet, a friend. Being homesick that first time away. Concepts make good poems: frustration, boredom, time, distance, anger, loneliness. Paint pictures of these abstract emotions and concepts. "Loneliness is a faded lilac against a gray rock wall." "Anger is a burst of a red-hot lava in your head." Fear is a powerful emotion, and scary poems can be fun to read. How does it feel to have to walk past a haunted house or face a bully? Or to be lost in the woods or in a department store? Most writers find it easier to write about joyous feelings such as anticipating Christmas or a visit with a loved relative, getting a puppy or kitten, or finally having a room of one's own. Even simple feelings that foster security and warmth are good poetry material.

MOTHER'S PURSE

My mother has a great big purse
She calls her "bag of tricks"
From which she pulls out chewing gum
And sometimes space food sticks.

She always has a handkerchief,
A pencil, and a pen;
And once she had a counting book
To help me count to ten.

Her purse is like a magic hat
Where little rabbits stay;
Oh, there is always something new
In Mother's purse each day!

—Barbara Steiner

HALLOWEEN

Halloween is gold
  As a harvest moon,
Just like honey you could
  Eat with a spoon.*
            —Barbara Steiner

CHRISTMAS

Christmas is gold
  As the manger's sweet hay,
Softening the bed
  Where the Baby lay.*
            —Barbara Steiner

*Excerpt from a longer poem.

The religious publications as well as many of the secular
magazines buy simple prayers that children can learn to say
at bedtime or before meals. Prayers that are nondenominational
have the best chance of acceptance. This one has been passed
along from parents to children for nearly 75 years:

GRATITUDE

God gives me joyous days to live;
  God guards and shelters me.
God's love is mine, and God is all;
  How grateful I should be.

For fun and friends I will be glad,
  For food by spoon or plate full;
For birds and dogs and pussy cats
  I will be truly grateful.
            —John Martin

Make a list of words that are particularly musical to your ear—your favorite "hears"—but words this time, not sounds. Edgar Allen Poe is reported to have said that the most beautiful word in the English language is "cellar-door." Make your choices and play with arranging some of these into verse. Some words are funny to the ear and make us laugh. A word may be the basis for a humorous poem. Google (the number 1 followed by 100 zeros), riffraff, bogy (a goblin).

Remember the importance of rhythm. The poem must *sing*. Too often the would-be poet sacrifices meaning to get a rhyme. You must work until meaning, rhyme, and rhythm are integrated.

CHICKADEE

Chick-a-dee-dee-dee,
Do you see-see-see
The seeds and suet for you to eat?
I put them out for a winter treat.
—Barbara Steiner

GOOD NEWS

Out in the orchard
    Where the apple trees grow,
A robin perched,
    Unaware of the snow,
He sang this song
    We love to hear:
"Spring is coming—
    Have no fear."
—Barbara Steiner

Rhyme can sometimes be a matter of personal taste, or should we say, ear, and as with all rules of writing is never universally binding. (Learn the rules, then break them *effectively*. Shelley's poem "Adonais" has forty-nine rhyme violations.) But some rules are well established:

The last accented vowels of the rhyming words must sound alike: *dough* and *so, beaver* and *weaver,* or *die* and *pacify* may rhyme, but not *though* and *do,* or *believer* and *endeavor.* The consonants before the accented vowels should not sound alike: *dough* and *doe,* for example, or *conception* and *deception.* These make what is called an identical rhyme, and fail to satisfy the ear. And finally, all the sounds after the accented vowel must sound alike; for example, *thorn* and *dawn, singer* and *finger,* or *moves* and *loves* do not rhyme. Sometimes changes in our language can cause a verse that rhymed when it was first written to do so no longer. It was not until I spent time in England that I realized that the verse

> Pussy cat, Pussy cat, where have you been?
> I've been to London to visit the Queen.

does rhyme if one speaks with an English accent.

When you're working on rhymes, don't overlook inner rhyme and spill-over rhymes in addition to end-word rhymes. Do avoid inversions, though, to create a rhyme. This device was once popular but is now out of favor. Don't write,

> When I go up in my swing so high
> Dizzy, oh, ever so dizzy am I.

Avoid obvious, overworked rhymes like *June* and *moon.* It's the fresh little surprises in rhymes that delight the reader.

Pay attention to the technique of tone-color. Use the sounds in our language to help you create a mood or image. Alliteration is the most common use of tonecolor. Keep in mind that poetry is going to be read aloud. Although "Theophilus Thistlethwaite thrust three thousand thistles through the thick of his thumb" is certainly alliterative, it is not easy to read aloud. But consider "lisp of leaves" and "ripple of rain" from Swinburne's "Atlanta."

Onomatopoetic words—words that imitate the sound they define—such as *crash, bang, tinkle,* and *splat*—are important to tone-color. Waves may "hush" or "lap." Bells "clang" and "bong." A cataract may "splash" or "crash." A stream may "murmur and whisper" or "bubble and chuckle" depending on the mood you wish to set.

FAIRY MAGIC?

The fairy tern, with unconcern,
Lays her egg on the branch of a tree.
Not me, said the weaver,
In a fever of lacing grasses
    into a swinging pouch
to receive *her* chicks.
Nor I, said the oriole,
Shaping her grassy bowl, leaving a peephole
For baby birds to eat worms whole.
Mother tern has no tricks to her act;
She claims no magic which might detract.
In fact, she admits, as she or father sits,
Intent upon their job,
That often she selects a dent on the limb,
Or a bent branch near a knob.
We cannot chance to guess what's best;
But mother tern, with unconcern
Would surely say, "Who needs a nest?"

—Barbara Steiner

If humor is your forte, try your hand at funny poems. One of the few books of poetry to land a spot on the best-seller list is Shel Silverstein's *Where the Sidewalk Ends*. One elementary school librarian says she has five copies and they are never on the shelf. It is one of the few hardback books that parents will buy at a school book fair. Another poet who writes humorous poetry is Jack Prelutsky, author of the popular book *The New Kid on the Block*.

Read other poets whose work appeals to children, to tune up your ear. Read the poems aloud over and over. Among the most popular authors are Myra Cohn Livingston, Aileen Fisher, and David McCord.

In addition to the traditional couplets, quatrains, cinquains, sonnets, and ballads, children like light verse and limericks, free verse, haiku and tanka, Scotch jingles and curlews. Another favorite is "shaped" poems such as the diamonte, so called because its shape is a diamond. Discover all of these forms and experiment to find those that you enjoy writing.

CHRISTMAS ORNAMENTS

Ornament
shiny, delicate
tinkling, swinging, swaying
bells, tinsel, cranberries, popcorn
falling, crashing, smashing
naughty, playful
kitten.

Sounds
happy, joyful
ringing, rustling, snapping
melody, laughter, bells, sleigh
listening, hushing, whispering
secret, expectant
silence.

Cookies
spicy, nutty
tasty, savory, snappy
fruit, sparkles, icing, butter
biting, chewing, crumbling
gobbled, sprinkled
crumbs.

Package
sparkly, ribboned
tied, stacked, tumbling
secret, rattle, bumps, box
tearing, teasing, opened
wished, welcomed
surprise!

—Barbara Steiner

As in children's stories, many poems have a second level. They say something. Ask these questions of your poems: What did I say? What did I mean to say? Did I try to say too much in one poem? Focus, zeroing in on fine detail, is very important. Will my poem communicate with a child, or have I been vague or esoteric? Children's poets should avoid writing about such subjects as life and death as abstractions. They should also avoid using emotional buzz words like "love" and "hate," and words that merely *tell*, such as "angry," "lonely," and "afraid." *Show* readers a picture of the emotion, and let them feel it for themselves. Don't make judgments for the reader.

HERONS

A breeze blows o'er the lake;
Against the heron's slender legs
The little ripples break.

If they had no voices, lo!
White herons would be
But a line of snow.
                    —Japanese Haiku

DAFFODILS

In spite of cold and chills
That usher in the early spring,
We have the daffodils.
                    —Japanese Haiku

PLUM BLOSSOMS

Far across hill and dale
The blossoms of the plum have cast
A delicate pink veil.
—Bashō

So sweet the plum trees smell!
Would that the brush that paints the flower
Could paint the scent as well.
—Japanese Haiku

I came to look, and lo,
The plum tree petals scatter down
A fall of purest snow.
—Reinko (1728-99)

Notice how the haiku around a single subject make a broader statement, a three-fold picture. In this case the three poems could be marketed as one, and with the art work, would make a lovely single magazine page.

In general, avoid adverbs. Adverbs modify fussily. They are seldom needed, and every word counts in a poem. A poem is a good place to learn about saying more with less. Word skills learned in writing verse inevitably carry over into writing prose and so make a writer's prose more beautiful and effective.

Let your subject lead you into the poem. A quiet subject needs quiet language. Rain on the roof may need stacatto words. A sloth needs slow words, long sentences. A monkey needs bouncy, sommersault words, funny, perhaps silly words. A pond in a forest needs shady, still words. A waterfall or a cataract needs roaring, fast-moving words. Think of writing a poem as play; you are playing with sound, rhythm, word arrangement. And you want to leave your reader with a feeling, an emotion.

Send poems out five at a time, one to a page. Put your name and address on each page. An editor may like only one and keep that single sheet. But even in the happy event that she takes all five, they will be separated and assigned to different issues of the magazine. A book of poems is difficult to sell and will probably happen only after you have established yourself as a poet whose work has child appeal. Pay for verse runs from 45¢ a word to $3.00 a line, or in some cases, from $5.00 to $15.00 per poem. Poems are often timeless, and an appealing poem may be sold many times over a period of many years, not only for magazine use but for school readers and anthologies.

POINTS TO REMEMBER:

1. Writing poetry will improve your prose style, since you will become aware of cutting, selecting the best words for rhythm and meaning, and the power of sensory image.

2. Subject matter for poetry must have sharp focus, detail, emotion, and a child's view of the world.

3. You must learn the craft of poetry before you attempt to write in this specialized field. Explore the different types of poetry as well as classic forms.

4. Poetry for children must be fresh, creative, playful, and original.

QUESTIONS AND EXERCISES

1. Find books of poetry by the poets mentioned in this chapter. Read the poetry aloud to tune your ear. See if you can locate examples of poems that children have written; children are imaginative and original and seldom write in clichés.

2. Make a list of sensory images that are pleasing to you and that would also be pleasing to a child. These may be images remembered from

your childhood. Make a list of your favorite words or of words that sound a. funny, b. beautiful, c. ugly, d. heavy, e. light.

3. Select a subject that you think has child appeal. Make a list of sensory image words that would make the subject come alive for a child.

4. Study a book of the poet's craft. Then select a subject and experiment with writing about the subject in a rhymed couplet, a quatrain, haiku, free verse, a limerick, a shaped poem.

5. Study the types and lengths of poems used in samples of children's magazines you have acquired. Ask yourself which magazines would like the type of poetry you discover that you can write.

22

Plays

Television and the expansion of community theater, puppetry, and drama in general have stimulated keen interest in plays for presentation by and for young people. Writers who learn the possibilities, demands, and limitations of this medium can find it rewarding. Although there are not a great many markets for plays, the competition is less here than in most other fields, and there are never enough good plays to meet the demand.

Whole books are written on playwriting, and we can do little more in this single chapter than present a few basic principles and show where playwriting fits into the profession of writing for young people. Whether or not you believe you are seriously interested in playwriting, you will find the experience of trying one or two plays helps to develop your skill in writing fiction. The necessity of telling a story entirely through action and dialogue, of "seeing" your characters on stage acting out their parts, of writing brisk, entertaining, realistic dialogue that moves a plot forward without sagging, of disciplining yourself to tell your story in definite scenes—all this will help you write better fiction. And if you ever want to write for the film or television media, you can have no better background than writing plays.

First let's consider briefly what a group of young persons and a play director—usually a busy teacher who has many other demands on his time—are up against in producing a play. The actors are tyros, often eager but inexperienced and self-conscious; the director, if the group is fortunate, has probably had some background in college drama, community theater, or other amateur productions. The play is to be produced in a school or church auditorium, with only limited possibilities for stage sets and props. The budget, if there is one, is probably too small to justify the term.

For these reasons, *simplicity* is the key word for the playwright. Staging must be simple and flexible, using only the barest necessities and what is likely to be on hand, procured easily, or quickly and inexpensively built. If at all possible, there should be just one setting for either a one-act or a three-act play; if a change is necessary, it should be as simple as possible and must be something that is easily shifted during the actual production of the play. Lighting effects, if any, must be the simplest possible.

Costumes, too, should be limited to what is likely to be readily available or can be easily assembled. Some purchasers of young people's plays say outright, "No costumes." Since period plays and plays with a foreign setting usually demand special props and costumes, they are difficult to sell. However, at the elementary-school level, historical plays that relate to the school curriculum are in demand, and the writer who can find ingenious ways to solve the problem of costumes and props without making outrageous demands on busy mothers and teacher-directors may find a ready market. At the elementary-school level, the plays are given essentially for other children the same age, and children are quite willing to use their imagination and ingenuity when it comes to props and costumes. They love "dressing up" and "pretending." A headband with a paper feather easily identifies an Indian. Hat or headdress, a wide bright-colored sash, a dagger (plastic, of course) thrust through a belt often comprise the only "costume" required. Similarly, a coat tree with a few leafy branches—or even green tissue paper—tied to it makes a fine "tree," and two such trees can make a forest.

By the time they have reached high school, students have lost interest in dressing up, and the plays are for a more adult audience. The writer must use common sense about costumes and props. Colonial costumes would be hard to come by; football gear or a cap and gown would be simple. A gas lamp or an old-fashioned kitchen range would present problems; equipment that might be borrowed from the chemistry or physics lab, or from the gymnasium or art department, would be easy.

Most wanted are one-act and three-act plays for high-school students. Light comedy is most popular, accounting for about 90 percent of the plays published for this age group. Some publishers also ask for mysteries, melodramas, and occasional fantasies. A few drama teachers have pointed out that today's children and teenagers are more knowledgeable and sophisticated than those of past generations, and beg for more realism in plays for young people. But most high-school casts and directors simply have not had the background to bring off a play that deals seriously, for example, with a major social problem; and the purchasers of plays for high-school production usually specify themes that are worthy and optimistic, and that contain no element that might be offensive to average American audiences. They reject reference to sex, except in its purely romantic sense, and want no profanity or vulgarity. There should be no smoking or drinking of alcoholic beverages on stage, and preferably no reference to these things or the use of drugs except to point a moral. There should be nothing that deals specifically with controversial aspects of politics, economics, religion, or morals.

Best subjects are the common, less serious problems of teenagers: family living, school situations, personal allowance and budget problems, meeting new situations that demand behavior or manners beyond the experience of the main character, teenage job and employment problems, and other maturing experiences. Light or humorous romance is also popular; no heavy romance, as high-school students are too self-conscious to play serious love scenes.

A three-act play should have a fairly large cast—perhaps six or seven female and four to six male parts. A one-act play may have a smaller cast—a total of six to nine, with the same proportion of male to female parts. Most parts should be for persons about the age of the actors themselves. A few parts for older or younger characters are often necessary and give some opportunity for those students who wish to play these "character" parts.

Plays for junior-high and elementary-school children are likely to be curriculum oriented—those dealing with historical events studied at these grade levels, dramatizations of pieces taken from their study of literature, special-day or special-occasion material such as plays for Thanksgiving and Christmas, as well as such lesser holidays as Columbus Day, Washington's and Lincoln's birthdays, Arbor Day, Book or Library Week, and so on. Also popular are plays that dramatize the values of good citizenship, democracy, patriotism, and safety; adaptations of classic stories and fables; and plays about other lands. Churches use Bible-oriented plays and special-occasion plays for Christmas, Easter, and some other holidays.

One-act plays are the general rule for this age group, and casts are limited to five to seven main parts distributed fairly evenly among boys and girls, and sometimes as many or more minor parts. Plays with a flexible cast that can provide a way to let every child in the group or classroom have a part are popular with persons planning a production. In addition to the main parts, there can often be a number of villagers, neighbors, singers, bell ringers, or flowers. Boys' and girls' organizations and camps sometimes need plays for all-boy or all-girl casts—though young people also have fun trying to play parts of the opposite sex.

Some drama teachers are opposed to use of published plays for children under twelve to fifteen; they feel that memorizing a part and rehearsing action directed by an adult achieves little for the child and inhibits creativity; they prefer to have children this age exercise their imagination by writing their own plays and acting them out. There is some demand for outlines for such projects—the bare framework on which the children themselves may hang a play; these are found generally in education magazines, and are usually by teachers who have actually used the material and can give a brief account of how they carried out the project.

Other related fields, outside the scope of this book, are plays for children's theater—that is, plays written for adults to give for children—plays for puppets, and material for tableaux, pantomime, pageants and festivals for special occasions, and musical plays. There is also some need for material for declamatory speeches and other monologues. Writers seriously interested in drama should study these possibilities further.

From a plot standpoint, a play is exactly like a story; the basic plot patterns are also the foundations on which plays are built. The three acts of a three-act play are the beginning, middle, and ending; generally the one-act play will have three scenes that break down into the same three components. The other techniques of fiction writing that you have been learning also apply to playwriting. There will be a main character with a clearly defined problem and goal about whom the plot revolves.

The play should begin with immediate drama involving the main character; this is no time to give the audience background material through having minor characters talking about the situation. The story must be easy to follow and simple enough to move swiftly, with little necessity for explanation. Any necessary explanatory material should be woven in skillfully with the dialogue.

As with a story, the suspense must grow as the play progresses. The beginning is very important; it must set the mood and establish rapport between cast and audience. The first-act curtain closes on the highest dramatic point thus far in the story; it should leave the audience wondering, *Now* what will he do?

The second act should continue the complication and suspense, and end with the main crisis of the whole play, with the main character in the worst possible situation. This is the Black Moment. The third act, usually the shortest, is the climax. It must be a true climax, and give the audience even more than the first two acts have promised in the way of entertainment.

One of the first problems you will become aware of when you start to plan a play is having to limit the action to what can take place on stage. A short story—and within certain limitations, a screen or television play—can present one scene in a schoolroom, jump to the playground, show the characters riding their bicycles home, and so on. To tell a whole story against just one or two stage settings requires some real ingenuity!

Largely it's a matter of adjusting your thinking to stage limitations. Some study of published plays to see how other writers have handled the problem will help. The characters can, of course, talk about what has happened and what is happening offstage. It is best, however, not to have the characters carry on a conversation about another character whom the audience has not yet met. Try to find a way to bring the character on stage, even momentarily, and identify new characters just before they come on stage or immediately after.

Exits and entrances can be used to keep the audience aware of what is happening offstage. If a character says, "Lois's plane is due in half an hour—I've got to go," the audience will project his activity mentally when he leaves the stage. If a character's first lines on entering are "The show was terrific and we ran all the way home to beat the rain," the audience has been given a good deal of information about what took place in this individual's immediate past.

Speeches in plays, though generally short, will be somewhat longer than in fiction; occasional speeches that run to four or five lines help to give cadence, variety, and naturalness to the dialogue. The dialogue must be brisk and entertaining, and must keep the story moving forward swiftly. Truly clever lines that provide lots of laughs without distorting the story line are the lifeblood of a play. They must be in the spoken language, and it is helpful to practice saying the lines aloud and *listening* to them—even to act out the part while saying the lines.

Cleverness in supplying entertaining action is also essential. The audience comes to *see* a play as well as hear it, and the writer who puts a good share of the entertainment into the action is using the medium properly.

Let's think of a play about the erratic course of a teenage boy's first love affair—a theme so familiar that it seems threadbare. The girl with whom he's felt so secure has suddenly tired of the relationship and ended it. It is Saturday evening. Normally Ken would have a date with Debbie. Hurt, bewildered, restless, he moves about the living room— which is our stage—switching on TV but not watching it, thumbing through a magazine, staring out the window. Turning off the TV, he comes to stand before his older sister, who sits on the couch, knitting.

>   KEN *(Watching her a moment)* What do you do when your heart is broken?
>
>   VIRGINIA *(Continues knitting, without looking up)* I knit.
>
>   KEN *(Incredulous)* You—you mean—*you*——?

VIRGINIA Everyone has problems, Ken. It's not getting thrown over that matters. It's what you let it do to you.

KEN *(Sits on couch on* VIRGINIA'S *left, not too close, picks up piece of knitting, studying it. He watches her hands a few moments, then moves impulsively to sit close to her)* Teach me to knit.

Curtain

When the curtain rises on the second act, we see Ken knitting, awkwardly, intently, with a bright-colored yarn. As the play progresses, he alternately gets on top of his trouble a bit, then backslides. Whenever things are going badly, we see him knitting. In the last act, he enters working on the bright-colored piece, which hangs, like a long scarf, nearly to his knees. At the end of the play, he brings home a new girl friend, who sees the piece and picks it up, asking, "What's this?" Laughing, he says, "Something I made just for you," and wraps it tenderly around her neck.

This kind of action—the idea of a big, virile boy knitting— gains immediate audience interest and holds it. It's a kind of action that wouldn't do much for a short story, but can be the making of a play.

One thinks of the length of a play in terms of playing time rather than number of words. Ordinarily, plays for junior- and senior-high-school students will have a playing time of 25 to 45 minutes; some three-act plays run as long as 50 minutes. The script for such a play would be 20 to 25 pages, plus the several pages that precede the actual opening of the play, which are not numbered. Plays for elementary-school-age children should have a playing time of 15 to 25 minutes and will have 12 to 18 numbered pages; plays for children in the lowest grades should not run more than 15 minutes and will have 6 to 10 numbered pages.

Several different formats are used for amateur plays, one just as "right" as another. Some publishers print stage directions in italics, some in caps, some just in regular printing;

all use parentheses around stage directions. Some put the character's name on a line alone in the middle of the page; others at the left of the page followed by stage directions and the character's speech, as in the brief example in this chapter. Almost always the characters' names are in caps, but there are exceptions.

There should be a title page similar to that used for any other script where a title page is included; under the title the author may type "A Contemporary Three-Act Play," or similar brief identification. This page should be followed by a page that lists the characters in the order of their appearance, with brief identification of each as needed, such as "Horace's older brother" or "baseball coach." Then comes a page of production notes, giving the playing time, props, costumes if any, sets, lighting if any. Some publishers want a brief synopsis of the story. The next page gives the time and locale and describes the scene as the curtain rises, telling who is present, where each is, and what he is doing. Some publishers like a rough sketch of the stage and setting.

The main thing is to be consistent. Editorial offices of publications that publish plays exclusively usually have a manuscript specification sheet which they will send free on request. If you are interested in writing plays, collect several of these sheets from different publishers and compare them, and study the format used in several recently published books of plays for young people, comparing these with the specification sheets. Then you can arrive at a format most nearly like that of publications for which you wish to write and use it consistently.

Amateur plays are almost always bought on an outright purchase rather than a royalty basis. If you believe you are seriously interested in writing plays, you should study one or more books on playwriting, as well as recently published plays for young people in both books and magazines. A number of the magazines that publish young people's fiction also publish occasional plays, as do several of the education magazines.

POINTS TO REMEMBER

1. Writing plays is valuable practice to improve fiction-writing skills, whether or not one wishes to write plays professionally.

2. Because actors and director are amateurs, working with limited stage settings and props, plays for young people must be simple in concept, staging, costuming, and every other respect.

3. One- and three-act comedies or other light dramas for high-school students are most wanted. Plays for younger children are usually curriculum oriented or for special days and occasions.

4. Plays are built on the same plot patterns as are short stories, and follow all other fiction techniques.

QUESTIONS AND EXERCISES

1. Collect and read at least ten plays for young people of various ages. Identify the plot pattern of each, and try stating each as a story-in-one-sentence.

2. Find out if any plays are to be given in your community by any group of young people, and try to attend. If possible, arrange with the director to attend a rehearsal or two. Borrow a copy of the play to read and study. The more you can familiarize yourself with plays and theater procedures, the better.

3. Study the plays you have collected to see how the author has overcome the limitations of having to tell the whole story against one or two settings. Analyze the dialogue for its appeal. What about the action? Does it carry its share of the entertainment, help to make the play fresh, unique? Study the format of each play, noting similarities and differences.

4. Plan a special-day or special-occasion one-act play for children under 12, with a playing time of not more than 15 minutes. Use the plot pattern of your choice, and state your story-in-one-sentence. Write the play.

5. Plan a contemporary one-act or three-act play for junior-high or high-school students, with a playing time of not more than 40 minutes. Use the plot pattern of your choice, and state your story-in-one-sentence. Write the play.

6. Look up play publishers in the market lists with which you are now familiar and send for specification sheets. Study these before writing the final draft of a play.

VII

Becoming a Pro

23

Marketing, Rights, and Records

You have gained a fair understanding of several young people's magazines and the specialties of some book publishers. You are also familiar with the books listing markets for writers that are mentioned in Chapter 2. If you've been working out the assignments in the first half of this book, you have built up an inventory of at least ten stories and perhaps several articles. A good inventory is an asset whose value you will appreciate more and more as your experience grows. Not only have you gained strength and breadth and quality in your writing—and a more professional attitude toward your work—but you have put yourself in a strong position from which to start marketing.

To most beginning writers, marketing is both exciting and frightening. The goal is in sight, but can you reach it? Some writers are so eager for sales that they try marketing before they've mastered the craft of writing; others so fear rejection that they seem unable to face marketing at all. Whichever way you tend to lean, entering the marketplace will help you gain a more realistic concept of writing as a profession. The very act of evaluating your own stories from the viewpoint of an editor will help you become a better writer. And the necessity for careful analysis and study of the markets, and your contacts with editors, will teach you a great deal that you can learn in no other way.

Get out all of your stories and reread each one with fresh objectivity. You're an editor now, and this story has come from someone you've never heard of. Would you buy it, just the way it is? If it's a seasonal or special-day story, is this the right time to market it? Magazine editors buy six to eight months in advance, sometimes more. As a general rule, submitting a Christmas story after June is futile; shelve it until at least March 1.

From your inventory choose one story you think will sell just the way it is. Note the length, age group, subject, and appeal. Then, using a market book or list, write down every possible market for the story. Your first consideration must be how well your story fits editorial needs; so think first of the magazines you are familiar with. You can find out about the others later.

Make it a rule never to submit a manuscript to an editor whose publication you have not held in your hands and studied. One of the prime complaints among editors is that they receive great quantities of material that is not at all suited to their publication, no matter how good it may be of its kind. To send unsuitable material is a waste of postage and of your own and the editor's time; it damages your image if you should have something that *is* right for this editor later, and is a threat to the whole free-lance system because it makes unreasonable demands on short-handed editorial staffs.

But you must think about other things, too, in planning your market list. Payment varies considerably, and so do purchase practices. As a new writer your main objective is to *sell*, and at first you may have to settle for some terms that would be unacceptable to established writers. Don't let this bother you now; soon *you'll* have some sales to your credit and will be in a stronger bargaining position. But before sending manuscripts to magazines there are several things you should know about and consider.

First, the market lists will tell you whether a magazine pays "on acceptance" or "on publication." In spite of vigorous protest by authors and authors' organizations, some magazines—including some of the best paying and most prestigious—persist in the basically unfair practice of deferring payment until the piece is published. Since there is no promise as to when this may happen and one really has no guarantee that the story will ever be used, most writers prefer to avoid these markets until they have exhausted other possibilities. A few periodicals have another insidious policy of asking to hold a story for later consideration. In most such cases the sale is eventually consummated, but certainly a straightforward payment on acceptance is much more businesslike and satisfactory.

Second, and more important, the market information tells you what "rights" the magazine buys. The Copyright Act of 1976, which became effective in 1978, puts the author in a much stronger position than he had under the old law. Properly, the intent of the new act is to give the *author* all rights to his own work for the rest of his life, plus fifty years. The purchaser must state in writing exactly what rights he is buying, and the author must agree in writing to those he is willing to sell. There is no justification for the buyer's ever having any rights that he is not in a position to use—such as radio, television, film, and in most cases, book rights.

Yet a number of magazine editors and/or their policymaking boards have been reluctant to end what has always been the unfair practice of arbitrarily insisting on having "all rights." Many new or timid authors think they have no alternative to accepting such terms, and in their eagerness to make a sale readily sign away rights that are justly their own.

Other publications have tried to take advantage of the "work made for hire" provision of the new law. This, in effect, claims that the author is an "employee" of the magazine, and also results in the magazine's owning all rights. Under no circumstances should an author accept this claim.

Doubtless there will be many court battles, some of which will drag on for years, over these and other provisions of the new law. For the vast majority of stories written and sold to young people's publications, these things are unlikely to make any difference—except in principle; very few of these stories have any further sales potential anyway. They will be used only one time, and it really doesn't matter who owns the remaining rights.

But some pieces certainly do have much greater possibilities—as the record on page 242 shows. Today exciting things are happening to children's stories. Several publications buy second or reprint rights—a few buy on a "multiple submission" basis. Films, filmstrips, and videotapes for schools and libraries, children's television programs, records and sound tapes, toys and other specialty or novelty items all offer possible extended uses of children's stories. Textbook publishers pay handsomely for book rights. Authors should consistently protest efforts of purchasers to buy any rights other than those they are actually going to use. If the purchaser insists, then the author should receive substantially more for these additional rights, and should *ask* for more. For the good of all authors, as well as his own interests, he should do everything he can to see that the spirit and intent of the Copyright Act of 1976 are upheld. And let us emphasize that many editors are as eager to do this as writers are, and have accepted it as their way of doing business. The market lists tell you what is the practice with each magazine.

With these thoughts in mind, then, you're ready to list the markets for your story in the order of your choice—and to send it to the magazine that tops your list. (Instructions for manuscript preparation and mailing are in Appendix B of this book.) The story's first journey will give you time to find and examine copies of other magazines on your list. Then you'll be prepared to send to these markets—if they prove to be right—if your story is returned by the first market.

This brings us to the matter of rejections. A rejection, of course, is always a disappointment, but should not be a cause for discouragement. Editors are as individual as other human beings, and the story that one doesn't like may be a real find to the next. But there are many possible reasons for rejection other than that the story is poor or that the editor doesn't like it. It may not fit the overall plan he is trying to work out for the coming year and about which you have no way of knowing. He may have published recently a story he feels is too similar, or may have such a story in his files. If it's seasonal, he may already have completed his purchases for that issue. If he says he's "overstocked," believe him—and avoid this market for the next few months. If your story comes back with a printed rejection slip, it could mean you've missed the mark by a hundred miles, but it doesn't necessarily mean this. Don't expect an editor to tell you why he didn't buy your story; this is not his job.

Perhaps an editor sees promise in your writing but can't use the story you sent. He might write a hurried "Sorry" or "Please try again" on the rejection slip, and may sign or initial it. *Any*thing more than a printed slip may be considered an invitation to send something else—*immediately*.

This is where your inventory is a blessing. If you've built up an inventory before you ever started to market, chances are you have another story similar to the one rejected. If you haven't built up an inventory, you may be caught flatfooted. Most editors are far more interested in finding a *writer* than finding a *story,* and even if your second submission also proves unacceptable, at least you've indicated that you're serious about writing and not a "one-story author." Keep trying as long as the editor keeps the invitation open, but don't get so eager that you send something inferior to what has been rejected. Again, *keep your inventory up,* in both quality and quantity.

In the meantime, of course you have sent the rejected story to the second market on your list, *immediately*—the same day it came home. This is one reason for making the list; you already know where it's to go next. It's very easy to look at a rejected manuscript, feeling a little low because it brought only a printed rejection—or because it's brought two or three such slips—and decide it just isn't any good. But manuscripts don't sell lying idle in a file. By now you should *know* whether a story is marketable. You don't send out a story at all that is not; and if it is, you keep sending it, and sending it, and sending it.

Most beginning writers give up far too easily. Every writing teacher knows students who are not superior writers, but who make many and constant sales because they really study the market, keep up on changes and trends, keep their manuscripts circulating. And the teacher knows other students who are much better writers, but who are timid or indifferent, or whose confidence in their work is easily shaken, and who silently envy their less capable but more aggressive classmates who make the sales. A group of selling writers kept records over a three-year period and discovered that they averaged one sale for each twelve submissions! No one should send a good story to only four or five markets and feel that he has "tried."

But let's suppose you have an unusual and early success. The first or second or third editor who sees your story wants to buy it. You will receive a letter or form to this effect, stating the amount offered, when the payment will be made, and which rights the editor wishes to buy. You will be asked for your social security number, and possibly another question or two.

Of course you're excited by your first sale! Your family is excited, too, and at least briefly will have a new respect for you. Your friends are impressed. But what's next?

First, you respond promptly to the offer, in the affirmative. Maybe the amount offered is a little less than you had secretly hoped—though it may well be more. And you may be expected to part with rights that should be yours. But whatever you receive, in addition to the money you have also earned a "credit." It may be the first step toward qualifying for membership in a professional writers' organization, and it has strengthened your position for all future manuscript submissions. You can now state on your title page of future submissions, when appropriate, "Have sold to _____." (See Appendix B.)

If you have sold only the first rights, *after the story has appeared in the magazine that bought these rights* you may try to resell it to a publication that buys "second rights." Some of these will accept "tear sheets,"—or the pages containing your story torn from the first publication; others want a freshly typed or clean photocopied manuscript. In either case, indicate clearly, on the first page of the tear sheets or on page 1 of the typescript, immediately under the word count, that you are offering second rights, where and when the story was first published, and that you own all other rights. Your payment for the second rights will probably be somewhat less than for the initial sale, but the effort is still worthwhile. The second rights should not be offered to any magazine except one you *know* buys second rights, and one you know is not in competition with the one that originally published the story.

This is also the inviolable rule if you venture into the multiple submission of a manuscript—that is, submitting the same manuscript to two or more publications at one time. *Remember, there are only certain publications*—principally in the religious field—that accept manuscripts on this basis. Be *sure* you know that a magazine does buy on this basis before marketing this way; and when you do, make it clear on page 1 of your script, right under the word count, exactly what you have done. Type, "Submitted simultaneously to: ———" and then list the publications to which you are sending the script. You should not attempt multiple marketing of this kind until you have made several single sales.

Although you will not make the approach in trying to sell book reprint rights to one of your stories, a book publisher may approach *you*, usually through the magazine that first published the story, for purchase of the book rights. Here is the record of one 1,200 word story, "Harold and Burt and Sue and Amy, etc.," by Nancy (Casey) Garber. The original sale was to *Boys' Life*, a magazine that at the time bought "all rights" but negotiated sales of the book rights for the author:

1975—"Harold and Burt and Sue and Amy, etc." published in *Boys' Life*. Purchase price	$ 600
1976—Laidlaw Bros., a division of Doubleday & Co., for use in a fifth-grade reading text	100
Houghton Mifflin Co., for use in a 7th or 8th grade reader	100
1977—Harper & Row, Inc., for use in an 8th grade reader	100
Holt, Rinehart and Winston (Canada) for use in a reader	200
Houghton Mifflin Co. for use in "New Action Series" for junior high schools	100
1979—Houghton Mifflin Co., for use in a reader	250
1979—McDougal, Littell & Co., for use in a reader	150
1981—Houghton Mifflin, for use in a reader	250
1983—Houghton Mifflin, excerpt for use in a textbook	50
1983—Harcourt Brace Jovanovich, for use in a reader	250
1985—Houghton Mifflin, excerpt for use in a textbook	100
1986—Houghton Mifflin, for use in a reader	250
	$2,600

Clovernook Printing House for the Blind also asked for and was given permission to reprint the story in Braille; although no fee is paid for this use, it brings satisfaction and prestige to the author. In years to come this story may well be bought by still more editors for book reprint or use by other media, such as film or television. One never knows where book and other rights may lead. This same author, for example, sold a magazine story for $20. (That's right—twenty dollars!) But a book publisher paid $150 for the book rights. An author should secure and hold as many subsidiary rights as possible.

Marketing a book is somewhat different from marketing magazine material. Again begin by studying the market, trying to match your script to editorial requirements and specialties. You may pick out ten or a dozen likely prospects, and then at the library ask to look at catalogs of these publishers and study critically some of each publisher's recent books. A publisher does not, of course, want a book that will compete with one he has just published, but may welcome one that will complement this list. Try to understand which publishers use the *kind* of book you have written or are writing, which publish the most for the age group for which you write, and work toward these.

Mailing a book manuscript back and forth to various publishers can be expensive, time consuming, and very hard on the manuscript. Yet nearly all book editors agree that they want to see the whole book script, and not just a few chapters and an outline. More and more editors are asking for queries, however, even on fiction books, and this practice can save both time and mailing expense.

We've already discussed using a literary agent, in Chapter 1; if you happen to have some personal contact with a reputable agent who will offer your young people's manuscript to publishers, this may be an advantage. But unless the agent really knows the young people's field and takes a real interest in placing the book, you are probably better off working on your own—at least until you have made a significant sale or two. A writer should not pay an agent a fee to market a book; reputable agents work on a percentage basis, receiving 10 percent of what the author receives.

A book manuscript, like a magazine piece, may sell quickly or may make the rounds of a great many publishers. The author's only course of action is perseverance and a continuing study of the markets; some books have sold after 18 or 20 rejections.

Acceptance of a book results in a contract, which is a printed document of 2 or 3 to several pages with all the terms of the sale spelled out in legal-sounding jargon that the writer may not readily understand. It will state all the obligations of both writer and publisher, specify what rights are purchased and how money from sale of other than the book rights will be divided between author and publisher, and set a time limit within which the book will be published. This may be as much as two years; scheduling, manufacturing, and publishing a book is a major undertaking, especially if it is to have illustrations.

If you receive a book contract, you may want to have it looked at by someone who knows more about such things than you do. Lawyers are usually very little help; most of them have had so little experience with literary property matters that they don't know whether the offer made to you is usual or unusual, good or bad. A writer who has had books published would be a better adviser, or a professional writers' organization will be glad to review the contract for you. Actually, if the publisher is a well-established and reputable firm, you have no need to worry; the contract will be fair.

Just one caution: Don't be taken in by one of the "vanity" or "subsidy" publishers; in other words, don't ever *pay* anything to have your book published, no matter what lures are offered—unless you are prepared to pay the total cost of printing the book without any expectation of ever recovering even part of this cost. Reputable royalty publishers pay *you* to publish your book.

Almost always one of the terms of a book contract is that the author will receive a certain amount on signing the contract—anywhere from about $500 to $2,400—as an "advance against royalties." This is simply an advance payment of the first money the book will earn for the author. How much the book will earn altogether depends on how well it sells; the author practically always receives a "royalty"—usually 10 percent of the book's retail price—rather than an outright purchase price as with magazine material. If the book is a picture book, the royalty is divided with the artist. Royalty statements are sent to the author by the publisher, usually twice a year, telling how many copies of the book have been sold, and a check for the writer's share is sent with the statement or shortly thereafter. Thus payment for a book may be spread over many years.

Whether you are selling magazine material or a book, from the day you send your first manuscript for the first time, you are in business—the business of free-lance writing. Orderly, accurate record keeping is absolutely necessary, not only to the businesslike performance of your work, but for tax purposes.

You will establish your own method of record keeping that works best for you. It may be a card file or a notebook with a separate page for each manuscript. It should be accessible, easily kept up-to-date, and comprehensive. Here is a form that works well:

Title _____

Words _____ Age group _____ Postage—out _____ back _____

Date Submitted _____ Market _____ Results and Remarks

1. _____

2. _____

3. _____

When the script sells, you should note these items:

Date of sale
Name and address of publication or book publisher
Editor
Rights sold
Publication date
File copy received (if magazine publication)
Note of any correspondence
All subsequent resales

To support these records, in your regular office file you will have a folder for each manuscript, containing a copy of the manuscript, tear sheets of published magazine material, and any correspondence connected with the manuscript, including release of rights other than those used. The copy of a book script, of course, does not fit handily in the file; it should be boxed and labeled and shelved where it may be located easily.

A few miscellaneous tips may be helpful: Whether you are marketing a magazine story or a book script, submit your manuscript to only one market at a time—except for the few exceptions among the religious magazines that buy on a multiple-submission basis. Any other plan is unethical and could result in serious trouble. And send just one manuscript to an editor at one time; this too is a matter of ethics—and common sense, for if you send two, one is almost sure to be returned, whereas if sent at different times, both may be accepted.

Ordinarily it is probably better not to submit material to an editor who already has one of your stories in his files, though there are exceptions to this policy. If the second story is very different from the first—or if the first is a Thanksgiving story and the second is about summer camping—there's no reason for not sending it. But best wait until *one* of them is published before sending any more.

When an editor asks you to revise, think over the request carefully. Be sure you understand not only what you are asked to do, but why the editor thinks the change will improve the piece. Decide whether you agree. If you do—and can make the change without violating your own feeling about the piece—do it promptly and return it to the editor, with a letter thanking him for the suggestion and stating that you have made the revision. *Do only what is asked.* Editors groan about writers who, when asked for a specific revision or two, decide to make other changes also and may take out what the editor liked most!

When you submit a manuscript, how long should you expect to wait for a response? Some editors are very prompt, others inexcusably slow. If no word is forthcoming in six to eight weeks, a courteous inquiry is in order. Some authors hesitate to write, fearing that an inquiry may bring home a script that might have sold if they had been more patient. But if an editor thinks so little of a story that a polite inquiry shakes it loose, the writer is better off not selling it there. No writer should want an editor to take a story that he's not enthusiastic about; he will put it in his file and every time he sees it will wonder why he accepted it—and this doesn't help the writer's image! So go ahead and inquire, and if the script comes home, send it somewhere else.

When will your magazine piece be published? It may be within a few months, or it may not be for a year or more. Once a piece is sold, try to forget it, and give your attention to turning out and marketing new work, so that when the publications do start, they'll keep on in a steady stream. Normally you will receive a copy of the publication, or at least tear sheets, when your piece is published. If you have not received such copy within a year after sale, it may be well to write a polite inquiry, just to make sure you haven't missed your copy, which you want for your permanent files.

Probably you still have many "What if's" and "Should

I's" about marketing. Don't worry about them. Your objective *now* is to *sell*. Ninety-nine percent of editors and publishers are trustworthy; the long-established ones are the soul of integrity. The offer they make you is their standard offer, and does not seek to "catch" you or take advantage of your inexperience. Accept the terms offered and be grateful for your first successes, no matter how small. As you gain experience you will learn new angles of marketing that will meet your current needs. And if you reach the point where professional advice is needed on matters of motion picture and television sales, you may be sure a good, reputable agent who knows all about these things will welcome you with open arms.

If you believe in a story, and have had enough experience to judge your own work objectively, keep sending your manuscript out. Of course, repeated submissions will not sell a fundamentally poor story, but repeated submissions of a good story will almost certainly result in a sale. As a morale builder, it's a good idea to keep several manuscripts out all the time. Then when one or two come home, you can hold onto the hope that the others may *not* come home. But in spite of everything, like even the best and most seasoned writers, you will have "blue Mondays," when everything comes home at once and there's the temptation to chuck the whole lot in the wastebasket and forget writing. Don't do it! Some editors use your return envelope to send their acceptance—sometimes with a request for more and information about other of their publications. So open your returned envelopes promptly!

POINTS TO REMEMBER

1. Build up an inventory before you start to market magazine material, and then keep it up.

2. Study your market thoroughly, submitting only to those markets you know from having studied copies of their publications.

3. Use rejections intelligently, responding promptly to any requests for revision or for another submission.

4. Try to retain for yourself all rights except those actually to be used by a magazine. Then see if you can find ways to use them.

5. Books are usually bought on a royalty basis, with a contract stating terms of the purchase.

6. Records of submissions and sales must be kept systematically, regularly, and accurately. Work out a system that will be easy to maintain.

7. Trust editors and publishers, for most are entirely trustworthy.

8. *Perseverance* is the key to successful marketing. Keep scripts out and circulating.

QUESTIONS AND EXERCISES

1. Reread all the stories you have written and select the one you feel is most salable, taking into consideration the season of the year.

2. Study your market guides and make out a list of all possible markets for this story.

3. If you are familiar with one of these publications, prepare your manuscript properly by checking Appendix B, and send to this market. Write for sample copies to any of your markets whose publications you have not seen, enclosing 50 cents for postage and handling.

4. If you are working on a book, study your market guides and make out a list of ten or twelve possible publishers. At the library, study these publishers' catalogs and look at some of their recent books. Then reduce your list to the five best possibilities.

5. Prepare a permanent record, either a card file or a notebook, for your manuscript submissions and sales. Begin by making out a card or page for each manuscript you now have on hand.

24

Where Will You Go from Here?

By now you have gained a reasonably accurate view of the world of writing for young people. If you've been working out many of the assignments as you read, you have perhaps begun to feel at home in this world. A book or a teacher can take you only so far; the rest of the way you must walk alone. Where you will go from here only you can say. And you cannot say with certainty until several years have passed.

But you *can* reach a decision *now* about where you would like to be a year, five years, ten years from now. Probably you have decided what kinds of writing you want most to do and you have some idea of how well able you are to meet the requirements. Taking into consideration your own inclinations, talents, and special abilities, you should be able to plan your goals intelligently.

The important thing is that you make a plan and determine to follow it. A widely quoted management consultant says that although about 15 percent of the employed population are incapable of doing their job properly, 85 percent can work on a project if it is planned for them and if they are under constant supervision to see that they do not stray from the plan. A much smaller number, just 14 percent, can carry out a project if the work is just planned for them, without constant supervision. But only two out of every hundred employed persons are capable of creating a plan, laying out the work, and then doing it without benefit of supervision. Since this performance is required of the writer, he must be in that rare 2 percent.

We have mentioned setting goals. You should have three: first, a distant goal, one you probably will not reach for years; second, a nearer, more readily attainable goal that will mark a milestone on the road to your main goal; and third, a close-at-hand goal that you plan to reach in a few months or a year. If you have only the distant goal, at times it will seem too difficult and too far away. You may become discouraged and quit when a sustained effort would have brought success. So don't set impossible, or even too difficult goals to be achieved quickly. Take it easy. Climb the foothills first, then the near ranges, and leave the high mountain peaks until you are trained and toughened by experience. But while climbing the foothills, never forget that the lofty mountains are waiting to be conquered. Then you will enjoy each victory, each step upward, but you will never become self-satisfied, lazy, content with the laurels you have won.

Keep your mind alert. Learn to recognize the names of other writers in your field. Read their work and the work of new writers whose by-lines are appearing for the first time. Be specific in your judgment. Ask of each selection you read, Is this excellent, good, or mediocre? And then analyze why you think so.

Read reviews of children's books in *The New York Times Book Review* and *The Christian Science Monitor*. *The Horn Book Magazine*, published bimonthly, and the *School Library Journal* are devoted wholly to children's literature. Watch for the prize winners. The "grand prize" is the Newbery Medal, which has been awarded annually since 1922 for "the most distinguished contribution to American literature for children." Equally prestigious is the Caldecott Medal, awarded annually to "the artist of the most distinguished American picture book" of the preceding year. Winners are selected by the Children's Services Division of the American Library Association. Other prizes are awarded by publishers and various organizations. Talk with your librarian about books that have won these prizes and about other outstanding new books.

But never let reading or talking about the writing of others take the place of your own writing. Set a pace you can keep up with, and let nothing interfere with your daily output. Don't let adverse criticism or extravagant praise of your work depress or unduly exhilarate you. If either comes from nonprofessional critics, discount it altogether. If it comes from editors or professional writers *in your field,* consider it carefully and objectively. If you agree with suggestions for revisions, make necessary changes. If you don't agree, try to understand why the individual suggested the changes and see if you can remedy weaknesses without violating your own feeling about the piece. Revision made against your judgment will almost certainly be badly made, for your heart will not be in it.

If your story is dramatically sound, properly put together, and written with freshness and sparkle, some editor will like it and buy it. Editors—and seasoned writers, too—are unanimous in their assertion that no really good manuscript will fail ultimately to find a market. So keep your really good manuscript in the mail until you find an editor who likes it and needs it.

Don't be afraid to invest money in your career. Writing requires a smaller capital outlay in its training period than any other profession, but there are some tools that every writer should have. The first is, of course, a good typewriter—at least good enough to turn out clean, professional-looking manuscripts. Be generous in keeping yourself supplied with typewriter ribbons, paper of appropriate quality, and other necessary equipment. Subscribe to at least one writers' magazine. Editors and editorial policies change, publishing houses merge, new magazines are born, old magazines suspend publication; the writers' magazines keep you informed of these changes. Each issue has up-to-the-minute information on editorial needs, comments by editors and professional writers, and many tips to help you.

Build up your own professional library of books on writing and selected children's books; be choosy, for neither space nor time allows room for books that are not really and continuously helpful as references. Join a writers' organization as soon as you qualify for membership, but be choosy here, too. Find out who belongs and what the members do; you haven't time for mere "socializing." But an organization respected and supported by other professional writers can offer valuable and stimulating contacts; some organizations send helpful newsletters to their members and offer other useful services. The National Writers Club and The Society of Children's Book Writers provide membership classifications for new writers who cannot yet qualify for professional status. Think not only of what you can get from such an organization, but of what you can give to other members and to the writing profession.

Attend an occasional writers' conference, but again, be very selective in your choice, and don't become a chronic "conference-goer"; it's easy to mistake the pleasantries of attending conferences and dashing around to meetings for constructive work!

Finally, respect the profession of writing for children and young adults, and respect yourself as a privileged member of this profession. Set your goals high, so that you can inspire young readers to set *their* goals high. Pablo Casals said: "Each second we live is a new and unique moment of the universe, a moment that never was before and never will be again. And what do we teach our children? We teach them that two and two make four and that Paris is the capital of France. When will we also teach them what they are? We should say to each one of them: Do you know what you are? You are a marvel. You are unique. In all of the world there is no other child exactly like you. In the millions of years that have passed, there has never been a child like you. . . . You may become a Shakespeare, a Michelangelo, a Beethoven. You have the capacity for anything. Yes, you are a marvel. And when you grow up, can you then harm another who is, like you, a marvel? You must cherish one another. You must work—we must all work—to make this world worthy of its children."

What nobler or more important work could engage your time, your talents, your efforts than writing for young people?

Make your plans carefully, then work consistently and with assurance that you will succeed. The rewards are there; you have only to make yourself worthy to claim them. The path is not easy, but it is pleasant, ever changing, never dull. May yours lead to successes beyond your fondest hopes.

Suggested Reading

For Further Help

Much has been written about young people's books, as well as the books themselves. Because it is impossible to find specific back issues of magazines, I have chosen appropriate and readily available *books* for young people to illustrate various principles applicable to both books and magazines. To present even a cross section of the thousands of good books in the young people's section of any city library, however, is presumptuous; and the following lists should be seen as one-of-a-kind samplers, and not a comprehensive guide to literature for young people. Some of the authors have written a dozen or more books, and the one mentioned may not be your favorite. Use the lists as trail marks, to start you on your own path of discovery.

Part I—Young People and You

Books about Writing and Children's Literature
May Hill Arbuthnot and Zena Southerland, *Children and Books* (Scott Foresman, 4th edition, 1972).
Celebrating Children's Books, edited by Betsy Hearne and Marilyn Kaye (Lothrop, Lee & Shepard, 1981).
Annis Duff, *Bequest of Wings* (Viking, 1954).
Mollie Hunter, *Talent Is Not Enough* (Harper & Row, 1976).
Jacqueline Jackson, *Turn Not Pale, Beloved Snail* (Little, Brown, 1974).
Jean Karl, *From Childhood to Childhood: Children's Books and Their Creators* (John Day, 1970).
Nancy Larrick, *A Parent's Guide to Children's Reading*, revised 5th edition (Westminster, 1983).

Ivan Southall, *A Journey of Discovery: On Writing for Children* (Macmillan, 1976).

Triumphs of the Spirit in Children's Literature, edited by Francilia Butler and Richard Rotert (The Shoe String Press, 1987).

Magazines:

The Horn Book Magazine, published bimonthly in Boston.

The Kinderbook Newsletter, published 10 times a year by JCV Publications, St. Paul.

The Writer, published monthly in Boston. Also publishes *The Writer's Handbook*, annually.

Writer's Digest, published monthly in Cincinnati. Also publishes *Writer's Market*, annually.

Part II—Plans That Work

These monthly magazines are likely to have good fiction. Information about their needs can be found in the market books just mentioned.

Magazines for Children under 12:

Cobblestone (8-12-year-olds)

Cricket (6-12-year-olds)

The Friend (4-12-year-olds)

Highlights for Children (2-12-year-olds)

My Own Magazine (3-6-year-olds)

Ranger Rick (6-12-year-olds)

Wee Wisdom (3-12-year-olds)

Magazines for Teens:

Boys' Life (boys 8-18)

HiCall (readers 12-19)

Scholastic Scope (readers 15-18 with 6th grade reading ability)

Seventeen (young adults)

Sprint (junior high age readers)

TQ/Teen Quest (young teens)

YM (young women 14-18)

Part III—Skill with the Tools

Books about Writing and Young People:

Claudia Lewis, *Writing for Young Children* (Doubleday, 1981).

Uri Schulevitz, *Writing with Pictures: How to Write and Illustrate Children's Books.* (Watson-Guptill, 1985).

George Edward Stanley, *Writing Short Stories for Young People* (Writer's Digest, 1987).

Phyllis A. Whitney, *Writing Juvenile Stories and Novels* (The Writer, 1976)

Lee Wyndam/Arnold Madison, *Writing for Children and Teenagers*, (Writers Digest, 1985).

Beverly Cleary, *Dear Mr. Hinshaw* (Morrow, 1983).

Lois Duncan, *Stranger With My Face* (Little, Brown, 1986).

Belinda Harmence, *Tancy* (Clarion, 1984).

Irene Hunt, *The Everlasting Hills*, (Scribner's, 1985).

E. L. Konigsburg, *Up From Jericho Tel*, (Atheneum, 1986).

Ouida Sebestyen, *On Fire* (Atlantic Monthly/Little, Brown, 1985).

Barbara Steiner, *Oliver Dibbs and the Dinosaur Cause* (Macmillan, 1986).

Part IV—Expanding the Field

Books about Writing and Young People:

Barbara Baskin and Karen Harris, *Books for the Gifted Child*, The Serving Special Populations Series (Bowker, 1980).

Barbara Bader, *American Picture Books from Noah's Ark to the Beast Within* (Macmillan, 1976).

Bruno Bettelheim, *The Uses of Enchantment: The Meaning and Importance of Fairy Tales* (Vintage, 1976).

The Black Experience in Children's Books, compiled by Augusta Baker (New York Public Library, 1971).

Madelein L'Engle, *Trailing Clouds of Glory: Spiritual Values in Children's Books* (Westminster, 1985).

Human and Anti-Human Values in Children's Books, (Council on Interracial Books for Children, 1976).

Joan Lowery Nixon, *Writing Mysteries for Young People* (The Writer, 1977).

Ellen E. M. Roberts, *The Children's Picture Book: How to Write it, How to Sell It (Writer's Digest, 1981).*

Chapter 13—Fantasy and Science Fiction—Books for Young People:
John Christopher, *Dragon Dance,* (Dutton, 1986).
Andrew Glass, *My Brother Tries to Make Me Laugh* (Lothrop, Lee & Shepard, 1984).
Douglas Hill, *Exiles of Colsec* (Atheneum, 1984).
Elizabeth Starr Hill, *Fangs Aren't Everything* (Dutton, 1985).
Madelein L'Engle, *Many Waters* (Farrar, Straus & Giroux, 1986).
Ardith Mayhar, *Makra Choria* (Macmillan, 1987).
Robin McKinley, *The Hero and the Crown* (Greenwillow, 1985).
Willo Davis Roberts, *The Magic Book* (Atheneum, 1986).

Chapter 14—Picture Books
Judith Barrett, *Animals Should Definitely Not Act Like People* (Macmillan, 1980).
Barbara Helen Berger, *When the Sun Rose* (Philomel, 1987).
Claude Boujan, *The Fairy with the Long Nose* (McElderry/Macmillan, 1987).
Tomie de Peola, *The Clown of God* (Harcourt Brace Jovanovich, 1978).
Aileen Fisher, *The House of the Mouse* (Charlotte Zolotow, 1987).
Margaret Gordon, *Frog's Holiday* (Viking/Kestral, 1987).
C. S. Lewis, *The Chronicles of Narnia* (Macmillan, 1986).
Juliet and Charles Snape, *I'm Not Afraid of Ghosts* (Prentice Hall, 1987).

Chapter 15—Other Peoples, Other Places, Other Times—Books for Young People:
Aylesa Forsee, *They Trusted God—Bible Stories for Young Readers* (The Christian Science Publishing Society, 1980).
Nancy Luenn, *Arctic Unicorn* (Atheneum, 1986).
Gloria Miklowitz, *The War Between the Classes* (Delacorte, 1985).
Beverly Naidoo, *Journey to Jo'berg* (Lippincott, 1985).
Scott O'Dell, *Alexandra* (Houghton Mifflin, 1984).
Gary Provost, *Good If It Lasts* (Bradbury, 1984).
Elizabeth Shub, *Cutlass in the Snow* (Greenwillow, 1986).
Theodore Taylor, *Walking Up a Rainbow* (Delacorte, 1986).

Chapter 16—Five Special Kinds of Stories—Books for Young People:
Vivian Alcock, *The Sylvia Game* (Delacorte, 1984).
Jamie Gilson, *Hello, My Name is Scrambled Eggs* (Lothrop, Lee & Shepard, 1985).

Virginia Hamilton, *The Mystery of Drear House* (Morrow, 1987).

Lorle K. Harris, *Biography of a Mountain Gorilla* (P. G. Putnam's Sons, 1981).

Bill Martin, Jr., and Joh Archambault, *The Ghost-Eye Tree* (Holt Rinehart, 1985).

Harry Mazer, *Hey, Kid! Does She Love Me?* (Crowell, 1985).

Leo Rutman, *Five Good Boys* (Viking, 1982).

Peter Spier, *Peter Spier's Christmas!* (Doubleday, 1983).

Part V—The Nonfiction Skills

Books and Other Helps for Writers:

Administration for Children, Youth, and Families, Box 1182, Washington, DC 20013. Free media tip sheets specifically designed to provide writers with feature article or story ideas. One may be placed on mailing list by request.

A Complete Guide to Writing Nonfiction, edited by Glen Evans, American Society of Journalists and Authors, (Writer's Digest, 1983).

Reader's Guide to Periodical Literature, published annually by Wilson.

Ellen E. M. Roberts, *Nonfiction for Children: How to Write It, How to Sell It* (Writer's Digest, 1986).

F. A. Rockwell, *How to Write Nonfiction That Sells* (Regnery, 1975).

Magazines for Young People—Magazines listed for Part II, plus these nonfiction magazines. Further information available in market books mentioned in Part I.

Magazines for Children under 12:

Chickadee (for 2-8s) and *Owl* (for 8-12s) 10 times a year, outdoor and wildlife.

Happy Times (for 3-6s) monthly, general interest.

National Geographic World (8-12s) monthly, general interest.

Odyssey (8-12s) monthly, astronomy and outer space.

Stickers and Stuff (6-14s, "mostly girls") monthly, general interest.

3-2-1 Contact (8-14s) 10 times a year, current science interests.

YABA World (Young American Bowling Alliance) monthly, bowling.

Magazines for Teens:

Careers (High school juniors and seniors) 3 times a year, career and education opportunities.

Connections, The National Publication for High School Students, biweekly, general interest.

Current Consumer & Lifestudies, The Practical Guide to Real Life Issues, monthly during school year, consumer interests.

Exploring Magazine, 4 times a year, general interest for Explorer Scouts.

New Driver, quarterly, car maintenance and safe driving.

Purple Cow, monthly tabloid, general interest.

Scholastic Update, biweekly during school year, public affairs.

Tiger Beat Magazine, monthly, for girls; entertainers and entertainment.

Part VI—Looking to the Future:

Chapter 19—Fiction and Nonfiction Books:
Books and Other Helps for Writers:

AAAS Magazine, quarterly; and *AAAS Science Book List*, with supplement published from time to time by the American Association for the Advancement of Science, Washington, DC.

Joan Aiken, *The Way to Write for Children* (St. Martin's Press, 1982).

May Hill Arbuthnot, et al, *Children's Books Too Good to Miss* (University Press Books, 1980).

Books to Help Children Cope with Separation and Loss, compiled by Joanne E. Bernstein (Bowker, 1977).

Bulletin of the Center for Children's Books (University of Chicago Press, monthly).

Tipper Gore, *Raising PG Kids in an X-Rated Society* (Abingdon, 1987).

A Guide to Non-Sexist Children's Books, compiled by Judith Adell and Hilary Klein (Academy Press, 1976).

Notes from a Different Drummer—A Guide to Portraying the Handicapped (1977) and *More Notes from a Different Drummer* (Bowker, 1984).

Barbara Seuling, *How to Write a Children's Book and Get it Published* (Charles Scribner's Sons, 1984).

Irene Smith, *History of the Newbery and Caldecott Medals* (Viking, 1957).

Jane Yolen, *Writing Books for Children* (The Writer, 1983).

Contemporary Novels for Young Readers:
C. S. Adler, *Carly's Buck* (Clarion, 1987).
Sue Ellen Bridges, *Permanent Connections* (Harper & Row, 1987).
Robert Cormier, *Beyond the Chocolate War* (Knopf, 1985).
Jane Morton, *I Am Rubber, You Are Glue* (Beaufort, 1981).
Marguerite Murray, *Odin's Eye* (Atheneum, 1987).
Joan Lowry Nixon, *Maggie Forevermore* (Harcourt, Brace Jovanovich, 1987).
Marilyn Sachs, *Thunderbird* (Dutton, 1985).
Laurence Yep, *Liar, Liar* (Morrow, 1983).

Nonfiction Books for Young Readers:
Gail Anderson, *Fun Sports for Everyone (Westminster, 1985).*
Patricia Curtis, *Animal Rights: Stories of People who Defend the Rights of Animals* (Four Winds, 1980).
Russell Freeman, *Indian Chiefs* (Holiday House, 1987).
David C. Grass, *A Justice for All the People: Louis D. Brandies* (Dial, 1987).
James Jespersen and Jane Fitz-Randolph, *From Quarks to Quasars: A Tour of the Universe* (Atheneum, 1987).
Milton Meltzer, *Ain't Gonna Study War No More* (Harper & Row, 1985).
Christine Osinki, *I Can Be a Photographer* (Children's Press, 1986).
Ken Robbins, *Building a House* (Four Winds, 1984).

Chapter 20—Schoolbooks and Educational Materials—Books and Other Helps:
Curriculum Review, published 6 times a year by Curriculum Advisory Service, Chicago.
The Educational Marketer Yellow Pages, a directory of publishers of textbooks, workbooks, and audiovisual materials (White Plains, NY: Knowledge Industry Publications, annually).
Journal of Reading, The Reading Teacher (Newark, DE, International Reading Association, monthly during school year).
Literary Methods (Philadelphia, monthly during school year).
Kathleen C. Phillips and Barbara Steiner, *Creative Writing: A Handbook for Teaching Young People* (Libraries Unlimited, 1985).
Current catalogs of scores of education publishers and multimedia producers are available at the media center of your public library and/or public school system. The latter will also have actual materials that you can handle and inspect. *Publishers* and *School Supplies* in the Yellow pages

of city phone directories list local small publishers that publish specialized materials for schools.

Chapter 21—Poetry—Books to Help Writers:
Edward H. Hohman and Norma Leary, *The Greeting Card Handbook* (Harper and Row, 1981).
Judson Jerome, *On Being a Poet* (1984), and *The Poet's Handbook* (Writer's Digest, 1986).
Langford Reed, *The Writer's Rhyming Dictionary* (The Writer, 1985).
Ruth Whitman, *Becoming a Poet* (The Writer, 1982).

Poetry Books for Young People:
Nancy White Carlstrom, *Jesse Bear, What Will You Wear?* (Macmillan, 1986).
Aileen Fisher, *Rabbits, Rabbits* (Crowell, 1983), and *When It Comes to Bugs: Poems* (Charlotte Zolotow/Harper & Row, 1986).
Nancy Larrick, *When the Dark Comes Dancing: A Bedtime Poetry Book* (Philomel, 1983).
Myra Cohn Livingston, *Cat Poems* (Holiday House, 1987).
Pocket Poems: Selected for a Journey, edited by Paul Janeczko (Macmillan, 1985).
Jack Prelutsky, *The Random House Book of Poetry for Children* (Random House, 1983), and *The New Kid on the Block* (Greenwillow, 1984).

Chapter 22—Plays—Books about Plays and Playwriting:
Elizabeth Allstrom, *Let's Play a Story* (Friendship Press, 1957).
Sylvia Diane Borden, *Plays as Teaching Tools in the Elementary School* (Parker, 1970).
Raymond Hull, *How to Write a Play* (Writer's Digest, 1983).

Plays for Young People:
Sue Alexander, *Small Plays for Special Days* (Seabury, 1977).
Virginia Bradley, *Is There an Actor in the House?* (Dodd, Mead, 1975).
Aileen Fisher, *Year-Round Programs for Young Players* (Plays, Inc., 1985).
Plays Magazine, published monthly by Plays, Inc., Boston. Also publishes books of plays.

Part VII—Becoming a Pro

Books:

Judith Appelbaum and Nancy Evans, *How to Get Happily Published* (Harper & Row, 1978).

Richard Balkin, *A Writer's Guide to Book Publishing* (Hawthorne, 1977), and *How to Understand and Negotiate a Book Contract or Magazine Agreement* (Writer's Digest, 1985).

Michael Larsen, *How to Write a Book Proposal* (Writer's Digest, 1985).

Law and the Writer, edited by Kirk Polking and Leonard S. Meranus (Writer's Digest, 1985).

Organizations:

American Library Association, 50 East Huron Street, Chicago, Ill. 60611. Publishes *A.L.A. Booklist* and *Notable Children's Books,* annually.

Children's Book Council, 67 Irving Place, New York, N.Y. 10003. Leaflets: "Writing Children's Books" and "Illustrating Children's Books"; quarterly "Calendar" and other materials. A one-time nominal fee puts you on the mailing list indefinitely.

Council on Inter-racial Books for Children, 1841 Broadway, New York, N.Y. 10023. Helps writers who are members of ethnic minorities.

International Reading Association, 800 Barksdale Road, Newark, Del. 19711. Essentially for teachers and reading specialists, but has publications and local and regional chapters, meetings, and workshops helpful to writers. Free leaflet, "Good Books Make Reading Fun for Your Child." Send self-addressed, stamped envelope.

National Writers Club, 1450 South Havana, Suite 620, Aurora, Col. 80012. Newsletter, market lists, many aids and services.

Reading Is Fundamental (RIF), P. O. Box 23444, Washington, D.C. 20024.

Right to Read, U.S. Office of Education, Dept. of Health, Education, and Welfare, Washington, D.C. 20201.

Society of Children's Book Writers, P. O. Box 296, Los Angeles, California 90066. Has regional chapters, quarterly newsletter, and other material.

Appendix A

Sample Stories, with Commentary

The following stories are examples of the five basic plot patterns. Written for different age groups and drawn from secular, educational, and church-published magazines, they represent a wide spectrum. All are used with permission of the original publisher and/or author.

1.

WHAT DID YOU DO TODAY?*

by

Nancy Garber

Plot pattern: Incident-Excursion, projected to Incident-Adventure in the main character's imagination.   Approx. 500 words
Story-in-one-sentence: First-person character, imagining answers to the perennial question 'What did you do today?' decides there's too much to tell and settles on the usual answer, 'Oh, nothing.'

This appealing story has several features seldom found in stories for the very young: The main character doesn't go anywhere or do anything; all of the 'action' is purely in his imagination. Yet the dialogue—which is also simply imagined—is so realistic that the reader 'sees' the action vividly. Note that the first-person character—which is itself rare in a story for the youngest children—could be either a boy or a girl; he was pictured as a boy, however, by the magazine illustrator.

Every day when I come home from school, my mother asks me, "What did you do today, dear?"
Every day I say, "Oh, nothing."
And every day she says, "Oh."

* © *The Friend,* 1974. Reprinted by permission.

Maybe tomorrow when she says, "What did you do today, dear?" I'll tell her what I really did.

"When I left for school," I'll say, "a big lion chased me for two blocks."

"Really?" she'll say.

"Well," I'll say, "it was really the Johnsons' cat. But it looked like a big lion to me for just a minute."

"Oh," she'll say. "I'm glad it wasn't a real lion."

"And when I went out for recess," I'll say, "a giant came over to me. He wanted me to help him. He told me he was too big for the slippery slide. He asked me to give him a push. So I did."

"Really?" she'll say.

"Well," I'll say, "it was really Freddie. But he looked like a giant for just a minute."

"Oh," she'll say. "I'm glad it wasn't a real giant."

"And during school," I'll say, "a king came into our room. He said he wanted me to slay a dragon. Then he made me a knight."

"Really?" she'll say.

"Well," I'll say, "it was really the principal. He wanted me to take a note to Mrs. Smith's room. Then he told me I could be his messenger and take notes all over the school. But he looked like a king to me for just a minute.

"And then when it was lunchtime, we had a party. We had fancy foods and good things to drink. We had people standing behind our chairs and serving us."

"Really?" she'll say.

"Well," I'll say, "it was really hamburgers and milk today. And Jerry stood behind my chair waiting for me to leave something. But to me it tasted like fancy foods and good things to drink.

"And on the way home I rode in a golden coach. We had a driver in a fancy suit, and there were people all around wanting to do things for me."

"Really?" she'll say.

"Well," I'll say, "it was really the school bus. Sally wanted to carry my books for me. But I told her, 'No, thank you.'

"And then when I got off the bus, a monster was waiting for me. It made loud roaring and howling noises."

"Really?" she'll say.

"Well," I'll say, "it was really the Wilsons' dog. I guess he was glad to see me."

"I guess so," my mother will say. "But I'm glad it wasn't a monster."

"I'm glad, too," I'll say.

It would take me a long time to tell my mother all the things that happen to me at school in one day. So probably tomorrow when she says, "What did you do today, dear?" I'll probably say, "Oh, nothing."

2.

FIRE IN THE MOUNTAIN*

by

Corinne Bergstrom

Plot pattern: Purpose Achieved—by courage   Approx. 1,800 words
Story-in-one-sentence: With fireballs dropping around him and the flow of hot lava from erupting Helgafell imminent, Heldor risks his life, after

---

seeing to his mother's safety, to save his crippled friend Captain Ericson by wheeling him in his wheelchair to the dock and safety of the boats.

This story of physical courage in the face of life-or-death danger not only gives the reader a real and believable hero, but provides a glimpse of life in a fishing village and a vivid picture of a volcano in action and its effect on various individuals in the story. The problem may seem slow to emerge, but when one is writing of an unfamiliar situation in a foreign locale, he must take more time and words to establish these things than when writing of an everyday school or home situation that readers would recognize instantly. The author does hint at the problem in the fourth paragraph, and keeps the threat of the volcano alive and growing as she fills in the needed background.

In the dim light of a January afternoon on the island of Heimaey in Iceland, Heldor Arnason hurried home from school. The harbor had been free of ice floes that morning, and the fishermen had put out to sea. His father would need help on the dock when he returned. Heldor didn't mind the work. He loved the boats, especially his father's boat, <u>The Viking</u>, and someday he, too, would be a fisherman.

At home Heldor quickly changed out of his school clothes. His mother didn't ask where he was going--she knew. But she stopped him at the door and said, "Please take these rolls to Captain Ericson first."

Heldor frowned. Usually he enjoyed a visit with the Captain; today he didn't have time for an old man's tales. But it was useless to argue with his mother. "All right. I'll take them."

Outside, he turned up the road toward the volcano. Was there a faint trace of smoke at the top of Helgafell, or was it his imagination? The volcano had been inactive so long.

His thoughts were interrupted; someone was calling his name. "Heldor, come with us. We're going sliding." It was Magnus and his other friends from school.

Heldor wanted to go with them. They would climb the hillside and slide down the ice pockets in the gullies. But he had to hurry to the boats, so he walked on, carefully avoiding the deep puddles of the rutted road. "Not today," Heldor said. "I have to take these rolls to the Captain; then I'm going down to the docks."

Magnus groaned. "The boats. It's always the boats. Someday I'll leave Heimaey. Then I'll never have to see boats again."

The boys turned away when they reached the Captain's door. Heldor looked up at the volcano, so tall and menacing, and knocked to let the Captain know someone was there. Then he pushed the door open and walked in. "It's Heldor," he called.

"Heldor." It was more of a growl than a greeting. The Captain was in a bitter mood, as he was whenever the boats went out. Ever since his legs had failed, the Captain had been unable to go to sea.

"Mother sent some rolls."

"Thank her," said the Captain curtly, wheeling his chair closer to take them.

"Have you seen Helgafell today?" Heldor tried to get the old man's mind off the sea.

"Helgafell? She's always there. I see her whenever I look out the window."

"But today she is different. I can feel it. On the way here, I thought I saw smoke."

The Captain's eyebrows drew together. He

wheeled his chair to the window. "She looks the same to me." A sigh of relief ruffled his thick beard. "You scared me. I thought maybe she was about to pop open like Hekla."

Hekla was a volcano on the mainland, less than a hundred miles to the north of Heimaey. In 1947 she had erupted, sending tons of lava over a large piece of land. What was it the old men said? <u>Watch out for the quiet ones.</u> Helgafell had been quiet for a long time. As long as Heldor could remember, anyway.

"I must go," he said and moved toward the door.

"Not yet. You just came," the Captain growled. "We'll have a game of chess."

"I promised to help my father."

The old man's shoulders drooped. "You go to meet the boats."

Heldor nodded.

"Go. Go have a good time." The Captain waved him on his way.

Heldor grinned. "It's work," he said.

"But you have a good time doing it. I know."

"I'll come back later and tell you all about it," Heldor promised.

"Tomorrow." The Captain sounded sad. "Come tomorrow."

Heldor closed the door quietly behind himself and ran down the road to the docks. He felt better with Helgafell at his back.

"Heldor," his father called. "The unloading goes slowly. We need you."

Heldor reached for a barrel of fish rolling down the gangplank and off the boat.

He set it upright next to others on the dock. Barrel after barrel rolled down. After a while, he traded jobs with one of the crew. Now he heaved the heavy barrels down the gangplank.

Jokes rolled along with the barrels; the men were happy. The Captain had known it would be like this, and he missed it. Heldor would have, too, if he had gone sliding with his friends.

It was late when they finished. Every bone in Heldor's body hurt, and all he wanted was food and a hot bath. His bed would be welcome tonight. A hot mug of broth, cold sliced lamb on bread, a hot bath afterward, and Heldor was quickly asleep.

He dreamed--at least, he thought he dreamed--that the earth was rumbling. Earthquakes were not unusual in this land of fire and ice. The islands had been made from lava beds long ago, and the fires still burned underground. Earthquakes came and went, but in Heldor's dream, the rumbling sound didn't go away. It grew to a roar.

Heldor's eyes popped open. He shook his head. The roar was still there. Helgafell! Then the smoke hadn't been his imagination. He jumped out of bed and bumped into his mother, who had come to wake him. "It's a big one--like Hekla," she screamed. "Run, Heldor. Run to the boats!"

His father was calmer. "I have to go ahead, Heldor. I need to make room for our friends on the boat. See that your mother gets there."

Before the door shut behind his father,

Heldor saw Helgafell. A red glow reached high into the sky, and balls of fire began to spout from her mouth. Soon, boiling lava would pour over their village.

His mother screamed; then she was quite still. Heldor shook her. "Mother, put on your coat. We must run."

"We must run," she repeated woodenly, not moving.

Heldor found his mother's coat and his pants and jacket.

"It's too late," she said.

"No, Mother. We'll make it to the boats."

Outside he had to pull her away from their home. "What will happen to it?" she whispered. "Everything we have is inside."

"No, Mother," Heldor said, trying to hide his own fear. "We have each other. And we have the boat."

"But we were so happy living here." Tears came to her eyes, the stiffness left her body, and she was herself again. "Helgafell has been quiet all these years. Now look at her," she said sadly.

Heldor followed his mother's gaze and saw the Captain's small house on the hillside, the red glow raging behind it. "Captain Ericson!" he shouted. "We can escape, Mother, but he can't."

Magnus and his mother ran up to them. "May we go on your boat?" Magnus asked.

"Yes, Father is already there," said Heldor. "But the Captain, Magnus. We have to go get him."

Magnus stared at the fiery volcano. "We can't," he said flatly.

Heldor saw that Magnus would not go with him. "I'm going to try anyway," he said.

"You go to the boats and take my mother with you. I promised I'd get her there safely." Heldor started running up the hill before his mother could stop him.

"Heldor," Magnus called after him. "Save yourself. The Captain's old."

Heldor was too stunned to reply. Then he remembered how his mother had acted only moments before. At a time like this, people weren't themselves. Even he was different from last night. Then he, too, might have run. But now all he could think of was the Captain. What would it feel like to have a mountain of lava pour down on you?

Heldor's legs felt like wood. They refused to move as fast as he wanted them to. He darted right and left, dodging the fireballs. First the balls of fire, then the lava, the old men said. Could he get to the Captain in time?

When he reached the old man's house, he found the door locked. "Captain! Captain Ericson!" he shouted. There was no answer. Had someone helped the old man escape? Heldor could wait no longer. The fireballs were coming closer together now. He picked up a rock and threw it at a window, shattering the glass. Then he took off his jacket, wrapped it around his fist, and broke away the rest of the glass.

He climbed through the window. As his feet hit the floor, he heard someone shouting, "Helgafell, you mean old woman. You won't get me."

·The voice came from under the floor. Heldor suddenly remembered a root cellar the Captain had once shown him. He ran to it and lifted the trapdoor. There lay the old man, his eyes bright as fireballs. For a moment, Heldor thought that Captain Ericson did not recognize him. Then the Captain's face broke into a smile. "I don't know if you're real, but if you're not, it's a good dream, boy."

"Come on, Captain. I've got to get you out of here."

The old man waved a hand at Heldor. "You can't do it."

"There has to be a way. First let's move you out of this cellar."

"Don't know if I want to leave it," the old man said stubbornly. "Up there, I can see her coming."

Heldor didn't listen to the Captain's words, but climbed down into the root cellar. "You hang onto the upstairs floor, and I'll push," he instructed the Captain. "If we can't get you up, I'll stay down here with you."

The Captain laughed. "A real Viking, you are."

"All right. Now when I push, you pull," Heldor said. "Your arms are still strong."

Working together, they got the Captain out of the cellar and into his wheelchair.

"Now what?" the Captain shouted above the roar.

Heldor opened the front door. Hot air rushed into the room.

"Here it comes." The Captain's finger shook as he pointed to the top of Helgafell. Hot lava was beginning to ooze down her sides. "We'll never make it. Run, Heldor. I'll go back to the cellar."

There was no time to argue. Heldor pushed

the chair out of the house and down the
road. Once more he avoided the ruts. If
the wheelchair got stuck, they could go no
farther. He watched for the balls of fire,
too, but he forgot to watch for rocks.
Suddenly they hit one. The wheelchair
tipped over, and the Captain was sent
sprawling on the road.

Heldor set the chair upright. A ball of
fire rolled next to him and caught the
edge of the old man's pants. Heldor took
off his jacket and beat out the flames.

The Captain groaned and tried to sit up.
"My arm," he said. "I think it's broken."

Heldor bound the injured arm to the old
man's chest with his jacket. What would he
have done without that jacket? Then he
locked his arms around the Captain and
lifted him back into the wheelchair.

"We'll make it." His voice came in short
puffs as he wheeled the chair down the
road again. This time he watched for puddles, balls of fire, <u>and</u> rocks.

The roar of the volcano grew even louder.
Heldor looked back and saw that the lava
flow had almost reached the Captain's
house.

Then, miraculously, above the noise he
heard another sound. Voices. His father
and the crew from <u>The Viking</u> were coming
to help him. The men crossed arms to make
a chair for the old man, and together they
ran the rest of the way to the boat. Once
on board, Heldor looked back at Helgafell.
The lava had covered the Captain's little
house.

But they were safe. And one day Heldor
would return to live below Helgafell again.

He'd fish the waters around the island as his father had. Heimaey was his home.

3.

THE REAL CHARLIE BROWN*

by

J. F. Randolph

Plot pattern: Wish Fulfillment   Approx. 1,200 words
Story-in-one-sentence: Thwarted in his wish to borrow his neighbor's beagle to act as Snoopy in a school skit, Andy carries out his usual job of caring for the dog, washing its feet to remove salty chemicals after their romp in the park, thus winning the owner's approval and permission to use the dog after all.

In this story, Andy's one effort to solve his problem has taken place before the story opens. At the outset he has already abandoned hope, and concentrates instead on trying to think of a way out of the jam he's in.

Andy closed Mrs. Pierson's apartment door more loudly than he'd meant to. He hoped she didn't think he was mad; that certainly wouldn't help.

Baxter, Mrs. Pierson's beagle, tugged on his leash, urging Andy past his own apartment door toward the elevator. "Heel!" Andy ordered, and he jerked the leash-- harder than he'd meant to. Baxter obeyed, but he looked up as if he couldn't understand what had happened to his friend.

Andy stooped and hugged the dog. Baxter and Mrs. Pierson had been away for two weeks, and Andy had missed the daily romp in the park. It certainly wasn't Baxter's

fault that Mrs. Pierson had fouled everything up. Good grief--Andy had thought
she'd <u>want</u> Baxter to be in their play at
school. Baxter was to be the <u>star.</u> But
Mrs. Pierson wouldn't even listen. She
hadn't even let Andy explain how he
planned to get Baxter to school and home
again. She'd just said, "No."

What could he do, Andy asked himself as
he and Baxter stepped into the elevator.
For Character Costume Day everyone was
supposed to dress up like a fiction character and put on an act. Miss Shaefer had
said two or three could work together, and
Andy'd had a great idea. He'd be Charlie
Brown, and Baxter could be Snoopy. His
best friends, Mark and Susan, were to be
Schroeder and Lucy. They'd worked out a
really neat act, but without Baxter it
would just be dumb. And tomorrow was Character Costume Day!

As Andy and Baxter walked out the door,
little pellets of sleet bounced off the
sidewalk. Andy buttoned his jacket and
pulled on his mittens. He was glad it was
stormy; Mark and Susan probably wouldn't
be out. How could be explain to them about
Baxter? He felt like the real Charlie
Brown.

Slush on the pavement had begun to
freeze. The sand truck was already out,
Andy noticed as they waited for the WALK
light to cross the street.

When they reached the park, Andy let Baxter's leash go slack. Baxter gave a joyous
yip and started to run. It was for <u>running</u>
with Baxter that Mrs. Pierson gave Andy a
quarter every day. Andy would have done it

for nothing, even on days like this. It was the next best thing to having his own dog.

Baxter scattered a flock of pigeons and chased a squirrel up a tree. Andy wished <u>he</u> felt as happy as Baxter. He thought about how hard they'd worked on the skit. At first Susan didn't want to do it. She had a Bo Peep costume and a woolly lamb, and she was going to sing a song about Bo Peep. But Mark told her that was juvenile, and said Baxter was a lot better than a stuffed sheep.

Andy and Mark had spent all Saturday afternoon making a doghouse like Snoopy's out of a cardboard box. They'd made a cassette tape of a real neat piano piece, and Mark had practiced pretending to play along with it on his sister's toy piano. Mark knew how Baxter did whatever Andy told him to do, so Baxter didn't need to practice his part, which was to sit up and beg Schroeder to stop playing. Baxter would have <u>fun</u> being in the act. Andy just knew he would. What was the matter with Mrs. Pierson, anyway?

Andy tried to remember everything he could about her as he walked Baxter. She had moved into the apartment about the time school started, from some small town. She'd never lived in a city; she didn't like cities, she'd told Andy--or apartments. Yet she didn't leave the apartment often. Maybe she didn't feel well today. Maybe she was tired from her trip.

Andy saw the flashing blue light of the sand truck as it spewed salty sand across their path. That reminded him--one day last winter a man from the Humane Society had come to school to talk about caring for pets. He'd said that salt and chemicals scattered on the street to melt the ice and keep cars from slipping could make a dog's feet sore. And the dog would lick its feet and the chemicals could make him sick. Andy guessed he'd better wash Baxter's feet.

Back in the apartment he found a note saying his mother had gone to the store. In the kitchen he filled Mom's plastic cleaning pan with warm water and set it on the floor. Then he got soap and a piece of old bath towel from the bag of clean rags.

Baxter didn't seem to understand, but Andy didn't have too much trouble washing his front feet and drying them. He had just managed to stand Baxter with his hind feet in the pan when the doorbell rang. Good grief, Andy thought. Probably Mrs. Pierson.

"Stay!" Andy commanded, and went to open the door.

"Oh--you're here!" Mrs. Pierson seemed surprised. Good grief, where did she think he was?

"It's a quarter to five," Mrs. Pierson said sharply. "Where is Baxter?" She looked past Andy, to where Baxter stood with his back feet in the plastic pan. "What happened?" Mrs. Pierson shrieked, starting toward the kitchen. "What are you doing?"

Quickly Andy explained about the salt on the street. He knelt beside Baxter as he spoke, soaping the hind feet and rinsing them. "I thought you wouldn't know about this," he finished, "since you haven't ever lived in a city."

Andy didn't look up. He kept on drying Baxter's feet, and Baxter licked his ear. When Mrs. Pierson just stood there, not saying anything, Andy finally turned to look at her. And she had the oddest expression on her face--one he hadn't seen her wear before. A kind of soft look. She was almost pretty.

"You really care about Baxter, don't you?" she said.

"Almost as if he were my own dog," said Andy. "I certainly don't want Baxter to have sore feet. Or to get sick."

Mrs. Pierson smiled. "Tell me again," she said, "why you wanted to take Baxter to school."

Andy stood up, his hopes soaring. His words tumbled out as he told about Character Costume Day, his friends, and their skit. This time Mrs. Pierson listened, as if she really was interested. Andy finished by explaining that his mother would bring Baxter to school in a cab, after lunch, in time for their act; and then Andy would walk him home right after school.

"Well," Mrs. Pierson said thoughtfully. "It sounds as if you've planned for everything." She stooped to pat Baxter. "Baxter, would you like to be Snoopy tomorrow?"

Baxter licked her hand, and then Andy's. Andy and Mrs. Pierson laughed. "Boy," said Andy. "Thank you, Mrs. Pierson. Thank you

very much. I'll take good care of Baxter,
I promise." And to himself he added, Good
grief, I really <u>am</u> Charlie Brown.

4.

HARRY AND THE ANTS*

by

Jane Morton

Plot pattern: Misunderstanding, Discovery, and Reversal

Approx. 1,000 words

Story-in-one-sentence: After putting off his science project until it's nearly
due because he 'couldn't get started,' Harry has a miserable experience
trying to activate his ant farm, discovers that the ants start to work no
matter how big the job, and settles down to begin his own project.

This story, written in short, easy-to-read sentences and familiar words,
makes its point in a humorous way. As a 'plus value' it also gives the
reader some information about ants and the way they live.

"Harry, what are you doing for your science project?" Mark asked.

"I haven't decided," Harry said.

"Haven't decided!" echoed Mark. "Today is
Thursday, and the projects are due Monday.
We were supposed to work on them all se-
mester."

"I know," Harry said, "but I couldn't
seem to get started, and anyway I didn't
have time."

"Mr. Summers asked us to tell him what we
were working on. What did you tell him?"

"I said I was going to study insects, and
he suggested I study one particular kind.

So I've been thinking of ants."

"But it's late. What are you going to turn in?"

"I don't know. I'll think of something. We have an ant farm at home. I thought I might use that."

"Do you have ants?"

"No."

"Well, don't you think you had better get some?" Mark asked.

"I think there are some directions that came with the farm. I guess I had better read them," said Harry.

Mark shook his head. "Good luck," he said.

When Harry got home, he found the ant farm and he read the directions. There was an order blank at the bottom of the page. It told how to order the ants from the company that made the ant farm. Too late for that now, thought Harry.

The directions did say that it would be better to use black ants than red ones. So Harry went to the field behind his house to look for black ants. He walked and walked through the weeds. He got stickers in his socks and rocks in his shoes, and something in the field made him sneeze. There were red ants and more red ants, but no black ants.

It was time to go home and eat dinner. This was not as easy as Harry had thought it was going to be. Well, he still had time. He would look again tomorrow afternoon.

Friday after school, Harry went into the field again. He got stickers in his socks and rocks in his shoes, but he still

didn't find any black ants, just red ones.
Red ones would have to do. He did not have
the ant farm with him. He had to go back
to the house. By now it was dinnertime
again. So Harry decided to wait until Saturday to get the ants.

Saturday morning, Harry was getting ready
to go to the field when Mark came by.

"How are you coming on your project?"
Mark asked.

"Okay," said Harry.

"We're getting up a baseball game. Can
you play?

"No," said Harry. "I have to dig ants."

"Hey, that's too bad," Mark said. "Well,
if you finish in time, we'll see you at
the park."

Harry picked up the ant farm and a shovel
and headed for the field. He found an anthill. He scooped up some red ants and dirt
with his shovel and put the ants and dirt
in the top of the farm. The weight of the
dirt knocked the bottom out and the ants
escaped.

Harry felt something on his leg. It felt
as though someone stuck him with a pin,
then another, and another. The ants were
crawling up his leg and biting him. He put
the ant farm down and tried to brush off
the ants. He began to wish he had started
this project earlier. Then he could have
ordered the ants from the company.

These ants were so angry that Harry decided not to bother them any more. He went
on to the next anthill. He opened the ant
farm, scooped up some ants and dirt, and
the same thing happened. The bottom fell
out. Harry picked up his farm and moved

away from that hill fast. He did not want any more bites.

Well, he was getting nowhere. He went home to get some tape to close the bottom of the farm so that the ants could not escape. The field was hot. The stickers and the rocks and his sneezing and missing the baseball game made him miserable.

He found an anthill, scooped up some ants, and dumped them into the farm. This time he had them.

He left the ants in the garage while he rode his bike to the library to check out a book about them. He needed to know how to take care of them.

The book said they needed a wet sponge for water and a mixture of honey, water, and melted butter with a little egg white for food. It also said he needed a hump-backed queen. As he looked at his ants, he didn't think he had her. He read that ants organize into communities, just as people do. He began to feel sorry that he had disturbed them. He would not like it if someone had scooped him up and put him in a glass box and watched him work. He would take them to school on Monday, then put them back where he had found them.

He put the farm on his windowsill because he was sure ants needed air. He fixed their food and their sponge for water. By Monday the ants would have their tunnels dug and he would carry the farm to school. His project would be as good as if he had worked on it all semester.

Sunday afternoon Harry left the ants in his room and went upstairs to watch TV. He was in the middle of a program when he

heard a loud noise. It sounded as if someone had slapped a pile of paper. The sound
had come from his room. He raced down-
stairs and found the ant farm turned over
on its side. The wind must have blown it
over. The top had come off, and the ants
were crawling out. Some were already racing across the floor to what they must
have hoped was freedom. Harry had to be
careful where he stepped. He went after
them, and one by one he captured them and
dropped them back into the farm. He hoped
there were not any still loose that would
come to bite him in the night.

Now the tunnels that the ants had made
were ruined. There was hardly time for
them to build again before the project was
due on Monday. His project would not be
very good.

Harry rested his chin on his hand. He was
supposed to write a report to go along with
the project, telling what he had learned.
He was so discouraged that he could not
even start. He just sat there and watched
the ants. There was a steady stream of
workers going back and forth. Each one
carried a little piece of dirt from the
tunnel to the top of the hill. They were
all busy. Little by little, the tunnels
were beginning to take shape.

Harry had learned one thing, but he was
not sure it was what the teacher had expected him to learn. He knew now that he
should have started sooner. The ants had a
big project too, but they just kept plug-
ging away. And they were getting it done--
a little at a time. He picked up his pencil and started on his report.

5.

WHAT ARE FRIENDS FOR?*

by

Theresa Whitney

Plot Pattern: Decision   Approx. 3,000 words
Story-in-one-sentence: Troubled about her best friend Laurie's safety and
the violation of her own integrity, Katie decides to tell Laurie's mother
that Laurie is not at Katie's house, as Laurie had said—even though
she knows it means the end of the friendship.

This story that comes to grips with a common teenage situation is
similar to many adult stories in its 'open end' conclusion. Teenagers
like stories that don't wrap everything up neatly, but leave something
to the reader's imagination.

<u>I'm going to spend Friday night with
Teddy.</u> The words echoed in Katie McGrath's
ears, making it impossible to study. She
slammed the textbook shut and leaned back
in her chair, recalling the scene early
this afternoon with Laurie Nelson. They'd
been eating lunch in the school cafeteria,
comfortably silent as only two close
friends can be. Then Laurie had leaned forward, excitement lighting her normally
calm blue eyes, and whispered, "Katie, I'm
going to spend Friday night with Teddy."
  Katie, with a bite of cookie in her
mouth, could only sputter for a few sec-
onds. When she'd caught her breath she
could only think to squeal, "You're kidding!"
  Laurie had sat back, carefully smoothing

her long blond hair before answering, "No,
I'm not kidding. We made it final just before lunch."

Katie was impressed with Laurie's calm
and a little embarrassed by her own curiosity. "But how?" she asked. "What are you
going to do?"

Laurie had hesitated just a fraction of a
second before replying, "Well, we're not
actually doing anything, like a date, I
mean. We'll be spending the night at his
house."

Thinking back now, Katie smiled ruefully
as she realized how stunned she must have
looked. For Laurie had hurried to add,
just as the bell rang, that there was to
be an all-night party and she'd explain
more when she and Katie walked home after
school.

But Teddy, a senior at the same high
school where the girls were sophomores,
had decided at the last minute to take
Laurie to a track meet. So now Katie
waited impatiently for a phone call from
Laurie, finding it impossible to concentrate on anything until she found out exactly what was going on.

Ruffling her short dark curls, Katie
tried to sort through her thoughts. Her
main worry was what might happen when Laurie and Teddy spent the night at his
house. Laurie'd said there was going to be
a party. And then what? Katie wondered un-
easily. Laurie just turned fifteen a few
months ago. She's almost three years
younger than Teddy and she's said herself
a few times that he can be hard to handle
once in a while. Katie couldn't believe

she was actually planning on . . .

"No," Katie whispered fiercely, forcing herself not to even think along those lines. Besides, she reassured herself, his parents will be there. It isn't as if they'd be in the house alone.

Just then the phone beside her bed rang and Katie jumped to answer it.

"My, aren't we eager? Waiting for some boy to call?" Laurie's amused voice came over the wire.

Katie remained serious. "No, actually, I was waiting for you. I've been dying all afternoon, wondering what's going on. Can you talk?"

Laurie's laugh was faintly mocking. "The parents are nowhere around. They gave me the usual lecture about being out with Teddy on a school day and are leaving me alone to think it over. I don't know why they dislike him so much. Anyway, tell me what you want to know."

"Well," Katie said hesitantly, "I just want to know what's going on. All you've told me so far is that somehow you're staying overnight at Teddy's tomorrow night."

"Okay, it's like this." Laurie's normally soft voice grew even softer as she outlined her plans. "Teddy's parents are going away for the weekend, so Teddy's decided to have an all-night party for anyone in the senior class who wants to come. And me." Laurie giggled. "It's going to be a sort of open house with kids coming and going all night. And if anyone wants to stay, they can. I'm so excited I can't wait." She giggled again.

Then suddenly she grew serious. "But listen, I'm going to need your help."

"My help?" Katie repeated, not understanding.

"Yes," Laurie continued, "there's absolutely no way I could even ask my parents about going to this. They wouldn't even dream of letting me stay out all night with a boy they liked, and if I ever mentioned staying with Teddy they'd lock me up and throw away the key. So I'm going to have to tell them I'm spending the night at your house, if that's okay with you."

"Well . . . sure," Katie replied, not really sure at all.

Laurie went on, "I already told Teddy it would be okay. I mean, what are friends for? But to get back to my parents, I'll tell them I'm walking over to your house; then I'll meet Teddy with his car down the block and we'll go over to his place. The only hitch is, you know how my mother always invents a reason to call when I'm staying overnight at your house, just to make sure I'm really there. Well, you're going to have to stay near your phone so when she calls you can tell her I'm in the shower and you'll have me call her back. Then you can call me at Teddy's so I can call her at the right time."

Katie shook her head. "Wow, you really have this thing planned, don't you?" she said. "But what would have happened if I'd decided not to go along with it?"

"Oh, I knew you could be counted on," Laurie said airily.

"But what if I had turned you down?" Katie persisted.

"You wouldn't." Laurie's answer was sharp

and her tone cold. Then she softened. "Katie, we've been friends for five years. If I couldn't count on you, who could I count on?"

Katie's thoughts whirled. "You say Teddy's parents aren't going to be there?"

"That's right. They're going away," Laurie said warily, then added, "But it isn't like we'll be alone. Teddy says there will be kids there all night."

"But it won't be like having parents around," Katie said slowly. "What's to stop you from leaving the rest of the crowd and going off to one of the bedrooms?"

Laurie's cry of "Katie!" was so shocked that Katie was immediately sorry she had asked. She hadn't meant to pry, but she felt she had to know.

Her explanation was cut short by Laurie. "Listen, I guess I know why you asked. I know you worry about Teddy and me. He does have a wild reputation, but I'll be all right. Hey, I hear my mom coming upstairs. I'll see you tomorrow in school. Bye, Katie--and thanks."

Katie slowly cradled the phone. For several long minutes different scenes and snatches of conversation drifted through her mind. She remembered the day, over a month ago, when Laurie, at Teddy's urging, had skipped school. It had been up to Katie, after much pleading from Laurie, to tell the different teachers that Laurie had gotten sick on her way to school and returned home. None of them had bothered to check as was usually the case because Katie and Laurie had never been known as troublemakers.

Katie recalled another scene only last week in the Nelson home. She'd walked over to visit late one afternoon and had met Laurie just as Teddy was dropping her off down the street from her house. Laurie had run to catch up with her and the two of them had entered the house to find Laurie's parents waiting anxiously.

Before Katie'd had time to speak, Mrs. Nelson had demanded, "Laura, where have you been? We've been frantic. We tried Katie's house four times but the line was busy. We even called the school and had you paged."

To Katie's astonishment, Laurie had replied smoothly, "I can't understand why you didn't reach me at school. Katie and I stayed late to help set up this month's display case. Mrs. Ward asked for volunteers and I guess I never thought to call. I didn't think we'd be this late."

Mrs. Nelson had turned then and looked searchingly at Katie, who could only manage a weak, "That's right."

Now, thinking back, Katie winced at these and several more memories like them. In the past few months Laurie had come to rely more and more on Katie to cover up for her. Katie had been struck by Laurie's bold assurance that Katie would go along with her lies.

To Katie, her friend seemed changed lately. True, her parents had always been over protective of their only child. But what was once mere irritation on Laurie's part had turned into defiance.

A defiance that involves me, Katie thought unhappily.

Katie spent a restless night. Her decision to go along with Laurie's deception tomorrow night lay heavy on her mind, and nothing made her feel easy about it.

When she met Laurie on the school steps the next morning her friend was glowing with excitement.

"You're certainly bright-eyed this morning," Katie said, a little sourly. It didn't seem fair that she was the one doing all the worrying about this thing.

Laurie either chose to ignore her mood or just didn't notice it, for she squeezed Katie's arm. "I feel like we're a couple of conspirators," she said with a giggle.

"Yeah, but I'm the one doing most of the conspiring." It was out before Katie could stop it.

Laurie drew back. "What's that supposed to mean?" She seemed genuinely puzzled.

Katie shrugged. "I guess I'm just tired of doing your dirty work for you. Did it ever occur to you I might not like lying for you?" Katie was surprised at the anger in her voice.

Apparently Laurie was, too, for she stepped back before she said, in an attempt at lightness, "But it's all for a good cause, Katie."

"I'm not so sure," Katie answered. "I know you really like Teddy, but I'm not so sure this party is a good idea. And I'm not sure I want any part of it.

"No, wait," she ordered as she saw Laurie starting to protest. "I admit, at first, I thought it might be just a cover-up for you two spending the night together. But I really think I shocked you when I suggested you might wind up sleeping with Teddy. So I don't think you're planning it. But Laurie, it could happen. And if it did, I'd be partly to blame by lying for you. I don't want that."

Laurie's look was one of mixed anguish and anger. "Katie, I promise you, nothing will happen. You can't back out. You're the only one who'd do this for me."

"Oh, don't you see?" Katie wanted terribly for Laurie to understand. "You can't promise that. You might not be planning on it, but what about Teddy?"

Instantly Laurie was furious. "You're just like my parents. You only have bad things to say about Teddy. Well, he loves me and he wouldn't do anything to hurt me. Try to understand, we just want to have the chance to have some fun tonight without worrying about getting me home on time or having my father catch us kissing on the porch. And we need your help."

All of a sudden Katie felt very tired. "I know you just want to have a good time, and maybe, under different circumstances, I'd go along. But right now, I'm really tired of lying for you. I think it's a bad idea but go over to Teddy's. Only don't expect me to cover up for you."

Katie found herself looking into eyes that had turned ice blue. "You can't back out now," Laurie said, ominously controlled.

"I am backing out," Katie insisted. "It's not something I want to get involved in. Too many things could happen and too many people could get hurt."

"You'll do it," Laurie ordered very quietly. Then she turned and started up the steps.

"I won't," Katie called after her. But if Laurie heard she gave no sign.

Laurie ignored her the rest of the day. Twice Katie tried to talk to her, but Laurie turned her back.

After school Katie hurried through the crowds in hope of catching up with Laurie. She did, on the front steps again. But Laurie walked away from her suggestion that they talk the problem out. Finally, at Katie's anguished wail of "Laurie, please!" she halted on the bottom step.

As Katie neared, she whirled around. "What do you want?" she snarled.

"I just want to make sure you understand why I don't want to get involved anymore," Katie began earnestly.

"All I understand," Laurie cut in, "is that you think Teddy is some kind of sex maniac just because he asked me to his party and that I'm a sneak who lets you do all my lying for me."

"Laurie, that's ridiculous," Katie answered. "What I'm saying is I don't want to cover up for you anymore and especially with this party tonight. I never said you were a sneak."

Laurie tossed her hair. "Look. I've heard this already. All I want to know is whether or not I can tell my mom I'm at your house tonight."

Katie stared into a face that was almost like a stranger's. She tried to remember the laughter and the closeness she and Laurie had shared over the years. But all she seemed able to recall were the times she'd allowed Laurie to use her to cover up so many of her dates with Teddy.

"No," Katie said finally, "you can't say you're at my house."

"Then we have nothing more to talk about." Laurie turned and stalked away, leaving Katie to watch sadly.

Twenty minutes later Katie sat at her kitchen table reading a note from her mother. The woman across the street for whom Katie often babysat had called, wanting to know if Katie could possibly come over this afternoon so she and her husband could take in dinner and a movie. Katie considered a minute, then decided and quickly changed into jeans and a sweater.

The chore of playing with the three young children, getting their dinner, bathing them and putting them to bed kept Katie from dwelling too much on the scene with Laurie. She found herself wondering at odd moments, though, what Laurie had decided to do.

By the time Katie returned home about nine-thirty she had become frankly curious. She was sitting in the kitchen, having a snack and trying to decide whether to call Laurie's house, when she heard the phone in her bedroom ring.

"I'll get it," she shouted, taking the stairs two at a time. She caught it on the third ring and whispered a quick prayer that it might be Laurie calling to patch things up.

Instead she heard, "Hi, Katie? This is Mrs. Nelson. I was wondering if I might speak to Laurie, please."

Katie felt herself go weak. <u>I don't believe it</u>, she thought; <u>I don't believe she's done this.</u> She found herself repeating, "Laurie?"

"Why, yes." Mrs. Nelson sounded surprised. "She said she was spending the night at your house. Isn't she there?"

Katie began to shake. It was almost as if Laurie had told her right to her face how little she thought of her. Despite everything Katie had said, Laurie had gone ahead with her plan, sure that Katie would give in as she always had in the past. Katie felt a wave of fury wash over her, closely followed by a deep, flooding sadness.

Evidently Laurie thought friends were to be used. Even though she knew it would mean the end of a friendship that had meant a great deal to her, Katie could no longer go on lying for Laurie. Not if she wanted to keep her own self-respect. And while she honestly felt she was telling for Laurie's own good, she was sure her friend--her former friend--would not see it that way. What a mess!

She drew a long breath. "Mrs. Nelson, Laurie isn't here."

She heard Laurie's mother gasp, then ask quickly, "Do you have any idea where she might be?"

Katie squeezed her eyes shut to hold back tears. "I think she mentioned something about a party at Teddy's tonight."

Mrs. Nelson said a quick "Thanks," and hung up. With trembling hands Katie replaced her own phone.

In a few minutes Laurie would know that

her challenge to Katie had failed. Laurie
would finally realize that Katie had meant
what she said. But these thoughts brought
Katie no comfort, for she also knew that
as soon as Mrs. Nelson called the party
her friendship with Laurie would be over.

Thoughts filled Katie's mind. If only I
hadn't started lying for Laurie in the
first place . . . if Laurie just hadn't
told her mother she was here, none of this
would have happened.

The tears that had threatened started to
fall. With her head in her hands, Katie
wept for a long time--for herself, for
Laurie, and for what they had lost.

Appendix B

Manuscript Preparation and Mailing, and Copyright Notice

Your manuscript is *you* walking into an editorial office. It should be as neat, well groomed, correct, and businesslike as you yourself would be. To ensure such an appearance, use crisp white paper of good quality, sixteen-pound weight, 8½ × 11 inches. Use a fresh black typewriter ribbon, and keep type faces clean and sharp. No odd types; use elite or pica.

General Form

1. Double space all typing.
2. Indent paragraphs three to ten spaces.
3. Leave margins of 1 inch right and left, 1¼ inches top and bottom.
4. Number pages in upper-right-hand corner or top center of the page. (Identification, such as author's last name or a key word from the title, may be used in upper-left-hand corner of page 2 and following pages, but is not necessary. Do not distract reader by using such terms as **MORE** at the bottom of pages, but at the end type **THE END** or use a series of asterisks.)

Title Page (optional)

1. In upper-left-hand corner, your name, address, and if the piece is for a magazine, your copyright notice.*
2. In upper-right-hand corner the number of words in the manuscript,

---

* NOTE: An author's work is now copyrighted in his name from the moment of its "creation"—that is, from the moment it's written—whether the manuscript bears any copyright notice or not. This notice, however, *states* the author's ownership, and indicates to editors of *uncopyrighted* publications—of which there are several in the young people's field—that any printing of his piece is to bear his copyright notice. This consists of 3 items: the symbol © or the word "Copyright," the year of first publication of the work (or, if unpublished, year of "creation"), and the name of the copyright owner.

rounded out to the nearest 10 in short manuscripts, the nearest 50 in longer scripts: 570 words, 1,250 words. If you use the margins mentioned above, you will have about 250 words to a page if you use a pica typewriter, about 300 if your type is elite. You can estimate the number of words in a book manuscript by using these figures.

3. *Halfway down,* in the center of the page, the title of your story or article, in capital letters.

4. Double space and center the word "by."

5. Double space and center your name or pseudonym.

The First Page

1. Duplicate the instructions given for the title page.

2. Skip down 8 lines to begin the text. There will be only 6 to 10 lines of the text on page 1.

Envelopes and Mailing

1. Do not bind or staple the pages of your manuscript; use a paper clip.

2. Scripts of more than 10 or 12 pages should be mailed flat. Shorter scripts should be folded once crosswise through the middle.

3. Enclose a stamped, self-addressed envelope, the next size smaller than the outer envelope. For example, 9 × 12 envelope in a 9½ × 12½. Or for the folded script, a 6 × 9 in a 6½ × 9½.

4. Manuscripts should be sealed in the envelope and sent by first-class mail. Although manuscripts may legally be sent by fourth-class mail at a lower rate, this mail moves slowly and is so roughly handled that the manuscript often arrives in bad shape. (Sturdily packaged book manuscripts may be sent this way.)

When you register your copyright—or even whether you do so—is up to you. The law provides that it can be registered any time from the time of its creation up to five years after its first publication. However, if there's a reasonable expectation of significant further sales over which an ownership lawsuit might arise, you should register the copyright with the United States Copyright Office within three months after its first publication. This is a simple process, and there's no need for help from a lawyer or other "expert," or to pay any fee except the $10 fee for the registry. A letter to the Information and Publication Section, Copyright Office, Library of Congress, Washington, D.C. 20559, will bring you the information and forms you need, free of charge. In the vast majority of cases there's really no need ever to register your copyright; the piece will have had the usual one-time publication and lived its life—or may even be reprinted and paid for one or more other times. In the case of a book, the publisher will take care of registering the copyright, in the author's name.

5. Be sure the correct amount of postage is on both envelopes, and mark both FIRST CLASS, DO NOT BEND.

6. Address the outside envelope to the magazine's editor by name, if you know it, or simply Editor—or in the case of a book, Editor of Children's Books. If you are known to or have corresponded with an editor or someone in the editorial department, of course you should address your manuscript to that person by name.

Miscellaneous

1. Although a title page is not necessary, it does serve to protect the script itself and is simpler to replace for future mailings than a whole page of typing. It is a good idea when typing your script to make an extra title page or page 1, and an extra last page, for these take the brunt of hard wear. This practice ensures extra pages whose typing will match the original.

2. On the title page, or on page 1, under the word count, you may type, "Alternate title"—or "titles"—and list one or two other title suggestions. This is not necessary.

3. In the lower-right-hand quadrant of the title page, if you have published in or have sold to similar publications, it is appropriate to type, "Have sold to . . ." and simply list your credits of a similar nature.

4. Letters accompanying manuscripts are unnecessary and are not advisable unless you are known to the editor; if you have been corresponding with the editor about a particular project, of course a letter with the manuscript is appropriate. A manuscript that requires explanation is faulty, though if you have used material the authenticity of which might be questioned, it is advisable to include a brief note stating that you can verify all facts.

5. Always keep an accurate copy of all work. Loss in the mail or in editorial offices is rare, but is not unheard of.

Ellen Dean Chambers   Approx. 1,200 words
701 Lincoln Avenue
Hopewell, Arizona 85000   Alternate title:
                        FOOLSGOLD IS FOR FOOLS

Copyright Ellen Dean Chambers 1980

THE SECRET OF THE LOST MINE

by

Dean Chambers

Martin Summers slipped the extra canteen
of fresh water into his saddlebag and
buckled the strap. "Where we're going,
water may be the most important equipment
we're taking," he said to his cousin.
Easterners never seemed to understand how
dry the desert could be. Especially the
city kids.

"If it's so dry, I don't see why we have
to pack these slickers," Bob protested.
"The poor horses will be worn out before
we get to Cedar Gulch."

"They'll be tired enough to stay there
and graze while we hike up to the lost
mine," said Marty. "Where's that rope and
picket I had here?"

SAMPLE MANUSCRIPT

Appendix C

Some Pointers on Grammar, Punctuation, and Mechanics

Every writer should have on his ready-reference shelf a collegiate dictionary and a good, up-to-date college handbook of English usage—and *use* them. Correct grammar, sentence structure, punctuation, and usage are the hallmark of the professional writer. These are the tools of the trade, and editors have a right to expect letter perfection in their use.

The following points are those most often asked about by students, and those that crop up most frequently in student papers. Some are not covered in handbooks and should help with some of the commonest problems.

1. In counting words, everything with white space on both sides is considered a word: *a, the, I,* and *anthropomorphous* are all words; so is *1776. Able-bodied* is just one word.

2. In typing, underlining indicates *italics.* Italics should be used sparingly, for emphasis and for foreign words. The general practice now is to italicize a foreign word only the first time it appears in the script. Check your handbook for other uses of italics.

3. In typing, two hyphens indicate a printer's dash. No space should be left between the previous word and the two hyphens, or between them and the next word. The dash should be used correctly, to indicate an interruption in thought, and not lazily because the writer is not sure what punctuation is right.

4. Overuse of exclamation points is amateurish. Excitement and drama depend on phraseology and the situation itself, not on punctuation marks. The exclamation point should be reserved for exclamations, as its name indicates, usually only in dialogue: *"Watch out!" he shouted.* One should never use a double !! or ?? for added effect.

5. Capitalize *mother, father, dad,* and such words when they are used

as names but not otherwise: *"May I go with you, Dad?"* But, *Jim asked his father to help him.*

6. For the youngest readers, 3 to 8, most magazines use quotation marks for "thought" passages: *"I wish I had a sled," he thought. "I could take Spot for a ride."* But for older readers the quotation marks should be omitted: *If only I had a bicycle, he thought, I could get a paper route.*

7. The rules for using other punctuation marks with quotation marks are really simple, but students misuse them constantly.

a. The comma and period *always go inside* the quotation marks: *"No," she said, "I'm not going." If cooked too long, the fudge may "sugar."*

b. The colon and semicolon *always go outside* the quotation marks: *The fudge may "sugar"; if it is not cooked long enough, it will be syrupy.*

c. The question mark, exclamation point, and dash go inside the quotation marks when they refer to what is quoted, outside when they refer to the whole matter: *She asked: "Will you go with me?"* But, *Did she say, "I won't go with you"?*

d. Single quotation marks are used for a quotation within a quotation: *"We shall sing 'America the Beautiful,'" said Miss Wilson.*

8. Every change of speaker in dialogue means a new pragraph. The stories in this book contain virtually every possible dialogue situation and may be referred to as models.

9. The *so* that really means "very" is ungrammatical and should be avoided: not, *Jenny was so-o-o tired;* rather, *Jenny was very tired.* Or better, just *Jenny was tired.*

10. Proper syllabication of words is given in the dictionary; if in doubt about where to divide a word at the end of a line, one should check.

Appendix D

Checklists for Judging Your Stories and Articles

Just as airplane pilots have a written list of items to check routinely before each takeoff, most professional writers have a checklist against which to test their stories and articles before they go flying off to an editor. The following lists should help to insure a happy landing.

Checklist for Story Evaluation

What is the premise of my story?
Is my title fresh, provocative?

Opening

1. Is my main character the first one mentioned and the first to speak?
2. Have I begun my story at the right place—where something has got to give?
3. Have I established a character with a problem in the first 150 words?

Characterization

1. Is my main character appealing, sympathetic?
2. Are my characters believable, three-dimensional individuals? Do they really come alive?
3. What character growth takes place in my main character?
4. Have I given my main character real obstacles to overcome? (Made a tie-in with actual and alternate endings?)
5. Do my characters act from their own deep inner drive, or are they more like puppets carrying out the necessities of the plot?

Plot

1. Have I made suspense strong by making my reader hope for one ending but fear equally that something else (the alternate ending) is surely going to happen?

2. Does my plot rise steadily to a true crisis and climax?
3. Does my story build to a black moment? Does it come very near the end?
4. Does the climax bring suspense, relief, satisfaction, pleasure?
5. Does my main character solve his own problem?

Scenes

1. Have I told my story in scenes, with the main character in the spotlight in every scene?
2. Is my main character either nearer to or further from his goal for the story at the end of each scene?
3. Are my transitions between scenes smooth and swift?

Presentation

1. Have I handled viewpoint expertly, consistently, professionally?
2. Have I involved the reader emotionally? Will he care vitally what happens to my main character?
3. Have I given my story immediacy by showing rather than telling—by keeping it on stage?
4. Have I used as much dialogue and action and as little narration and exposition as possible? Does the dialogue characterize the story people? Move the plot forward?
5. Is the setting vivid but not too detailed?

Ending

1. Is the outcome of my story believable?
2. Is the problem solved in the ending the same one posed in the beginning?
3. Did I quit when my story was over? (Once the problem is solved, the story is over.)
4. Does the main character get the closing lines?

Mechanics

1. Is my story mechanically correct? Spelling? Punctuation? Grammar?
2. Is the story the right length for the age group and publication for which I planned it?
3. Is my manuscript properly prepared? Crisp, fresh, businesslike?

Checklist for Article Evaluation

CONTENT

1. Have I chosen an important subject? What am I trying to prove?
2. Is the material appropriate for the magazine to which I plan to send it? Can I direct its appeal more to this particular magazine?
3. Have I chosen the best age group for this material?
4. Does it appeal only to boys? Only to girls? To both girls and boys?

TITLE

1. Appropriate?
2. Does it intrigue, interest, arouse curiosity?

BEGINNING

1. Have I started at the right place?
2. Is the beginning swiftly paced? Will it immediately grip attention?
3. Do the first two paragraphs whet the reader's appetite for more?

BODY

1. Does my article contain enough fresh information?
2. Have I been careful with facts, double-checking each one? Have I presented them in a way that will entertain as well as inform?
3. Is my article plausible, logical? Can the reader follow the thought smoothly without losing interest?

ENDING

1. Is my ending a logical conclusion drawn from what I have said in the body?
2. Does the conclusion tie up all the threads referred to in the opening?
3. Does my article have one basic idea and leave the reader with a single emotion? How will he *feel* about it?
4. Is my ending strong—the strongest part of the whole article? Does it end on an upbeat?

GENERAL

1. What single point have I made?
2. Does my article show respect for law and for principles of good taste?

3. Does my article have a novel angle or twist? Will it entertain? Inform? Inspire?
4. Is my style simple, strong, sparkling?
5. Have I used the strongest verbs possible, throughout the article? Have I cut out all the deadwood?
6. Have I used words and terms that my readers will understand? Have I underestimated my audience by writing down to them?
7. Have I thought about what my reader wants to hear about this subject rather than what I want to say?
8. Have I said something that means something? If not, why not?

MECHANICS
1. Have I checked spelling? Punctuation? Grammar?
2. Does my manuscript look interesting? Have I broken up solid print with white space, used short paragraphs?
3. Is the manuscript neat, fresh, crisp?
4. Is the length right for the market to which I intend to send it?

Index

DATE DUE		
MAY 07 1991		
JAN 07 1992		